New Drug Development: A Regulatory Overview
Third Edition

New Drug Development: A Regulatory Overview
Third Edition

by
Mark Mathieu

with contributions from
Anne G. Evans, D.V.M.
and
Eric L. Hurden, M.Sc., Ph.D.

PAREXEL International Corporation
Waltham, MA
Publishers

New Drug Development: A Regulatory Overview
Third Edition

by
Mark Mathieu
PAREXEL International Corporation

with contributions from
Anne G. Evans, D.V.M.
and
Eric L. Hurden, M.Sc., Ph.D.

Joanna White: *Design and Production*
James Applebaum: *Cover Design*
Carolyn Newman: *Marketing*
Victoria Wong: *Fulfillment*

Acknowledgements

My sincerest thanks to the individuals who took time from their own demanding schedules to aid my efforts: Duncan Berkeley; Cori Doud; Anne Evans; Adrienne Garland; Vicky Gaudette; Alberto Grignolo, Ph.D.; David Hallinan, Ph.D.; Eric Hurden, Ph.D.; Karleen Kelley; John Kirchner; Cheryl Mathieu; Carolyn Newman; Steven Reich, M.D.; Jeff Packman; Barry Sall; Anne Sayigh, Ph.D.; Roberta Sensale; Josef von Rickenbach; Joanna White; Ann Whittaker; Vicky Wong; and Ed Zebrowski.

Also, special thanks to the Center for the Study of Drug Development, particularly Kenneth Kaitin, Ph.D., and Peg Hewitt.

Preface

A product of both science and society, the FDA's regulation of the drug development process evolves considerably over time. As the millennium approaches, several factors are shaping this evolution.

Perhaps no single factor will affect the FDA's new drug approval process more fundamentally than prescription drug user fees. FDA officials have pledged to act on most new drug applications within 12 months. To meet these goals, the agency will employ user fees collected from industry to hire roughly 300 new staffers for its drug review offices. The need to increase the pace of drug reviews will almost assuredly have other implications for the review process—among them, tighter standards for NDA submissions and increased agency experimentation with innovative review methods.

Like drug development, drug regulation has been affected by international initiatives. Efforts to harmonize the technical and regulatory requirements of the United States, Europe, and Japan have prompted the FDA to reexamine and, in some cases, revise its drug development and approval standards.

Meanwhile, the scourge of AIDS continues to challenge traditional ideas about medical risks and benefits. Largely because of this, recent years have brought a variety of new initiatives to expedite the availability and approval of new drugs designed to treat serious and life-threatening illnesses.

Obviously, much has happened in the three years since the last edition of *New Drug Development: A Regulatory Overview* was published. The new text has been expanded and updated to make it the most comprehensive and up-to-date work of its kind. New chapters analyze the FDA's prescription drug user fee program and the agency's various initiatives to speed drug approvals. In addition, the text's discussion of the Center for Drug Evaluation and Research (CDER) has been expanded to provide more in-depth analyses of the center's ten drug review divisions and their respective responsibilities.

The drug approval process outlined in *New Drug Development: A Regulatory Overview* applies to new molecular entities (NME), previously approved pharmaceuticals proposed for new uses, and all other medicines classified as new drugs. Excluded from the analysis are biologics, generic drugs, medical devices, animal drugs, and over-the-counter (OTC) drugs.

The nascent trends and movements specified above are not the only factors that make providing a comprehensive outline of the FDA's new drug approval process a particularly daunting challenge. Even when taken alone, that process is not a single, static process, but many different processes, each designed to ensure that critical questions regarding a new drug's safety and effectiveness are addressed before approval. Today, more than ever, the development and approval paths traveled by two new products are always different, sometimes considerably so. Similarly, each of the FDA's drug review divisions has its own internal policies, philosophies, and personality. Therefore, it is virtually impossible to provide all-encompassing descriptions of FDA policies, regulatory requirements, and review procedures that are entirely relevant to each new drug or to each FDA division or office. Inevitably, there are special cases and situations that make such descriptions inaccurate, and experiences and views that contradict even the most basic outlines of the drug approval process. Finally, it is important to note that this text does not necessarily, and does not claim to, represent the views of the FDA or any agency official or employee.

Contents

Chapter 1:

The New Drug Approval Process: A Primer

It is no mystery why the Food and Drug Administration's (FDA) new drug approval process is such a closely monitored government activity. After all, that process determines when and if patients are given access to new therapies that might end suffering or extend life. And as the gatekeeper to the world's most lucrative pharmaceutical market, the FDA, through that process, can determine the short-term financial destiny—in some cases, even the existence—of entire corporations.

But visions of the drug development and review process as a single, static process are myopic. To some degree, the FDA's new drug approval process reinvents itself for each new pharmaceutical.

Since new drugs present their own distinct risks and benefits, and because these risks and benefits are evaluated by different FDA reviewers, the development and approval paths traveled by two new products are always different, sometimes considerably so. The nature of the drug development and approval process is, in large part, a function of the drug being developed and the condition being studied, and is tailored to ensure that the key questions regarding the compound's safety and effectiveness in this use are addressed sufficiently before approval.

As a product of both science and society, the drug development process evolves considerably over time. In the early 1990s, several factors were influencing the evolution of that process:

- *Changing Attitudes Toward Risks and Benefits.* As the scourge of AIDS has grown, so, too, has the recognition that suffering individuals— particularly the desperately ill—should be given greater freedom to

1

accept risks proportionate to the severity of their conditions. Accompanying this are increased government efforts to provide the desperately ill with access to promising new therapies before those therapies have met traditional standards of safety and effectiveness. In recent years, this has produced a variety of new experimental drug accessibility programs and the first codified accelerated drug approval program for drugs designed to treat serious or life-threatening illnesses.

- *Prescription Drug User Fees*. Perhaps no single factor will affect the FDA's new drug approval process more fundamentally than the Prescription Drug User Fee Act of 1992. FDA commitments made in this law call for the agency to take action on most new drug applications (NDA) within 12 months. User fees collected from industry will allow the FDA's drug review offices to increase existing staffing levels by approximately 300 staffers from 1993 to 1997. The need to increase the pace of drug reviews will almost assuredly have other implications for the review process—among them, tighter standards for NDA submissions and increased agency experimentation with innovative review methods.

- *Cooperation Among International Regulatory Authorities*. To expedite global pharmaceutical development, national drug regulatory authorities are working more closely than ever before. The FDA and the Canadian Health Protection Branch (HPB) are conducting joint reviews of important new therapies. In addition, efforts to encourage international harmonization of scientific and regulatory requirements is clearly forcing regulatory authorities to reexamine, restate, and, in some cases, revise their regulatory standards.

- *The Integration of Computers Into the Drug Review Process*. By the early 1990s, computers clearly had earned a place as an FDA drug review tool. Not only had fully one-third of all 1991 new molecular entity (NME) approvals involved computer-assisted new drug applications (CANDA), but also FDA data suggested that computerized applications could reduce review time by a year or more. Meanwhile, the FDA was beginning to consider the regulatory implications of similar trends within industry: pharmaceutical companies were reengineering their drug development processes to further integrate computers, particularly in the collection of clinical data and the management of regulatory documentation.

• *Migration From the "Honor System" to the "Trust, But Verify" System of Regulatory Surveillance and Enforcement.* The FDA's protracted response to fraudulent practices within the generic drug industry continues to bring changes in all areas of regulation, from NDA submission requirements to the nature of inspectional activities undertaken before and following drug approval.

The FDA and the Food, Drug and Cosmetic Act

Despite the new legislation and emerging trends outlined above, the foundations of the new drug approval process remain intact within the provisions of the Federal Food, Drug and Cosmetic Act (FD&C Act). Seen by many as the most complex law of its kind, the FD&C Act has at least three provisions that shape the new drug development and approval process:

1. The FD&C Act defines the term "drug," thereby identifying the universe of products subject to regulation as drugs. The statute defines drugs as "articles intended for use in the diagnosis, cure, mitigation, treatment, or prevention of disease in man..." and "articles (other than food) intended to affect the structure or any function of the body of man...."

2. The FD&C Act defines "new drug," thereby identifying which products are subject to the requirements of the new drug approval process. The law defines "new drug" as: "(1) Any drug (except a new animal drug or an animal feed bearing or containing a new animal drug) the composition of which is such that such drug is not generally recognized, among experts qualified by scientific training and experience to evaluate the safety and effectiveness of drugs, as

safe and effective for use under the conditions prescribed, recommended, or suggested in labeling thereof, except that such a drug not so recognized shall not be deemed to be a 'new drug' if at any time prior to the enactment of this Act it was subject to the Food and Drugs Act of June 30, 1906, as amended, and if at such time its labeling contained the same representations concerning the conditions of its use; or (2) Any drug (except a new animal drug or an animal feed bearing or containing a new animal drug) the composition of which is such that such drug, as a result of investigations to determine its safety and effectiveness for use under such conditions, has become so recognized, but which has not, otherwise than in such investigations, been used to a material extent or for a material time under such conditions."

3. The FD&C Act identifies, in the broadest possible terms, the criteria that all new drugs must meet to gain marketing approval. Before a new drug can be marketed in the United States, it must be the subject of a FDA-approved NDA, which must contain adequate data and information on the drug's safety and "substantial evidence" of the product's effectiveness.

But as similar laws do in other areas, the FD&C Act merely establishes the basic framework and essential principles of new drug approval. The statute must be interpreted, implemented, and enforced. Since the early 1900s, these responsibilities have fallen on the FDA.

It is the interpretive and discretionary powers granted to the FDA under the FD&C Act that give the agency wide-ranging authority. Perhaps the most significant of these powers is the FDA's role in interpreting the legal requirement that a sponsor present substantial evidence of effectiveness prior to a drug's approval. While this is a statutory requirement, it is the FDA that decides what constitutes substantial evidence for each new drug. In doing so, the agency also determines what scientific testing and data submissions are needed to obtain marketing approval.

As a drug regulator and the interpreter of the FD&C Act, the FDA has a responsibility to communicate its policies and standards so that industry may

4

address these in developing new pharmaceuticals. The agency does this primarily by developing and publishing regulations, which are compiled in the *U.S. Code of Federal Regulations* (CFR). These regulations describe premarketing requirements and approval procedures that are, at least in theory, binding on both the FDA and drug sponsors. Although federal regulations often provide this information in broad rather than specific detail, they are significantly more specific than the provisions of the FD&C Act.

The FDA supplements federal regulations through several means, including agency guidelines. Unlike regulations, guidelines are not legally binding, but are designed to provide drug sponsors with informal and more detailed guidance on specific methods through which they might satisfy regulatory requirements. Further, the FDA corresponds directly with drug applicants on specific drug testing and approval processes. It also maintains an active communication program involving speeches by FDA officials and the publication of talk papers, information sheets, staff manual guides, and other materials designed to explain agency requirements, philosophies, policies, and internal practices.

New Drug Development and Approval: The Principal Steps

New drugs face a reasonably well-defined development and approval process that has been refined over several decades. The more recent and significant changes notwithstanding, the drug approval process is probably one of the more widely understood of the FDA's product approval processes.

Each stage of the drug development and approval process falls within one of three types of activities: (1) scientific testing designed to provide data on a product's safety or effectiveness; (2) the preparation and submission of these data and other information in regulatory applications; and (3) the FDA's review of regulatory submissions. While all drug development programs involve these core activities, it is important to note how fundamentally different each can be for any two products. Testing and submission requirements, for example, will be shaped by many factors, including the drug's proposed indication, the amount and nature of data already available on the drug and on compounds similar in molecular structure, and the availability of therapeutic alternatives for the target indication.

These factors also affect the FDA's premarketing review. Under the provisions of the Prescription Drug User Fee Act of 1992, for example, a drug's therapeutic importance will dictate, beginning in October 1996, whether the FDA must attempt to act on the product's NDA within either 6 or 12 months. Similarly, a drug's proposed indication will directly influence the nature and amount of testing necessary and, therefore, the quantity of data that the FDA must review.

Stage 1: Preclinical Testing

Clearly, clinical trials represent the ultimate premarketing proving grounds for new pharmaceuticals. Because of the costs and risks inherent in using an untested new drug in clinical testing, however, drug sponsors do not leap headlong into a clinical program once chemical screening, molecular modeling, or some other discovery method identifies a promising compound. Prior to clinical studies, the sponsor wants some evidence that the compound is biologically active, and both the sponsor and the FDA want data showing that the drug is reasonably safe for initial administration to humans. According to U.S. Pharmaceutical Manufacturers Association (PMA) statistics, developing this evidence absorbs 3.5 years on average.

Under FDA requirements, the sponsor first must submit data showing that the drug is reasonably safe for use in initial, small-scale clinical studies. Depending on whether the compound has been studied or marketed previously, the sponsor may have several options for fulfilling this requirement: (1) compiling existing nonclinical data derived from past *in vitro* laboratory or animal studies on the compound; (2) compiling data from previous clinical testing or marketing of the drug in the United States or another country whose population is relevant to the U.S. population; or (3) undertaking new preclinical studies designed to provide the evidence necessary to support the safety of administering the compound to humans.

Sponsors lacking clinical or nonclinical data will face the last of these alternatives. During preclinical drug development, a sponsor evaluates the drug's toxic and pharmacologic effects through *in vitro* and *in vivo* laboratory animal testing. Genotoxicity screening is performed, as well as investigations on drug absorption and metabolism, the toxicity of the drug's metabolites, and the speed with which the drug and its metabolites are excreted from the body. At the preclinical stage, the FDA will generally ask, at a minimum, that sponsors: (1) develop a pharmacological profile of the drug; (2) determine the acute toxicity of the drug in at least two species of animals; and (3) conduct short-term toxicity studies ranging from two weeks to three months, depending upon the proposed use of the substance.

Nonclinical animal testing is not discontinued once the preclinical phase is complete. Lengthier and more specialized studies—including chronic toxicity, carcinogenicity, and reproductive toxicity studies—are conducted throughout the clinical development process, providing the data on long-term drug effects needed to support the safety of lengthier clinical studies and, ultimately, commercial marketing.

Because preclinical drug development does not involve human exposure to an experimental compound, drug developers have considerable flexibility in manufacturing, shipping, and testing new substances. Virtually the only regulatory limitations facing sponsors are the general animal welfare provisions contained in current federal and state animal protection statutes and regulations, and little more than a single FDA requirement detailed in federal regulations: "A person may ship a drug intended solely for tests *in vitro* or in animals used only for laboratory research purposes if it is labeled as follows: Caution: Contains a new drug for investigational use only in laboratory research animals, or for tests *in vitro*. Not for use in humans."

However, when a sponsor begins to compile safety data for submission to the FDA, a set of regulations called Good Laboratory Practice (GLP) apply. Because it will base important regulatory decisions on these data, the FDA uses GLP standards to ensure the quality of animal testing and the resultant data.

The Investigational New Drug Application

When a sponsor believes that it has sufficient data to show that a new drug is adequately safe for initial small-scale clinical studies, the company assembles and submits an investigational new drug application (IND). The IND is the vehicle through which a sponsor seeks an exemption from the statutory requirement that prohibits unapproved drugs from being shipped in interstate commerce. As such, the IND is essentially a proposal through which a sponsor obtains the FDA's permission to begin testing a drug in human subjects.

In the IND, the sponsor submits information in three principal areas: (1) the results of all preclinical testing and an analysis of what implications these results have for human pharmacology; (2) an analysis of the drug's chemical composition and the manufacturing and quality control procedures used in producing the pharmaceutical; and (3) protocols describing the sponsor's plans for the initial-stage clinical studies proposed in the IND, and information describing the relevant qualifications of the investigators who will carry out these studies.

The FDA's Review of the IND

Perhaps due to the federal government's respect for the scientific research process, the FDA's IND review process has changed little despite significant evolution in other areas of federal regulation. Indeed, the IND review process is a curious, and at times delicate, balance between the FDA's responsibility to protect clinical subjects and its desire not to impede the advance of scientific progress.

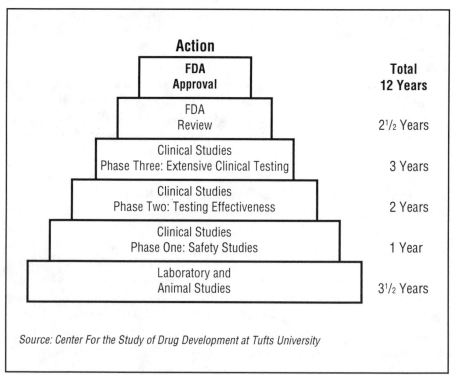

Action	Total
FDA Approval	**12 Years**
FDA Review	2¹/₂ Years
Clinical Studies Phase Three: Extensive Clinical Testing	3 Years
Clinical Studies Phase Two: Testing Effectiveness	2 Years
Clinical Studies Phase One: Safety Studies	1 Year
Laboratory and Animal Studies	3¹/₂ Years

Source: Center For the Study of Drug Development at Tufts University

Current regulations give the Center for Drug Evaluation and Research (CDER) 30 days in which to review an IND and decide whether the drug is sufficiently safe for clinical administration under the conditions outlined in the application. This review focuses primarily on three areas:

Pharmacology/Toxicology Review. The reviewing pharmacologist examines the results of animal pharmacology and toxicology testing, and attempts to relate these results to potential effects in humans.

Chemistry Review. The reviewing chemist evaluates both the chemical nature of the compound and the sponsor's manufacturing processes and control procedures to ensure that the compound is reproducible and is stable in its pure form. If a drug is either unstable or not reproducible, then the validity of any clinical testing would be undermined and, more importantly, the studies may pose significant risks.

Clinical Review. The reviewing medical officer, generally a physician, evaluates the clinical protocols to ensure: (1) that subjects will not be exposed to unreasonable and significant risks during clinical trials; and (2) that Phase 2 and Phase 3 trials (generally not submitted in the initial IND filing) are adequate in design to provide scientifically valid data.

If the FDA does not contact the applicant within 30 days of the IND submission, the sponsor may initiate clinical trials. In this way, the FDA never approves an IND, but allows clinical testing to proceed through its silence.

When the FDA decides that a certain clinical trial should be delayed, the agency contacts the sponsor within the 30-day period to initiate what is called a "clinical hold"—the delay of the clinical trial until potential problems or unanswered questions are addressed. Aside from the conditions mentioned above, the FDA may issue a clinical hold for several reasons, including the following:

- the IND does not contain sufficient information to assess the risks of using the subject drug in clinical trials;

- the clinical investigators named in the IND are not qualified by reason of their training and experience to conduct the investigation described in the IND; or

- the investigator's brochure—an information package designed to inform each investigator about the drug and its benefits and risks—is misleading, erroneous, or materially incomplete.

Clinical Trials

Clinical trials are clearly the most critical and demanding stage in the drug development process. If the drug survives the rigors of clinical testing, the FDA's ultimate approval decision will be based primarily upon data derived from these studies—the agency estimates that as much as 80 percent of the average NDA consists of clinical data and analyses alone.

Naturally, the FDA has much tighter standards regarding the conditions under which new drugs are shipped for and used in clinical investigations. The principal restrictions facing an IND holder are fairly straightforward: an investigational drug may be shipped and supplied only to those clinical investigators detailed in an IND for use exclusively in those experiments described in the clinical protocols section of the application or in IND amendments subsequently submitted to the FDA. In addition, sponsors and other parties involved in the clinical investigation must conform to standards commonly known as Good Clinical Practices (GCP), which are designed to protect the rights of the patients and the integrity of the clinical data.

Generally, clinical studies begin and proceed cautiously. As long as the results are favorable, an investigational drug is tested in progressively larger population groups and, in some cases, over longer periods and in higher doses. Although there is no statute or regulation that mandates a specific clinical trial structure and design, a clinical drug development program most often proceeds in at least three stages, or phases:

Phase 1: The cautious use of a drug in a few patients or normal human volunteers—20 to 80 patients—to gain basic safety and pharmacological information. Specifically, these pharmacology studies help the sponsor to determine toxicity, metabolism, absorption, elimination, and other pertinent pharmacological actions, and to find a preferred route of administration and safe dosage range. The FDA estimates that Phase 1 studies last an average of six months to a year.

Phase 2: The use of the compound in a small number of subjects—100 to 200 patients—who suffer from the condition that the drug is intended to treat or diagnose. Phase 2 trials give additional safety data, and provide the first indication of a drug's clinical effectiveness in its proposed use.

Phase 3: Use of the drug in a significantly larger group of subjects who suffer from the condition that the drug is proposed to treat or diagnose. Phase 3 trials are designed to assess a drug's safety and effectiveness and to help determine the best dosage in a larger and more varied patient population. The trials may involve several hundred to several thousand patients enrolled at several sites, and may include both controlled and uncontrolled studies. Because certain Phase 3 trials, called "pivotal" trials, will serve as the primary basis for the drug's approval, these studies must meet more rigorous standards.

The type and amount of clinical testing needed for new drugs can differ significantly. A sponsor seeking approval for a drug for which there exists relevant foreign clinical data may, under certain conditions, use this information to circumvent the need for much—in some cases, all—of the newly developed clinical data.

The dire need for therapies for AIDS, cancer, and other illnesses compelled the FDA to develop alternative models for clinical drug development. For medicines designed to treat life-threatening and severely debilitating illnesses, the agency works closely with sponsors to develop compressed Phase 2/3 trials designed to serve as the basis for the product's approval. In a December 1992 regulation, the agency announced its willingness to approve drugs for serious and life-threatening illnesses based on "surrogate endpoints," whose therapeutic relevance can then be verified through mandatory postmarketing clinical studies.

Throughout all clinical phases, sponsors generally maintain close communications with the FDA through periodic update reports and meetings. When not discontinued due to unfavorable results, clinical testing of a single drug is a complex and costly multi-year project. According to FDA estimates, clinical drug development programs consume an average of five years, but range from two to ten years.

The New Drug Application

The NDA is the vehicle through which drug sponsors obtain FDA authorization to market a new pharmaceutical in interstate commerce. In the NDA, the sponsor proposes that a compound be approved, and uses clinical data, nonclinical data, and other information to show that the drug is safe and effective for the proposed indication.

Although an NDA may consist of as many as 15 distinct sections, the core of any application consists of the nonclinical and clinical data on the drug's safety and effectiveness, and a full description of the methods, facilities, and quality controls employed in the product's manufacture and packaging.

FDA initiatives in the early 1990s brought several subtle changes to, and some further agency clarification of, NDA content and submission requirements: (1) NDAs must include certifications that the sponsor did not and will not use the services of any person that has been debarred by the FDA; (2) sponsors must submit a "field" copy of the NDA to their "home" district offices, and must certify in the NDA that they have done so; (3) applicants must include certain information about the batches of the drug product used to conduct the "pivotal" bioavailability and bioequivalence studies and the "primary" drug stability studies; and (4) NDAs must include analyses of drug effects in key demographic groups, including gender, age, and racial groups.

The NDA Review Process

The length of the FDA's NDA review process has been, for many years, perhaps the most contentious issue between the agency and regulated industry. Recognizing the need to reduce approval times, the FDA has promoted the use of computer-assisted new drug applications (CANDA), and encouraged its divisions to experiment with other innovative drug review methods in recent years.

Although such efforts have proven successful in many cases, none stands to affect the drug review process as fundamentally as the Prescription Drug User Fee Act of 1992. Under the provisions of this landmark statute, the FDA agreed to fulfill a series of aggressive new review goals, beginning with NDAs submitted in fiscal year (FY) 1994 (October 1993 to September 1994). To provide the agency with the resources to meet these goals, the pharmaceutical industry agreed to pay fees for each NDA and certain NDA supplements, and to pay annual fees for manufacturing facilities and marketed products. With revenues generated from these fees, CDER will hire an estimated 300 new staffers, and will make other investments designed to help speed drug reviews.

Obviously, this legislation has many implications for the drug review process and the FDA's own practices and standards. For example, the FDA repeatedly has warned the pharmaceutical industry that the quality of NDAs must improve and that the agency must apply its NDA refusal-to-file (RTF) criteria more consistently and rigorously if the review goals are to be met. Even without the influence of the user-fee legislation, annual CDER RTF decisions—under which deficient NDAs are returned to sponsors before a substantive review is initiated—more than doubled from 1990 to 1992. However, more recent data suggest that CDER may have used RTF less frequently in 1993.

NDAs are forwarded to one of CDER's ten drug review divisions—specifically, the division that handles the therapeutic area relevant to the submission. Within 45 days of the NDA's submission, FDA reviewers—including the lead medical, chemistry, and pharmacology reviewers—will meet to determine if the application is sufficiently complete for a full review. NDAs that meet minimum submission criteria are "filed" or accepted for review, while the FDA issues RTF decisions for deficient applications, which are returned to their sponsors.

Once the review team decides that an NDA is fileable, it begins the "primary" review of the application. During this evaluation, each member of the review team sifts through volumes of research data and information applicable to his or her expertise:

Clinical Reviewer: Evaluates the data from, and analyses of, clinical studies to determine if the drug is safe and effective in its proposed use(s).

Pharmacology/Toxicology Reviewer: Evaluates the entire body of nonclinical data and analyses, with a particular focus on the newly submitted long-term test data, to identify relevant implications for the drug's clinical safety.

Chemistry Reviewer: Evaluates commercial-stage manufacturing procedures (e.g., method of synthesis or isolation, purification process, and process controls), and the specifications and analytical methods used to assure the identity, strength, purity, and bioavailability of the drug product.

Statistical Reviewer: Evaluates the pivotal clinical data to determine if there exists statistically significant evidence of the drug's safety and effectiveness, the appropriateness of the sponsor's clinical data analyses and the assumptions under which these analyses were used, the statistical significance of newly submitted nonclinical data, and the implications of stability data for establishing appropriate expiration dating for the product.

Biopharmaceutics Reviewer: Evaluates pharmacokinetics and bioavailability data to establish appropriate drug dosing.

The filing decision also triggers a division request that FDA field offices conduct what is called a preapproval inspection of the sponsor's manufacturing facilities. During such inspections, FDA investigators inspect a sponsor's production facilities to audit sponsor statements and commitments made in the NDA against actual manufacturing practices employed by the sponsor. Ultimately, the FDA wants to conduct preapproval inspections within 45 days of the FDA's acceptance of an NDA for filing. As of this writing, however, preapproval inspections are, on average, being conducted six or seven months after the filing decision is reached.

During the drug review process, the FDA may seek advice and comment from one of its 15 prescription drug advisory committees. When called upon, these expert committees provide the agency with independent, non-binding advice and recommendations.

Under the user-fee program, the FDA must "act on" 55 percent of NDAs submitted in FY-1994 within 12 months. The agency can fulfill this requirement by issuing any one of three "action letters"—either an approval, approvable, or not-approvable letter. While an approval letter means that the drug has been formally approved for marketing, an approvable letter will most likely indicate that the sponsor must make minor revisions or submissions to the NDA and probably submit final printed labeling before marketing authorization is granted. A not-approvable letter states that the NDA cannot be approved, and identifies the relevant deficiencies.

Chapter 2:

Nonclinical Drug Testing

by Anne G. Evans, D.V.M.

For most new molecular entities (NME) and other drugs whose clinical safety and efficacy have not been established previously, preclinical *in vitro* and *in vivo* animal testing represents the first major step toward regulatory approval. According to some estimates, only one in every 1,000 compounds studied in preclinical testing progresses beyond this phase. Preclinical screening and testing will show that the remaining compounds are unsafe, are poorly absorbed, lack pharmacological activity, or have some other flaw that makes them unworthy of further development.

For those drugs that are researched further, animal studies play several roles in drug development. First, the studies provide the basic toxicological and pharmacological information needed to obtain the FDA's permission to begin clinical trials. While the FDA's decision to approve a new pharmaceutical for marketing is based largely on the results of clinical studies, the agency will not allow an entirely unknown and uncharacterized compound to be administered to human subjects. Before clinical work begins, the agency requires that the drug be administered to, and its short-term effects be studied in, laboratory animals. The FDA uses data from these studies to decide if the drug is sufficiently safe for initial administration to humans.

Once clinical trials begin, further *in vitro* and *in vivo* animal studies provide information essential to the continued clinical use and, ultimately, the approval of the drug (see exhibit below). Long-term and specialized animal tests are needed to support the safety of testing the compound in larger patient populations and over longer periods. These tests also allow researchers to evaluate effects that are impractical or unethical to study in humans, such as drug effects over an entire animal life span, effects over several generations of species, and effects on pregnancy and reproduction.

Although nonclinical research results are imperfect predictors of clinical responses, laboratory animals remain the best practical experimental models for identifying and measuring a compound's biological activity, and for predicting the drug's clinical effects (because animal studies are performed before and during clinical studies, the term "nonclinical" generally is preferable to "preclinical" when discussing the full spectrum of *in vitro* and non-human *in vivo* tests associated with drug development). By studying a drug's dose-response characteristics, adverse and residual effects, and mechanism, site, degree, and duration of action, drug sponsors and the FDA gain valuable insights on the compound's probable action and effects in humans.

The FDA plays at least three principal roles in the nonclinical testing of drugs:

- the agency determines, sometimes on a case-by-case basis, what nonclinical test data are needed to show that a drug is sufficiently safe for initial and continued testing in humans;

- the agency, when asked, provides advice to drug sponsors on the adequacy of nonclinical testing programs developed for specific drugs before the animal studies are initiated; and

- the agency sets minimum standards for laboratories conducting nonclinical toxicity testing through good laboratory practice (GLP) regulations (see Chapter 3).

FDA Guidance on Nonclinical Testing Requirements

Until fairly recently, FDA nonclinical testing requirements were described only in very general terms in two now outdated guidelines, one published in 1968 by the FDA and the other in 1977 by the U.S. Pharmaceutical Manufacturers Association (PMA). In the late 1980s and early 1990s, FDA

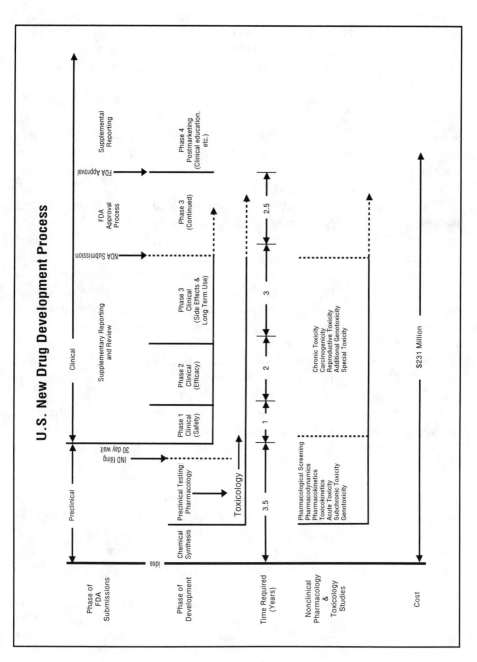

U.S. New Drug Development Process

toxicologists and pharmacologists were developing several guidance documents to address subjects ranging from animal-testing requirements for specific classes of drugs to the use of computer technology for nonclinical data submissions.

Concurrent with the FDA's efforts to produce guidance in this area, the European Community (EC) and Japan were developing testing standards that were often similar in principle but different in detail. In an effort to harmonize these and other testing standards, the regulatory authorities and pharmaceutical industries of these three regions organized the International Conferences on Harmonization (ICH).

The harmonization initiative has had fundamental effects on the agency's own efforts to develop recommendations for nonclinical testing. Most importantly, the FDA has sought to revise its guidelines to reflect the consensus to which the agency has contributed as part of the ICH process.

The ICH process and its effects on the FDA's efforts will continue for some time. By early 1994, the FDA had accepted harmonized recommendations on acute toxicity testing and the duration of chronic toxicity testing in rodents, as well as a harmonized guideline on reproductive toxicity studies. However, final ICH guidelines on toxicokinetic studies, genotoxicity testing, and dose selection for carcinogenicity studies were not expected before 1994 or 1995. The following discussion analyzes the specific effects the ICH process is expected to have on FDA nonclinical testing requirements.

FDA officials are always careful to stress the limitations of guidelines, no matter how current. As with any guidelines, the agency's nonclinical guidelines are designed only to provide general direction for typical situations; they cannot be applied universally to all drugs and all situations. Therefore, the FDA remains willing to advise sponsors, particularly about unusual cases. FDA staffers will discuss nonclinical testing strategies during the development of these plans, but can usually offer more useful insights if a sponsor develops a nonclinical study program and submits the plan for agency review. Recommendations obtained from such reviews supplement drug sponsors' own expertise, and the more general suggestions provided by FDA and ICH guidelines.

Whether or not a sponsor chooses to initiate a dialogue with FDA reviewers, the types and amount of nonclinical testing ultimately required by the agency will depend on several factors, including:

- a drug's chemical structure, and the similarity of that structure to existing compounds with safety profiles known to the FDA;

- a drug's proposed use in humans;

- a drug's target patient population (e.g., elderly, infants, women, etc.);

- special characteristics of a drug's use pattern (e.g., if a drug is likely to be prescribed as a concomitant medication);

- a drug's proposed route of administration; and

- a drug's proposed duration of administration (i.e., whether for chronic or short-term use).

Types of Nonclinical Studies

When drug sponsors initiate a nonclinical testing program, their first goal is to conduct the studies and collect the data necessary to support the safety of early clinical trials. In the past, these data generally have been limited to short-term animal test results. Today, however, *in vitro* and *in vivo* genotoxicity testing is assuming greater importance during the preclinical phase.

As stated above, preclinical studies represent only part of a drug's nonclinical development. The comprehensive nonclinical testing program needed to support marketing approval for most new drugs involves years of work and several different types of studies. For the purpose of analysis, nonclinical testing is often divided into two areas: pharmacology and toxicology. Together, pharmacology and toxicology studies are designed to provide an integrated overview of a drug's effects in various animal species.

Pharmacology Studies   Because insights gained from pharmacological studies—particularly those regarding adverse effects—can influence the direction of later toxicological testing, pharmacologic work is generally conducted first.

Pharmacological Screening. The pharmacological study of a new drug proceeds in phases. The first phase, pharmacological screening, is really part of the drug discovery process. It involves the use of *in vitro* and *in vivo* assays designed to determine if a compound has any pharmacological activity. Hundreds of compounds may be subjected to these screenings, with those exhibiting measurable pharmacological effects being selected as "lead chemicals" (i.e., substances to be tested further).

Pharmacodynamics. Once a lead chemical is selected, the sponsor generally begins to compile a more complete qualitative and quantitative pharmacological profile of the compound. This profile consists primarily of pharmacodynamic studies, which provide an indication of the drug's action on various receptors or physiological systems in animals.

Pharmacodynamic studies should be sufficiently extensive to determine dose-response relationships and the drug's duration and mechanism of action. Researchers explore the drug's effects on major physiological systems and activities (i.e., neurologic, cardiovascular, respiratory, gastrointestinal, genitourinary, endocrine, anti-inflammatory, immunoreactive, chemotherapeutic, and enzymatic). Studies are designed to investigate all primary and secondary effects related or unrelated to the desired therapeutic effect, extensions of the therapeutic effect that might produce toxicity at higher doses, and effects related to interactions with other drugs.

Pharmacokinetics. The pharmacology component of preclinical development also includes pharmacokinetic testing, which is designed to obtain information on the extent and duration of systemic exposure to the drug. Generally, these studies are performed in multiple species. The results are then compared to identify species-to-species drug-response differences that might affect later nonclinical and clinical studies or their interpretation. Today, these data are considered to be a much more important aspect of preclinical drug development than they were previously, and serve as the basis for subsequent toxicokinetic assessments (see discussion on toxicity studies below).

Pharmacokinetic studies are designed to yield information about the drug's absorption, distribution, metabolism, and excretion (ADME) pattern. Analytical methodology employed to generate these data may include ultraviolet absorption, fluorescence, high-pressure liquid chromatography, gas chromatography, radioimmunoassay, and mass spectrometry analysis of parent and/or major metabolites in tissues or fluids.

Absorption studies generally involve serial determinations of drug concentration in blood and urine after dosing to indicate the rate and extent of absorption (e.g., following oral administration). Typically, studies using the intravenous route are conducted to serve as a reference. Common pharmacokinetic parameters employed in these assessments include plasma area under the curve (AUC), maximum (peak) plasma concentration (C_{max}), and plasma concentration at a specified time after administration of a given dose ($C_{(time)}$). Bioavailability (i.e., the amount of drug that reaches the systemic circulation) is dependent, in part, on the extent of absorption, but is also influenced by other factors such as the extent of a drug's metabolism by the liver before it enters the general circulation.

Distribution studies provide information on the extent and time course of tissue accumulation and the elimination of a drug and/or its metabolites. Distribution patterns can be assessed by sacrificing animals at predetermined intervals after dosing, and then measuring the concentration of the drug and/or its metabolites in selected tissues. The "volume of distribution" represents another parameter that is useful in assessing drug distribution. The volume of distribution relates the amount of drug in the body to the concentration of drug in the blood or plasma. For drugs that are extensively bound to plasma proteins but not to tissue components, the volume of distribution will approach that of the plasma volume.

The assessment and quantification of a drug's metabolic pattern is essential for a complete understanding of efficacy and toxicity, since species differences in toxicity may be related to differences in metabolism. To assess the metabolic profile of a drug, the concentration of the drug and its major metabolites are measured in plasma, urine, feces, bile, and/or other tissues as a function of time following dose administration. In some cases, toxicological testing of pharmacologically active metabolites may be necessary in addition to testing on the drug itself.

"Clearance" is a measure of an organism's ability to eliminate a drug. This concept represents the rate of a drug's elimination in relation to its concentration (CL = Rate of elimination/C). This excretion parameter can be determined for individual organs and when added together will equal total systemic clearance. In general, decreased toxic potential is associated with rapid and complete excretion.

Toxicity Studies   *In vitro* and *in vivo* animal toxicity studies are undertaken to identify and measure a drug's short- and long-term functional and morphologic effects. Depending on the nature of a drug, its intended use, and the extent of its proposed study in clinical trials, a toxicity testing program may consist of some or all of the following elements:

- acute toxicity studies;

- subacute or subchronic toxicity studies;

- chronic toxicity studies;

- carcinogenicity studies;

- special toxicity studies;

- reproductive toxicity studies;

- genotoxicity studies; and

- toxicokinetic studies.

Because many of the ongoing ICH initiatives focus on toxicity testing, drug sponsors are advised to keep abreast of harmonization developments and subsequent regulatory changes as they affect these types of studies in particular.

Acute Toxicity Studies. Acute (single dose) toxicity studies are designed to measure the short-term effects of a drug when administered in a single dose, or in multiple doses during a period not exceeding 24 hours. Results from acute toxicity studies should provide information on the following:

- the appropriate dosage for multiple dose studies;

- the potential target organs of toxicity;

- the time-course of drug-induced clinical observations;

- species-specific differences in toxicity; and

- the potential for acute toxicity in humans.

To determine initial toxicity levels, researchers should study the investigational drug in at least two mammalian species, including a non-rodent species when reasonable. These studies should involve dosages that are intended to cause no adverse effects and those intended to cause major (life-threatening) toxicity. The route(s) of administration should include an intravenous route and the route intended for human administration. When intravenous dosing is proposed in humans, use of this route alone in animal testing is sufficient. The animals are then observed for 14 days after drug administration.

The FDA indicates that investigators need to obtain more than just mortality data from acute toxicity studies. At a minimum, researchers should observe and record test animals' clinical signs, and the time of onset, the duration, and the reversibility of toxicity. Gross necropsies should be performed on all animals.

In the past, one type of data derived from acute toxicity studies was the drug's "lethal dose" (LD). LD_{50}, which is calculated using a specific statistical formula, represents the dosage level that kills 50 percent of the test animals. In recent years, the value of the "classic" LD_{50} has been widely criticized for ethical and scientific reasons. In accordance with ICH recommendations for single dose toxicity testing, the FDA no longer requires or recommends that sponsors determine the "classic" LD_{50}. The LD_{50} has been replaced by single-dose administration, increasing dose tolerance studies that measure toxic response as a function of dose. When relevant, major and pharmacologically significant metabolites should be tested in acute toxicity studies. The tests, which replace the determination of LD_{50}, should employ a testing protocol that maximizes the amount of information that can be derived from the smallest number of animals.

As of this writing, the FDA had adopted these ICH recommendations and was preparing to publish its *Guidance on Acute Toxicity Testing*. The new guidance document indicates that acute toxicity studies, when appropriately designed and conducted, may provide the primary safety data to support single–dose pharmacokinetic studies in humans, although nonclinical studies of this nature will require a more comprehensive study design. Clinical pathology, histopathology, and pharmacokinetic data may also prove useful, as might data necessary to assess dose-response relationships. These studies will help sponsors develop a more comprehensive characterization of adverse effects.

Subacute or Subchronic Studies. Subacute, or subchronic, toxicity testing allows investigators to evaluate a drug's toxic potential and pathologic effects over a longer period. These studies range from 14 to 90 days, with the duration generally dependent on the proposed term of clinical use and the duration of proposed clinical trials.

Subacute studies are designed to assess the progression and regression of drug-induced lesions. However, the studies are generally of insufficient duration to identify all secondary effects that may arise during chronic toxicity and carcinogenicity testing.

Typically, the test compound is administered daily to at least one rodent and one non-rodent species at three or more dosage levels. The highest dose used in these studies should be selected to deliberately induce toxic reactions. The lowest dosage should be selected to identify a no-observed-effect level (NOEL) and, when possible, should represent a multiple of the projected average daily clinical dosage. Additionally, each study should employ appropriate control groups (i.e., untreated, vehicle, positive, comparative). During such studies, researchers should collect the following data, as appropriate, for the specific test compound:

- observed effects;

- mortality;

- body weight;

- food/water consumption;

- physical examinations;

- hematology/bone marrow/coagulation;

- blood chemistry/urinalysis;

- organ weights;

- gross pathology; and

- histopathology.

Chronic Toxicity Testing. Chronic toxicity studies, which are tests of 180 days in duration or longer, are intended to determine the following:

- the potential risk in relation to the anticipated dose and period of drug treatment;

- the nature of drug toxicity;

- the no-observed-effect level (NOEL);

- the no-adverse (toxic)-effect level (NOAEL) (i.e., that dose demonstrating only pharmacological effects); and

- the maximum tolerated dose (MTD) (i.e., the dose just high enough to elicit signs of minimal toxicity without significantly altering the animal's normal life span due to effects other than carcinogenicity).

The FDA generally requires that sponsors conduct these studies in one rodent (usually rat) and one non-rodent (usually dog) species for both chronic-use drugs and for drugs intended for intermittent use where the total cumulative lifetime exposure may exceed three months. Because there is flexibility in this requirement, sponsors should consult the relevant review division for a product-specific assessment.

In accordance with an ICH consensus, the FDA has reduced its recommended maximum duration of chronic toxicity studies in rodents from 12 to 6 months. However, the agency continues to recommend 12-month studies when rodent carcinogenicity bioassays are not performed as part of the drug toxicity profile.

The duration of non-rodent studies remains 12 months, although the adequacy of 6-month toxicity studies in non-rodents was considered by ICH and was subsequently offered for comment as a proposal by the FDA. When an FDA reviewing division concludes that data from longer studies may not contribute significantly to risk-benefit analyses, non-rodent studies of 6 months or less may be appropriate for drugs with certain indications. In early 1994, the FDA was preparing to release a *Statement on the Duration of Chronic Toxicity Studies in Rodents and Non-rodents*.

Dose selection criteria are similar to those described for subacute and subchronic studies, and must reflect the results of range-finding studies, structure-activity relationships, pharmacology studies, and pharmacokinetic data. Interim sacrifice subgroups are typically included. As specified above for subacute and subchronic studies, researchers must collect the data listed, as appropriate, for the drug under investigation.

Chronic studies are often initiated when Phase 2 trials provide indications of a drug's effectiveness, and are conducted concurrently with Phase 3 trials. Data obtained from chronic toxicity tests may be used to support the safety of late-phase clinical trials and, ultimately, the approval of the drug for general marketing.

Carcinogenicity Studies. As are chronic toxicity studies, carcinogenicity studies are generally required for any drug intended for chronic use, and for drugs intended for intermittent use where the total cumulative lifetime exposure may exceed three months. The FDA generally requires carcinogenicity studies of two years in both the mouse and the rat.

Ideally, the route of administration selected for these studies should be the intended clinical route. When there is more than one route or there is a change in the proposed clinical route, the carcinogenicity test route should be that which provides the greatest systemic exposure. Similar to chronic toxicity studies, carcinogenicity investigations are not usually initiated until a drug shows some indication of effectiveness in Phase 2 clinical trials.

Carcinogenicity testing has been discussed as part of the ICH initiative. As stated in ICH proceedings, "...a carcinogenicity study is one of the most resource-consuming in terms of animals and time. In the interests of decreased animal use and protection, but without prejudicing safety, such studies should only be performed once.... This could be achieved through harmonisation of the requirements of different regulatory systems."

A *Draft Consensus Text on Carcinogenicity: Guidance for Dose Selection for Carcinogenicity Studies of Therapeutics* is now under review by the three ICH participants. As stated in this document, the doses selected should provide exposures "to the agent that (1) allow an adequate margin of safety over the human therapeutic exposure, (2) are tolerated without significant chronic physiological dysfunction and are compatible with good survival, (3) are guided by a comprehensive set of animal and human data that focuses on the properties of the agent and the suitability of the animal, (4) and permit data interpretation in the context of clinical use."

The guidance proposes that any one of several approaches may be appropriate for dose selection in carcinogenicity studies: (1) pharmacodynamic endpoints; (2) toxicity-based endpoints; (3) pharmacokinetic endpoints; (4) saturation of absorption; and (5) maximum feasible dose. In all cases, appropriate dose-ranging studies are necessary.

In the United States, dose selection based on the MTD has been the only acceptable practice. Because the approaches for dose selection proposed by ICH are under discussion within the FDA, sponsors should ask the agency for an assessment of appropriate dose selection criteria for individual cases. The threat of additional revisions to recommended study designs, as well as the expense associated with this aspect of nonclinical testing, should also motivate sponsors to obtain specific FDA guidance before initiating carcinogenicity studies. CDER offers consultation on dose selection and study design issues for carcinogenicity studies through the work of the Carcinogenicity Assessment Committee.

Special Toxicity Studies. Special toxicity studies include those studies appropriate for a particular formulation or route of administration (e.g., parenteral or topical irritation studies, *in vitro* hemolysis, etc.), and studies conducted in a particular animal model relevant to a human disease or age. As of this writing, formal FDA guidance pertaining to special toxicity testing is limited to a brief discussion provided in the FDA's *Guideline for the Format and Content of the Nonclinical Pharmacology/Toxicology Section of an Application.* Therefore, sponsors should ask the relevant CDER review division if special toxicity testing is considered applicable. Special toxicity testing is not currently a topic under consideration by ICH.

Reproductive Toxicity Studies. The FDA requires reproductive testing for any drug to be used in women of childbearing potential, regardless of whether the target population is pregnant women. Generally, these studies have been conducted in a three-segment testing protocol previously recommended by the FDA: (1) Segment I—fertility and general reproductive performance (involving the study of both the male and female rat); (2) Segment II—teratology (conducted in the rat and the rabbit); and (3) Segment III—perinatal and postnatal development (conducted in the rat to evaluate drug effects during the last third of pregnancy and the period of lactation).

In an effort to reduce differences in reproductive toxicity requirements between the EC, Japan, and the United States, the participating parties adopted an ICH *Harmonized Tripartite Guideline* in June 1993. As stated in the guideline, which was published in the *Federal Register,* "the aim of reproductive toxicity studies is to reveal any effect of one or more active substances(s) on mammalian reproduction." Therefore, the combination of studies selected should "allow exposure of mature adults and all stages of development from conception to sexual maturity." The integrated sequence of testing has been segregated into the following stages: (A) premating to conception; (B) conception to implantation; (C) implantation to closure of the hard palate; (D) closure of the hard palate to the end of pregnancy; (E) birth to weaning; and (F) weaning to sexual maturity.

The guideline suggests that the "most probable" option for investigating reproductive toxicity is a three-study design:

- Fertility and embryonic development. This study comprises stages A and B, and is conducted in at least one species, preferably the rat. Assessments should include maturation of gametes, mating behavior, fertility, preimplantation stages of the embryo, and implantation. In particular, sponsors should note that, in contrast to the previous Segment I study, this study design uses a histological evaluation of testes, epididymis, and sperm counts to assess drug effects on male fertility.

- Pre- and post-natal development, including maternal development. This phase comprises stages C to F, and is conducted in at least one species, preferably the rat. The study is designed to detect adverse effects on the pregnant/lactating female, and on the development of the conceptus and the offspring following exposure of the female from implantation through weaning. Assessments should include toxicity relative to that in nonpregnant females, pre- and postnatal death of offspring, altered growth and development, and functional deficits (e.g., behavior, maturation, and reproduction) in offspring.

- Embryo-fetal development. This study comprises stages C to D, and is usually conducted in two species: a rodent (preferably the rat) and non-rodent (preferably the rabbit). The goal is to detect adverse effects on the pregnant female and the development of the embryo and the fetus consequent to exposure of the female from implantation to closure of the hard palate. Researchers should assess toxicity relative to that in nonpregnant females, embryo-fetal death, and altered growth, including structural changes.

Genotoxicity Studies. Also referred to as "mutagenicity studies," genotoxicity studies (now the preferred term) are used to assess a drug's potential to induce cancer (i.e., somatic cell mutation) and/or heritable defects (i.e., germ cell mutation). These short-term studies include a battery of mammalian and non-mammalian, *in vitro* and *in vivo* tests designed to detect a compound's ability to cause an increase in genetic alterations (e.g., primary DNA damage, chromosomal aberrations). Although genotoxicity tests are not, at present, specifically listed by the FDA as requirements or described in an agency guideline, these screening tests are strongly recommended by the FDA, and are required by both the EC and Japan. FDA advice on genotoxicity studies is limited to a brief discussion on the appropriate tabulation and the order of study presentation in the agency's *Guideline for the Format and Content of the Nonclinical Pharmacology/Toxicology Section of an Application.*

The ICH is considering genotoxicity testing as a topic, and an ICH working group has written a draft position paper that addresses 11 issues relating to the protocols and the battery of tests appropriate for routine genotoxicity testing. Included among these issues is a definition of a minimal test battery, and a discussion of the timing of genotoxicity tests in relation to Phase 1 studies. This draft position paper will form the basis for an ICH harmonized guideline, and is expected to be reviewed by the ICH parties in 1994.

Sponsors should anticipate FDA adoption of the final tripartite harmonized guideline on genotoxicity testing.

Pending harmonization, however, the FDA recommends that sponsors conduct the battery of tests described in the draft revision of the FDA's *Toxicological Principles for the Safety Assessment of Direct Food Additives and Color Additives Used in Food* (Redbook). As of this writing, the genotoxicity tests recommended by the FDA include: (1) gene mutations in *Salmonella typhimurium*; (2) gene mutation in mammalian cells *in vitro*; and (3) cytogenetic damage *in vivo*. The Ames test is used to evaluate gene mutations in *S. typhimurium*. The *in vitro* mutation assay should employ a cell line(s) capable of measuring single gene point mutations, frame-shift mutations, and chromosomal mutations. To satisfy these criteria, the FDA recommends the use of the mouse lymphoma mutation assay. Alternatively, data from other *in vitro* mammalian cell tests, which detect both site-specific and chromosome mutations, are acceptable. The *in vivo* cytogenetic assay should provide concurrent detection of micronuclei and chromosome aberrations in the mouse bone marrow, although data from either mouse micronucleus or chromosome aberration tests using mouse or rat bone marrow are acceptable.

Toxicokinetic Studies. Toxicokinetics is defined "as the generation of pharmacokinetic data as an integral component in the conduct of nonclinical toxicity studies or in ancillary studies. These data may be used in the interpretation of toxicological findings and their relevance to clinical safety issues." A draft *Note for Guidance* and a draft *Consensus Text* addressing these studies are now being reviewed by the regulatory authorities of the three ICH parties.

As stated in ICH's *Note for Guidance on Toxicokinetics*, the primary objective of toxicokinetics is to describe the systemic exposure achieved in animals and its relationship to the dose level and the time course of the toxicity study. Secondary objectives are:

- to relate the exposure achieved in toxicity studies to toxicological findings, and to assist in the assessment of the findings' relevance to clinical safety;

- to support the selection of species and the treatment regimen in nonclinical toxicity studies; and

- to provide information that, in conjunction with the toxicity findings, contributes to the design of subsequent nonclinical toxicity studies.

These objectives may be achieved by deriving pharmacokinetic parameters from measurements made at appropriate time points during the course of the individual studies. Relevant measurements usually consist of plasma (or whole blood or serum) concentrations for the parent compound and/or its metabolite(s). For some compounds, it may be more appropriate to calculate exposure based on the concentration not bound to plasma proteins. Plasma AUC, C_{max}, and $C_{(time)}$ are the most commonly used parameters in assessing exposure in toxicokinetic studies, although studies involving measurements of organ tissue or urine drug levels may be advisable instead of or in addition to plasma measurements. Toxicokinetic studies should be selected on a case-by-case basis, and should be designed to provide information that may be integrated into the full spectrum of nonclinical toxicity testing and then compared to human data.

As of this writing, formal FDA guidance on toxicokinetics was limited to a brief discussion of ADME studies provided in the agency's *Guideline for the Format and Content of the Nonclinical Pharmacology/Toxicology Section of an Application.* The draft ICH *Toxicokinetic Guidelines*, which provide greater detail on the selection and design of appropriate toxicokinetic studies, will be finalized by the end of 1994.

References

Food and Drug Administration. Draft revised "Toxicological principles for the safety assessment of direct food additives and color additives used in food (Redbook)," 1993.

Food and Drug Administration. Guidance on acute toxicity testing (draft). Food and Drug Administration, Washington D.C., provided Jan.7, 1994.

Food and Drug Administration. FDA statement on the duration of chronic toxicity studies in rodents and non-rodents. Food and Drug Administration, Washington D.C., provided Jan. 7, 1994.

Food and Drug Administration. Guideline for the format and content of the nonclinical/pharmacology/toxicology section of an application. U.S. Department of Health and Human Services, Public Health Services, Food and Drug Administration, Washington D.C., 1987.

Food and Drug Administration. International conference on harmonization: Draft guideline on detection of toxicity to reproduction for medicinal products: Availability. Federal Register. 1993; 58:21074-21080.

Food and Drug Administration. US FDA's proposed implementation of ICH safety working group consensus regarding new drug applications: Availability. Federal Register. 1992; 57:13105.

International Conference on Harmonisation. Draft consensus text on carcinogenicity: Guidance for dose selection for carcinogenicity studies of therapeutics. The second international conference on harmonisation. Orlando, Florida, Oct. 27, 1993.

International Conference on Harmonisation. Draft consensus text on toxicokinetics: Guidance for repeated dose tissue distribution studies. The second international conference on harmonisation. Orlando, Florida, Oct. 27, 1993.

International Conference on Harmonisation. Draft position paper on genotoxicity. The second international conference on harmonisation. Orlando, Florida, Oct. 27–29, 1993.

International Conference on Harmonisation. ICH harmonised tripartite guideline: Detection of toxicity to reproduction for medicinal products. The second international conference on harmonisation. ICH Steering Committee. June 24, 1993.

International Conference on Harmonisation. Note for guidance on toxicokinetics: The assessment of systemic exposure in toxicity studies. The second international conference on harmonisation. Orlando, Florida, Oct. 27, 1993.

International Conference on Harmonisation. Proceedings of the second international conference on harmonisation. Orlando, Florida, Oct. 27–29, 1993; 2, 9-11, 15.

Pharmaceutical Manufacturers Association. Pharmaceutical Manufacturers Association guideline for the assessment of drugs and medical device safety in animals. 1977; PMA, Washington, D.C.

Pharmaceutical Manufacturers Association. Reporter's handbook for the prescription drug industry. 1993.

Roberts SA. Overview and history of toxicology requirements. In: Pharmaceutical Manufacturers Association education and research institute pharmaceutical toxicology training course. Washington D.C., Nov. 14–17, 1993.

Roberts SA. Toxicology study design (range-finding to chronic). In: Pharmaceutical Manufacturers Association education and research institute pharmaceutical toxicology training course. Washington D.C., Nov. 14–17, 1993.

Taylor AS, Assistant Director for Pharmacology at CDER, FDA. Personal communication directed to A. Evans. Jan. 31, 1994.

Taylor AS, Assistant Director for Pharmacology at CDER, FDA. Personal communication directed to M. Mathieu. Nov. 5, 1993.

Chapter 3:

FDA Standards for Nonclinical Testing: Good Laboratory Practice (GLP)

Drug manufacturers are given a great degree of freedom during the preclinical screening and testing of new drugs. Provided that they do not violate the U.S. Animal Welfare Act and related laws, nonclinical laboratories at drug companies and private contractors are not restricted in their use of animals to screen and measure the activity of drug compounds.

However, when the sponsor begins to compile safety data for submission to the FDA, a set of standards called Good Laboratory Practice (GLP) apply. To ensure the quality of animal testing and the resultant data, the FDA requires that all key nonclinical laboratory studies designed to provide data for an IND or NDA meet GLP standards.

The FDA's GLP regulations, which were modified in October 1987 to ease the regulatory burden on nonclinical laboratories, specify requirements in the following areas:

- the organization and personnel of the laboratory conducting non-clinical studies, including the facility's management and the appointment of a study director and quality assurance unit;

- the physical structure and contents of the facility, including the calibration and maintenance of equipment;

- the facility's standard operating procedures and the protocol used for the study;

- safeguards used in the storage of test specimens and records; and

- methods used to record and communicate test results.

GLP: A Short History

GLP standards first became a requirement on June 20, 1979. They were the FDA's reaction to finding, in the mid-1970s, that some nonclinical studies submitted to support the safety of new drugs were not being conducted according to accepted standards. Because the FDA was basing important regulatory decisions on these data—specifically, whether clinical trials could be initiated or continued, or whether new drugs should be approved—the agency saw this as a serious problem.

After establishing the initial GLP regulations in 1979, the FDA's confidence in the work of preclinical laboratory facilities increased markedly. As a result, the agency revised its GLP regulations in October 1987 to reduce regulatory and paperwork burdens facing laboratories conducting animal studies.

The FDA's 1987 GLP regulations brought changes in such areas as quality assurance, protocol preparation, test and control article characterization, and specimen and sample retention. In virtually all cases, the changes were designed to ease GLP requirements.

The revisions in no way affected the scope of GLP regulations. GLP still applies to all "definitive" nonclinical safety studies, including key acute, subacute, chronic, reproduction, and carcinogenicity studies.

Preliminary pharmacological screenings and metabolism studies need not meet GLP standards. Initial pilot studies, such as dose-ranging, absorption, and excretion tests, are among those exempt from GLP requirements.

Significant deviations from GLP during the conduct of key studies can result in the rejection of nonclinical data (see discussion below). Repeated deviations by a drug sponsor can result in an FDA clinical hold order for an IND or the rejection of an NDA.

Major Provisions of GLP

The core provisions of GLP can be grouped into seven general areas:

- organization and personnel;

- testing facility;

- testing facility operation;

- test and control article characterization;

- the protocol and the conduct of the nonclinical laboratory study;

- records and reporting; and

- equipment design.

Organization and Personnel   GLP regulations address four areas of a nonclinical laboratory's organization and personnel: general personnel, testing facility management, the study director, and the quality assurance unit. While it establishes general requirements for the qualifications and responsibilities of personnel and management, this aspect of the GLP regulations focuses primarily upon the study director and quality assurance unit. It is worth noting, however, that the agency continues to scrutinize facility management's role in assessing how effective the study director and quality assurance unit are in addressing GLP compliance issues.

Study Director. GLP requires that the management of the testing facility conducting a nonclinical program designate a scientist or other professional to serve as the study director. This individual has overall responsibility for the "technical conduct of the study, as well as for the interpretation, analysis, documentation, and reporting of results...." The FDA does not require that the study director be technically competent in all areas of a study, however.

The study director and others involved in conducting and supervising animal experiments should possess the education, training, and experience necessary to perform their assigned functions. Current training, experience, and job-description profiles must be maintained for each of these individuals. These documented profiles must be stored by the facility and made available to the FDA if the agency has any questions about personnel qualifications.

Quality Assurance Unit. GLP also requires that each testing facility have at least a one-person quality assurance unit (QAU) that is directly responsible to facility management. The QAU monitors each study to "assure management that the facilities, equipment, personnel, methods, practices, records, and controls" are consistent with GLP.

To ensure that their evaluations are made objectively, QAU members may not be involved in any animal study that they are responsible for monitoring. However, the FDA has stated that the QAU does not necessarily have to be a separate entity or a permanently staffed unit. In addition, the agency does not require that the QAU be composed of individuals whose only duties are in quality assurance. Provided that quality assurance activities are separated from study direction and conduct activities, a trained and qualified person who works on one study can perform quality assurance duties on any other study in which he or she is not involved.

GLP regulations specify seven major QAU responsibilities, including record maintenance, study inspections, and developing reports for facility management. Current regulations require that the QAU inspect a nonclinical study at intervals the unit considers to be adequate to ensure the study's integrity. However, the FDA advises that each study, regardless of its length, be inspected in-process at least once, and that, across a series of studies, all phases be inspected to assure study integrity. At the conclusion of each study, the QAU ensures that the study was conducted under GLP.

Testing Facility   The laboratory facilities in which testing programs take place are also a primary focus of GLP. The regulations include detailed requirements for animal care and supply facilities, test substance handling areas, laboratory operations, specimen and data storage areas, administrative and personnel facilities, methods of dosage preparation, and test substance accountability. Facilities must maintain records indicating compliance with these requirements.

In general terms, a testing facility and its equipment must be of suitable size and construction to allow for the proper conduct of the nonclinical study.

Animal care areas, for example, must provide for the sufficient separation of species/test systems and individual projects, the isolation of animals, protection from outside disturbances, and routine or specialized animal housing. Regulated environmental controls for air quality (i.e., temperature, humidity, and air changes) and sanitation are needed as well.

Testing Facility Operation   Each laboratory must have, and base its operations upon, standard operating procedures (SOPs). SOPs, which are extensions of preclinical protocols in some respects, are written study methods or directions that laboratory management believes are adequate to ensure the quality and integrity of data obtained from animal tests. The description of research procedures provided by protocols and SOP documents makes it possible to verify and reconstruct studies.

The detailed written procedures contained in the SOPs must be maintained for all aspects of the study, including animal care, laboratory tests, data handling and storage, and equipment upkeep and calibration. Each laboratory area must have immediately available laboratory manuals and standard operating procedures relative to the laboratory procedures being performed. Determining the degree to which SOPs are observed is another of the QAU's duties.

Any deviations from established SOPs must be authorized by the study director and noted in the raw data. However, major SOP deviations first must be approved by the laboratory's management.

Test and Control Article Characterization   Under the 1987 GLP revisions, testing facilities were no longer required to characterize test and control articles before toxicity studies begin. This allows companies to screen out many of the useless compounds before investing money and other resources in characterizing test and control articles. According to the FDA, "characterization of test and control articles need not be performed until initial toxicology studies with the test article show reasonable promise of the article reaching the marketplace. In arriving at this conclusion, the agency considered that prior knowledge of the precise molecular structure is not vital to the conduct of a valid toxicology test. It is important, however, to know the strength, purity, and stability of a test or control article that is used in a nonclinical laboratory study." Either the sponsor or a contract testing laboratory may handle the article characterization tasks. GLP permits facilities to conduct stability testing for test and control articles either before study initiation or through periodic analyses of each batch.

The Protocol and the Conduct of a Nonclinical Laboratory Study
A protocol, or testing plan, is a vital element in both clinical and nonclinical studies. GLP states that a nonclinical program must have a written protocol that "clearly indicates the objectives and all methods for the conduct of the study."

Included in the 12-item protocol, which the sponsor must approve, should be descriptions of the experimental design and the purpose of the study, and the type and frequency of any tests, analyses, and measurements involved in the study. Changes made to the protocol during the course of the study call for an official protocol amendment signed and dated by the study director. The study director's approval of protocol amendments assures the FDA of the data's integrity.

Although protocols and SOPs may seem similar, the two have different purposes. The protocol is specific to the study being conducted, while laboratory SOPs are standards used for all research projects at a given facility. For example, SOPs would provide "how to" instructions on a facility's repeatedly used procedures for obtaining animal blood samples, caring for animals, and using and maintaining equipment.

For a particular study, the protocol would specify how often and from what animals blood samples are to be taken, what tests are to be conducted, and the number, species, sex, age, and weight of the animals to be tested. These factors would probably differ for each nonclinical study, while the facility's SOPs would remain the same. In many ways, the protocol identifies what tasks must be performed, and SOPs instruct a facility's employees on how these should be carried out.

GLP regulations allow facilities to use "umbrella protocols." By revising the definition of "nonclinical laboratory study" as part of its 1987 revision of GLP, the FDA allows facilities to conduct multiple studies using the same test article under a single, comprehensive protocol. According to the preamble of the 1987 GLP final rule, "a single 'umbrella protocol' may be used for concurrent testing of more than one test article using a single, common procedure, e.g., mutagenicity testing, or for a battery of studies of one test article conducted in several test systems." Although the FDA recognizes that a longer, more complex protocol might be more difficult to manage than a simpler one, the agency believes that using an "umbrella" protocol is more efficient than using several closely related protocols.

Records and Reporting   A final report must be prepared for each nonclinical laboratory study. Comprehensive reports typically include the summary, testing methods, results, and conclusions of a study, as well as all raw data on each of the test animals. These final reports, along with all raw data, documentation, protocols, and specimens (except specimens obtained from mutagenicity tests and wet specimens of blood, urine, feces, and biological fluids) generated during the toxicology study, must be stored in an archive or repository to preserve their safety and integrity for specific periods as designated in GLP regulations. Although these regulations state that two to five years is adequate, the FDA sometimes recommends that records be stored indefinitely, and that specimens (e.g., slides, tissues, and blocks) be stored as long as they can be used to validate data.

Equipment Design   GLP regulations specify requirements for the design, maintenance, and calibration of equipment used in nonclinical tests. Equipment used for facility environmental control and automatic, mechanical, or electronic equipment used in the generation, measurement, or assessment of data must be: (1) of appropriate design and adequate capacity to function according to the protocol; (2) suitably located for operation, inspection, cleaning, and maintenance; and (3) adequately tested, calibrated, and/or standardized. To provide guidance on the use of computers in nonclinical studies, CDER published a guideline entitled *Computerized Data Systems for Nonclinical Safety Assessment: Current Concepts and Quality Assurance* in 1988.

SOPs are required to define, in sufficient detail, the methods, materials, and schedules to be used in the routine inspection, cleaning, maintenance, testing, calibration, and/or standardization of equipment. The facility must maintain written records of routine and certain nonroutine procedures involving equipment.

FDA Inspections: Enforcing GLP

CDER performs on-site inspections to ensure that toxicology laboratories are meeting GLP requirements and to verify that submitted data are accurate.

Because of budgetary and other constraints, the FDA concentrates on U.S. laboratories. The agency performs only 10 to 12 foreign inspections each year.

Although the agency sometimes conducts announced inspections, CDER began to place a greater emphasis on unannounced GLP inspections in late 1991. According to CDER officials, virtually all GLP inspections ordered since that time have been unannounced. CDER's *Compliance Policy Guide* 7348.808 (October 1991) provides the most detailed discussion of the center's GLP inspectional policies and practices.

During an inspection, an FDA field investigator will usually audit both a completed and an ongoing trial to determine a laboratory's GLP compliance. Surveillance (i.e., routine) GLP inspections are nondirected, meaning that they involve the random review of studies to provide some assurance that nonclinical data supplied by a specific facility are valid. The less common directed inspections typically involve a comprehensive audit of nonclinical studies submitted in a specific IND or NDA. Following inspections, the FDA monitors corrective action for those facilities for which it proves necessary.

The FDA does not certify that nonclinical laboratories are in compliance with GLP. In other words, a laboratory that passes an inspection does not receive permanent or temporary certification. No such certification exists.

The Rejection of Nonclinical Studies   If FDA inspectors find GLP violations within a facility, agency officials review the violations and decide on a course of action. When severe compliance problems are discovered, the FDA may refuse to consider data from an entire nonclinical study. According to federal regulations, the purposes of the agency's right to reject nonclinical data are: "(1) To permit the exclusion from consideration completed studies that were conducted by a testing facility which has failed to comply with the requirements of the good laboratory practice regulations until it can be adequately demonstrated that such noncompliance did not occur during, or did not affect the validity or acceptability of data generated by, a particular study; and (2) to exclude from consideration all studies completed after the date of disqualification until the facility can satisfy the Commissioner that it will conduct studies in compliance with such regulations."

As stated above, the FDA may also disqualify nonclinical laboratories. For the FDA to take such action, the agency must find that: "(a) The testing facility failed to comply with one or more of the regulations....; (b) The noncompliance adversely affected the validity of the nonclinical laboratory studies; and (c) Other lesser regulatory actions (e.g., warnings or rejection of individual studies) have not been or will probably not be adequate to achieve compliance with the good laboratory practice regulations."

An Analysis of GLP Violations
(October 1987–March 1993)

CDER conducted 372 GLP inspections from October 1987 (the effective date of the current GLP regulations) to March 1993. The following table provides an analysis of the number of nonclinical laboratories (i.e., sponsor, contract, university, foreign, and government laboratories) found to be deficient in one or more areas of GLP.

Type of Violation	Number of Laboratories	Percentage of Laboratories
Personnel/Management/ Study Director	128	34%
Quality Assurance Unit and Operations	78	21%
Animal/Testing Facilities	34	9%
Equipment Maintenance/Calibration	87	23%
Standard Operating Procedures	110	30%
Animal Care	58	16%
Test and Control Articles	69	19%
Protocol and Conduct	112	30%
Final Report	66	18%
Records	45	12%

Source: CDER Office of Compliance

Chapter 4:

The IND

In many respects, the investigational new drug application (IND) is the main product of a successful preclinical development program. The IND is also the vehicle through which a sponsor seeks regulatory authorization to advance to the next stage of drug development—clinical trials.

During a new drug's early preclinical development, the sponsor's primary goal is to determine if the product is reasonably safe for initial use in humans, and if the compound exhibits pharmacological activity that justifies commercial development. When a product is identified as a viable candidate for further development, the sponsor then focuses on collecting the data and information necessary to establish, in the IND, that the product will not expose human subjects to unreasonable risks when used in limited, early-stage clinical studies. Generally, this includes data and information in three broad areas:

Animal Pharmacology and Toxicology Studies. Preclinical data to permit an assessment as to whether the product is reasonably safe for initial testing in humans.

Manufacturing Information. Information pertaining to the composition, manufacture, and stability of, and the controls used for, the drug substance and the drug product to permit an assessment as to whether the company can adequately produce and supply consistent batches of the drug.

Clinical Protocols and Investigator Information. Detailed protocols for proposed clinical studies to permit an assessment as to whether the initial-phase trials will expose subjects to unnecessary risks. Also, information on the qualifications of clinical investigators—professionals (generally physicians) who oversee the administration of the experimental compound—to permit an assessment as to whether they are qualified to fulfill their clinical trial duties.

The IND is not an application for marketing approval. Rather, it is a request for an exemption from the federal statute that prohibits an unapproved drug from being shipped in interstate commerce. Current federal law requires that a drug be the subject of an approved marketing application before it is transported or distributed across state lines. Because the sponsor will probably want to ship the investigational drug to clinical investigators in many states, it must seek an exemption from that legal requirement. The IND is the means through which the sponsor obtains this exemption from the FDA.

Types of INDs

This chapter focuses on applications that are sometimes called "commercial INDs," which are applications submitted principally by companies whose ultimate goal is to obtain marketing approval for a new product.

There are, however, several types of applications that may be grouped within a second class of filings broadly known as "noncommercial" INDs. Interestingly, the vast majority of INDs are, in fact, for noncommercial research (see chart below). These include the following types of INDs:

Investigator IND (also called research INDs). The investigator IND is submitted by a physician who both initiates and conducts an investigation, and under whose immediate direction the investigational drug is administered or dispensed. In most cases, an investigator IND proposes clinical studies on previously studied drugs. A physician might submit a research IND to propose studying an unapproved drug, or an approved product for a new indication or in a new patient population. Generally, however, the physician's motivation is not commercial in nature—in other words, the goal is not to develop data to support marketing approval for an unapproved product or to support new labeling for an approved product. For example, the investigator may simply want to treat patients or obtain data to publish a paper.

Emergency Use IND. The emergency use IND is a vehicle through which the FDA can authorize the immediate shipment of an experimental drug for a

Number of IND Submissions 1982-1992

Year	Original INDs		
	Total	Commercial	Non-Commercial
1982	1467	297	1170
1983	1798	402	1396
1984	2112	391	1721
1985	1904	326	1578
1986	1596	330	1266
1987	1346	302	1044
1988	1337	363	974
1989	1345	308	1037
1990	1530	376	1154
1991	2116	374	1742
1992	2576	370	2206

desperate medical situation. According to FDA regulations, "Need for an investigational drug may arise in an emergency situation that does not allow time for submission of an IND.... In such a case, FDA may authorize shipment of the drug for a specified use in advance of submission of an IND."

Emergency use INDs are generally reserved for life-threatening situations in which no standard acceptable treatment is available, and in which there is not sufficient time to obtain institutional review board (IRB) approval. In an FDA *Clinical Investigator Information Sheet* (February 1989) on emergency drug use, the agency states that, "The usual procedure is [for the investigator] to contact the manufacturer and determine if the drug or biologic can be made available for use (in this one patient) under the company's IND. Should the company elect not to name the physician as an investigator [under its existing IND] the physician can contact FDA directly for an IND. The physician will be placed in contact with an FDA physician familiar with the drug or biologic to review the proposed circumstances for use and the information to be submitted in the IND." If the FDA decides to approve the emergency use, the agency immediately provides authorization for the investigator to receive a shipment of the drug.

Treatment IND. Although the treatment IND has a history dating back to the 1960s and 1970s, the FDA took steps to formalize the treatment IND concept in a 1987 regulation. Through the FDA's treatment IND program, experimental drugs showing promise in clinical testing for serious or life-threatening conditions are made widely available, while the final clinical work is conducted and the FDA review takes place (for more on treatment INDs, see Chapter 17).

The Applicability of the IND

The IND is a requirement for all persons and firms seeking to ship unapproved drugs over state lines for use in clinical investigations. The agency offers exemptions from IND submission requirements for certain types of clinical testing and products, including the following:

• Clinical investigations of a drug product that is lawfully marketed in the United States, provided that all of the following conditions apply: (1) the investigation is not intended to be reported to the FDA as a well-controlled study in support of a new indication for use, or is not intended to be used to support any other significant change in the drug's labeling; (2) the investigation is not intended to support a significant change in the advertising for a prescription drug; (3) the investigation does not involve a change in the route of administration, dosage level, patient population, or other factor that significantly increases the risks (or decreases the acceptability of the risks) associated with the use of the drug product; (4) the investigation complies with institutional review board (IRB) evaluation and informed consent requirements; and (5) the sponsor of the investigation does not represent in a promotional context that the drug is safe or effective for the purposes for which it is under investigation. The FDA has stated that this exemption is intended primarily for practicing physicians.

- Drugs intended solely for testing *in vitro* or in laboratory research animals, provided the drug shipments are made in compliance with FDA regulations.

- Clinical investigations involving the use of a placebo, provided that the investigations do not involve the use of a new drug or otherwise trigger IND submission requirements.

- Certain *in vivo* bioavailability and bioequivalence studies in humans. FDA regulations state, however, that INDs are required for *in vivo* bioavailability or bioequivalence studies in humans if the test product is a radioactively labeled drug product, is a cytotoxic drug product, or contains a new chemical entity. Further, INDs are required for the following types of human bioavailability studies that involve a previously approved drug that is not a new chemical entity: (1) a single-dose study in normal subjects or patients when either the maximum single or total daily dose exceeds that specified in the labeling of the approved product; (2) a multiple-dose study in normal subjects or patients when either the single or total daily dose exceeds that specified in the labeling of the approved product; or (3) a multiple-dose study on a controlled-release product on which no single-dose study has been completed.

In addition to IND exemptions, FDA regulations provide a mechanism through which individuals and firms can seek an agency waiver from IND requirements. Also, there are alternatives to the IND in some circumstances. Under FDA regulations, for example, a person or company seeking to export an experimental drug product for foreign-based clinical trials can apply for FDA authorization either through an IND or through a less formal written request. The FDA sets minimum standards for such requests, including a cover letter, documentation from the foreign government that it has decided to permit the import of the experimental drug, and a protocol or protocol summary.

IND Content and Format Requirements

Until the late 1980s, the FDA had less-than-exacting content and format requirements for INDs. A 1987 revision to FDA regulations changed this, however, as the FDA sought better organized and more standardized INDs to help expedite reviews. According to FDA regulations, an IND will consist of between 8 and 11 sections:

1. Cover Sheet (Form FDA 1571).

2. Table of Contents.

3. Introductory Statement.

4. General Investigational Plan.

5. Investigator's Brochure.

6. Clinical Protocols.

7. Chemistry, Manufacturing, and Controls Information.

8. Pharmacology and Toxicology Information.

9. Previous Human Experience with the Investigational Drug (if applicable).

10. Additional Information (if applicable).

11. Relevant Information (if applicable).

The nature of the drug and the available product-related information will affect the number of sections included in an IND submission. These and other factors will also determine the quantity of information to be included in the application. "Sponsors are expected to exercise considerable discretion... regarding the content of information submitted in each section [of the IND], depending upon the kind of drug being studied and the nature of the available information," FDA regulations state. "The amount of information on a particular drug that must be submitted in an IND...depends upon such factors as the novelty of the drug, the extent to which it has been studied previously, the known or suspected risks, and the developmental phase of the drug." The following sections discuss the content requirements for each section of the IND.

IND Cover Letter Although not included in the formal listing of IND content requirements above, many INDs start with a cover letter. By providing a general introduction to the submission and identifying any previously reached sponsor/FDA agreements, cover letters are often extremely useful to drug reviewers.

Cover Sheet Form FDA 1571 serves as the cover sheet for the entire IND submission (see sample form below). In completing and signing, or having an authorized representative complete and sign, this form, the sponsor: (1) identifies itself, the investigational drug, the clinical investigators and monitors, and the phase(s) of investigation covered by the application; (2) identifies any responsibilities that have been transferred to a contract research organization (CRO); and (3) agrees to comply with applicable regulations, including those requiring the sponsor to refrain from initiating clinical studies "until an IND covering the investigations is in effect." A completed copy of Form FDA 1571 is also required with each amendment submitted to the IND.

Sponsors seeking to transfer any obligations for the conduct of a study to a CRO must include with the cover sheet a statement providing the CRO's name and address, identifying the relevant clinical study, and listing the specific obligations transferred. Companies transferring all study obligations to a CRO may submit "a general statement of this transfer—in lieu of a listing of the specific obligations transferred...."

Sponsors lacking both a U.S.-based residence and place of business must have an authorized representative sign the IND cover sheet as well. In such cases, the cover sheet must provide the "name and address of, and be counter-signed by, an attorney, agent, or other authorized official who resides or maintains a place of business within the United States."

Table of Contents FDA regulations offer no guidance on the IND's table of contents. However, the agency does state that sponsors should follow the

New Drug Development: A Regulatory Overview

<table>
<tr><td colspan="2">
DEPARTMENT OF HEALTH AND HUMAN SERVICES
PUBLIC HEALTH SERVICE
FOOD AND DRUG ADMINISTRATION
INVESTIGATIONAL NEW DRUG APPLICATION (IND)
(TITLE 21, CODE OF FEDERAL REGULATIONS (CFR) PART 312)
</td><td>
Form Approved: OMB No. 0910-0014.
Expiration Date: November 30, 1995.
See OMB Statement on Reverse.

NOTE: No drug may be shipped or clinical investigation begun until an IND for that investigation is in effect (21 CFR 312.40).
</td></tr>
</table>

1. NAME OF SPONSOR

2. DATE OF SUBMISSION

3. ADDRESS *(Number, Street, City, State and Zip Code)*

4. TELEPHONE NUMBER *(Include Area Code)*

5. NAME(S) OF DRUG *(Include all available names: Trade, Generic, Chemical, Code)*

6. IND NUMBER *(If previously assigned)*

7. INDICATION(S) *(Covered by this submission)*

8. PHASE(S) OF CLINICAL INVESTIGATION TO BE CONDUCTED. ☐ PHASE 1 ☐ PHASE 2 ☐ PHASE 3 ☐ OTHER_____ *(Specify)*

9. LIST NUMBERS OF ALL INVESTIGATIONAL NEW DRUG APPLICATIONS *(21 CFR Part 312)*, NEW DRUG OR ANTIBIOTIC APPLICATIONS *(21 CFR Part 314)*, DRUG MASTER FILES *(21 CFR 314.420)*, AND PRODUCT LICENSE APPLICATIONS *(21 CFR Part 601)* REFERRED TO IN THIS APPLICATION.

10. *IND submissions should be consecutively numbered. The initial IND should be numbered "Serial Number: 000." The next submission (e.g., amendment, report, or correspondence) should be numbered "Serial Number: 001." Subsequent submissions should be numbered consecutively in the order in which they are submitted.*

SERIAL NUMBER: ___ ___ ___

11. THIS SUBMISSION CONTAINS THE FOLLOWING: (Check all that apply)

☐ INITIAL INVESTIGATIONAL NEW DRUG APPLICATION (IND)   ☐ RESPONSE TO CLINICAL HOLD

PROTOCOL AMENDMENT(S):   INFORMATION AMENDMENT(S):   IND SAFETY REPORT(S):
☐ NEW PROTOCOL   ☐ CHEMISTRY/MICROBIOLOGY   ☐ INITIAL WRITTEN REPORT
☐ CHANGE IN PROTOCOL   ☐ PHARMACOLOGY/TOXICOLOGY   ☐ FOLLOW-UP TO A WRITTEN REPORT
☐ NEW INVESTIGATOR   ☐ CLINICAL

☐ RESPONSE TO FDA REQUEST FOR INFORMATION   ☐ ANNUAL REPORT   ☐ GENERAL CORRESPONDENCE

☐ REQUEST FOR REINSTATEMENT OF IND THAT IS WITHDRAWN, INACTIVATED, TERMINATED OR DISCONTINUED   ☐ OTHER_____ *(Specify)*

CHECK ONLY IF APPLICABLE

JUSTIFICATION STATEMENT MUST BE SUBMITTED WITH APPLICATION FOR ANY CHECKED BELOW. REFER TO THE CITED CFR SECTION FOR FURTHER INFORMATION.

☐ TREATMENT IND 21 CFR 312.35(b)   ☐ TREATMENT PROTOCOL 21 CFR 312.35(a)   ☐ CHARGE REQUEST/NOTIFICATION 21 CFR 312.7(d)

FOR FDA USE ONLY

CDR/DBIND/OGD RECEIPT STAMP | DDR RECEIPT STAMP | IND NUMBER ASSIGNED:

DIVISION ASSIGNMENT:

FORM FDA 1571 (12/92)   PREVIOUS EDITION IS OBSOLETE

12.

CONTENTS OF APPLICATION

This application contains the following items: *(check all that apply)*

☐ 1. Form FDA 1571 [21 CFR 312.23 (a) (1)]

☐ 2. Table of contents [21 CFR 312.23 (a) (2)]

☐ 3. Introductory statement [21 CFR 312.23 (a) (3)]

☐ 4. General investigational plan [21 CFR 312.23 (a) (3)]

☐ 5. Investigator's brochure [21 CFR 312.23 (a) (5)]

☐ 6. Protocol(s) [21 CFR 312.23 (a) (6)]

   ☐ a. Study protocol(s) [21 CFR 312.23 (a) (6)]

   ☐ b. Investigator data [21 CFR 312.23 (a) (6)(iii)(b)] or completed Form(s) FDA 1572

   ☐ c. Facilities data [21 CFR 312.23 (a) (6)(iii)(b)] or completed Form(s) FDA 1572

   ☐ d. Institutional Review Board data [21 CFR 312.23 (a) (6)(iii)(b)] or completed Form(s) FDA 1572

☐ 7. Chemistry, manufacturing, and control data [21 CFR 312.23 (a) (7)]

   ☐ Environmental assessment or claim for exclusion [21 CFR 312.23 (a) (7)(iv)(e)]

☐ 8. Pharmacology and toxicology data [21 CFR 312.23 (a) (8)]

☐ 9. Previous human experience [21 CFR 312.23 (a) (9)]

☐ 10. Additional information [21 CFR 312.23 (a) (10)]

13. IS ANY PART OF THE CLINICAL STUDY TO BE CONDUCTED BY A CONTRACT RESEARCH ORGANIZATION? ☐ YES ☐ NO

IF YES, WILL ANY SPONSOR OBLIGATIONS BE TRANSFERRED TO THE CONTRACT RESEARCH ORGANIZATION? ☐ YES ☐ NO

IF YES, ATTACH A STATEMENT CONTAINING THE NAME AND ADDRESS OF THE CONTRACT RESEARCH ORGANIZATION, IDENTIFICATION OF THE CLINICAL STUDY, AND A LISTING OF THE OBLIGATIONS TRANSFERRED.

14. NAME AND TITLE OF THE PERSON RESPONSIBLE FOR MONITORING THE CONDUCT AND PROGRESS OF THE CLINICAL INVESTIGATIONS

15. NAME(S) AND TITLE(S) OF THE PERSON(S) RESPONSIBLE FOR REVIEW AND EVALUATION OF INFORMATION RELEVANT TO THE SAFETY OF THE DRUG

I agree not to begin clinical investigations until 30 days after FDA's receipt of the IND unless I receive earlier notification by FDA that the studies may begin. I also agree not to begin or continue clinical investigations covered by the IND if those studies are placed on clinical hold. I agree that an Institutional Review Board (IRB) that complies with the requirements set forth in 21 CFR Part 56 will be responsible for the initial and continuing review and approval of each of the studies in the proposed clinical investigation. I agree to conduct the investigation in accordance with all other applicable regulatory requirements.

16. NAME OF SPONSOR OR SPONSOR'S AUTHORIZED REPRESENTATIVE	17. SIGNATURE OF SPONSOR OR SPONSOR'S AUTHORIZED REPRESENTATIVE	
18. ADDRESS (Number, Street, City, State and Zip Code)	19. TELEPHONE NUMBER *(Include Area Code)*	20. DATE

(WARNING:A willfully false statement is a criminal offense, U.S.C. Title 18, Sec. 1001.)

specified IND format "in the interest of fostering an efficient review of the application." Obviously, the table of contents should be sufficiently detailed to permit FDA reviewers to locate important elements of the application quickly and easily. The table of contents should provide the location of items by volume and page number.

Introductory Statement   The IND's introductory statement must describe the drug, the goals of the proposed clinical investigations, and previous human experience with the drug. According to FDA regulations, this section should provide "a brief introductory statement giving the name of the drug and all active ingredients, the drug's pharmacological class, the structural formula of the drug (if known), the formulation of the dosage form(s) to be used, the route of administration, and the broad objectives and planned duration of the proposed clinical investigation(s)." The sponsor must also summarize all previous clinical experience with the drug, including "investigational or marketing experience in other countries that may be relevant to the safety of the proposed clinical investigation(s)." If a foreign regulatory authority discontinued the drug's testing or marketing for any reason related to safety or effectiveness, the sponsor must identify the country(ies) in which the withdrawal took place and must describe the reason for the withdrawal.

General Investigational Plan   The general investigational plan must provide a brief description of the overall plan for investigating the drug product for the following year. The FDA has stated that the goal of this section "is to give agency reviewers a very brief overview of the scale and kind of clinical studies to be conducted during the following year. This overview, which is general, should be no more than two to three pages in length...[and]...will provide the necessary context for the FDA reviewers to assess the sufficiency of technical information to support future studies and to provide advice and assistance to the sponsor."

According to federal regulations, the "plan should include the following: (a) the rationale for the drug or the research study; (b) the indication(s) to be studied; (c) the general approach to be followed in evaluating the drug; (d) the kinds of clinical trials to be conducted in the first year following the submission (if plans are not developed for the entire year, the sponsor should so indicate); (e) the estimated number of patients to be given the drug in those studies; and (f) any risks of particular severity or seriousness anticipated on the basis of the toxicological data in animals or prior studies in humans with the drug or related drugs."

The FDA does not require rigid adherence to the general investigational plan. Provided that it fulfills protocol and information amendment reporting requirements (see discussion below), a sponsor is free to deviate from the plan when necessary.

Investigator's Brochure   With the exception of investigator-sponsored applications, INDs must include a copy of the investigator's brochure—an information package in which a sponsor provides participating clinical investigators with available information on the drug, including its known and possible risks and benefits. Since it might provide insights relevant to drug administration and patient monitoring, the brochure must provide all relevant information that a sponsor has on a drug and its effects, including:

- a brief description of the drug substance and formulation, including the structural formula, if known;

- a summary of the pharmacological and toxicological effects of the drug in animals and, to the extent known, in humans;

- a summary of the pharmacokinetic and biological disposition of the drug in animals and, if known, in humans;

- a summary of information relating to the drug's safety and effectiveness in humans obtained from prior clinical studies (reprints of published articles on such studies may be appended when useful); and

- a description of possible risks and side effects anticipated because of past experience with the drug under investigation or with related drugs, and a description of precautions to be taken or special monitoring to be done as part of the drug's investigational use.

As clinical trials advance, the sponsor must inform investigators "of new observations discovered by or reported to the sponsor of the drug, particularly with respect to adverse effects and safe use." Such information may be distributed to investigators by means of periodically revised investigator's brochures, reprints of published studies, reports or letters to clinical investigators, or other appropriate means. Sponsors must relay important safety information to investigators through IND safety reports (see discussion below).

In serving as the "labeling" for the investigational drug, the investigator's brochure plays a key role in determining safety reporting requirements during clinical development. Since the brochure identifies which adverse experiences are expected, it determines, in part, which adverse experiences must be reported immediately to the FDA in IND safety reports (see discussion below).

Clinical Protocols FDA regulations state that, along with the general investigational plan, clinical protocols are "the central focus of the initial IND submission." Protocols are descriptions of clinical studies that identify, among other things, a study's objectives, design, and procedures. The FDA reviews clinical protocols to ensure: (1) that subjects will not be exposed to unnecessary risks in any of the clinical trials; and (2) that Phase 2 and Phase 3 clinical study designs are adequate to provide the types and amount of information necessary to show that the drug is safe and/or effective.

In the original IND submission, the sponsor must provide only protocols for the study or studies that will begin immediately after the IND goes into effect—that is, after the FDA's 30-day review period. The safety of initial Phase 1 studies is the FDA's principal concern in reviewing the IND. Since latter-phase clinical studies often are not fully developed until data from Phase 1 studies are obtained, Phase 2 and Phase 3 protocols may be submitted later in the development process.

According to FDA regulations, "protocols for Phase 1 studies may be less detailed and more flexible than protocols for Phase 2 and 3 studies. Phase 1 protocols should be directed primarily at providing an outline of the investigation—an estimate of the number of patients to be involved, a description of safety exclusions, and a description of the dosing plan including duration, dose, or method to be used in determining dose—and should specify in detail only those elements of the study that are critical to safety, such as necessary monitoring of vital signs and blood chemistries. Modifications of the experimental design of Phase 1 studies that do not affect critical safety assessments are required to be reported to FDA only in the annual report."

In contrast, the FDA requires that Phase 2 and 3 protocols include detailed descriptions of all aspects of the study. Federal regulations state that these protocols "should be designed in such a way that, if the sponsor anticipates that some deviation from the study design may become necessary as the investigation progresses, alternatives or contingencies to provide for such deviations are built into the protocols at the outset. For example, a protocol for a controlled short-term study might include a plan for an early crossover of nonresponders to an alternative therapy." About such contingency plans, which are optional, the FDA has commented that it "strongly encourages the submission of such plans as it believes there is much to be gained in thinking about the planning for possible alternative courses of action early in the protocol development process. Providing in the initial protocol for possible departures from the study design enhances the value or reviewability of study results. Such advance planning also permits both FDA and the sponsor to raise useful questions about study design and supporting information at the earliest possible time."

Although the components and level of detail found in a protocol will depend upon the phase covered and other factors, FDA regulations state that a protocol should include seven elements:

• a statement of the objectives and purposes of the study;

• the name and address of, and a statement of qualifications (résumé or other statement of qualifications) for each investigator, the name of each subinvestigator (i.e., research fellow, resident) working under the supervision of the investigator, the names and addresses of the research facilities to be used, and the name and address of each institutional review board (IRB) responsible for reviewing the protocols (this information may be submitted on Form FDA 1572, see sample below);

• the criteria for patient selection and exclusion, and an estimate of the number of patients to be studied;

• a description of the study design, including the type of control group to be used, if any, and a description of the methods to be used to minimize bias on the part of subjects, investigators, and analysts;

New Drug Development: A Regulatory Overview

DEPARTMENT OF HEALTH AND HUMAN SERVICES PUBLIC HEALTH SERVICE FOOD AND DRUG ADMINISTRATION **STATEMENT OF INVESTIGATOR** **(TITLE 21, CODE OF FEDERAL REGULATIONS (CFR) PART 312)** *(See instructions on reverse side.)*	Form Approved: OMB No. 0910-0014 Expiration Date: November 30, 1995 See OMB Statement on Reverse. NOTE: No investigator may participate in an investigation until he/she provides the sponsor with a completed, signed Statement of Investigator, Form FDA 1572 (21CFR 312.53(c)).

1. NAME AND ADDRESS OF INVESTIGATOR.

2. EDUCATION, TRAINING, AND EXPERIENCE THAT QUALIFIES THE INVESTIGATOR AS AN EXPERT IN THE CLINICAL INVESTIGATION OF THE DRUG FOR THE USE UNDER INVESTIGATION. ONE OF THE FOLLOWING IS ATTACHED:

       ☐ CURRICULUM VITAE   ☐ OTHER STATEMENT OF QUALIFICATIONS

3. NAME AND ADDRESS OF ANY MEDICAL SCHOOL, HOSPITAL, OR OTHER RESEARCH FACILITY WHERE THE CLINICAL INVESTIGATION(S) WILL BE CONDUCTED.

4. NAME AND ADDRESS OF ANY CLINICAL LABORATORY FACILITIES TO BE USED IN THE STUDY.

5. NAME AND ADDRESS OF THE INSTITUTIONAL REVIEW BOARD (IRB) THAT IS RESPONSIBLE FOR REVIEW AND APPROVAL OF THE STUDY(IES).

6. NAMES OF THE SUBINVESTIGATORS (e.g., research fellows, residents, associates) WHO WILL BE ASSISTING THE INVESTIGATOR IN THE CONDUCT OF THE INVESTIGATION(S).

7. NAME AND CODE NUMBER, IF ANY, OF THE PROTOCOL(S) IN THE IND FOR THE STUDY(IES) TO BE CONDUCTED BY THE INVESTIGATOR.

FORM FDA 1572 (12/92)   PREVIOUS EDITION IS OBSOLETE

8. ATTACH THE FOLLOWING CLINICAL PROTOCOL INFORMATION:

☐ FOR PHASE 1 INVESTIGATIONS. A GENERAL OUTLINE OF THE PLANNED INVESTIGATION INCLUDING THE ESTIMATED DURATION OF THE STUDY AND THE MAXIMUM NUMBER OF SUBJECTS THAT WILL BE INVOLVED.

☐ FOR PHASE 2 OR 3 INVESTIGATIONS, AN OUTLINE OF THE STUDY PROTOCOL INCLUDING AN APPROXIMATION OF THE NUMBER OF SUBJECTS TO BE TREATED WITH THE DRUG AND THE NUMBER TO BE EMPLOYED AS CONTROLS, IF ANY; THE CLINICAL USES TO BE INVESTIGATED; CHARACTERISTICS OF SUBJECTS BY AGE, SEX, AND CONDITION; THE KIND OF CLINICAL OBSERVATIONS AND LABORATORY TESTS TO BE CONDUCTED; THE ESTIMATED DURATION OF THE STUDY; AND COPIES OR A DESCRIPTION OF CASE REPORT FORMS TO BE USED.

9. COMMITMENTS:

I agree to conduct the study(ies) in accordance with the relevant, current protocol(s) and will only make changes in a protocol after notifying the sponsor, except when necessary to protect the safety, rights, or welfare of subjects.

I agree to personally conduct or supervise the described investigation(s).

I agree to inform any patients, or any persons used as controls, that the drugs are being used for investigational purposes and I will ensure that the requirements relating to obtaining informed consent in 21 CFR Part 50 and institutional review board (IRB) review and approval in 21 CFR Part 56 are met.

I agree to report to the sponsor adverse experiences that occur in the investigation(s) in accordance with 21 CFR 312.64.

I have read and understand the information in the investigator's brochure, including the potential risks and side effects of the drug.

I agree to ensure that all associates, colleagues, and employees assisting in the conduct of the study(ies) are informed about their obligations in meeting the above commitments.

I agree to maintain adequate and accurate records in accordance with 21 CFR 312.62 and to make those records available for inspection in accordance with 21 CFR 312.68.

I will ensure that an IRB that complies with the requirements of 21 CFR Part 56 will be responsible for the initial and continuing review and approval of the clinical investigation. I also agree to promptly report to the IRB all changes in the research activity and all unanticipated problems involving risks to human subjects or others. Additionally, I will not make any changes in the research without IRB approval, except where necessary to eliminate apparent immediate hazards to human subjects.

I agree to comply with all other requirements regarding the obligations of clinical investigators and all other pertinent requirements in 21 CFR Part 312.

INSTRUCTIONS FOR COMPLETING FORM FDA 1572
STATEMENT OF INVESTIGATOR

1. Complete all sections. Attach a separate page if additional space is needed.

2. Attach curriculum vitae or other statement of qualifications as described in Section 2.

3. Attach protocol outline as described in Section 8.

4. Sign and date below.

5. FORWARD THE COMPLETED FORM AND ATTACHMENTS TO THE SPONSOR. The sponsor will incorporate this information along with other technical data into an Investigational New Drug Application (IND). INVESTIGATORS SHOULD NOT SEND THIS FORM DIRECTLY TO THE FOOD AND DRUG ADMINISTRATION.

10. SIGNATURE OF INVESTIGATOR	11. DATE

Public reporting burden for this collection of information is estimated to average 84 hours per response, including the time for reviewing instructions, searching existing data sources, gathering and maintaining the data needed, and completing reviewing the collection of information. Send comments regarding this burden estimate or any other aspect of this collection of information, including suggestions for reducing this burden to:

Reports Clearance Officer, PHS	and to:	Office of Management and Budget
Hubert H. Humphrey Building, Room 721-B		Paperwork Reduction Project (0910-0014)
200 Independence Avenue, S.W.		Washington, DC 20503
Washington, DC 20201		
Attn: PRA		

Please DO NOT RETURN this application to either of these addresses.

FORM FDA 1572 (12/92)   PAGE 2 OF 2

- the method for determining the dose(s) to be administered, the planned maximum dosage, and the duration of individual patient exposure to the drug;

- a description of the observations and measurements to be made to fulfill the objectives of the study; and

- a description of clinical procedures, laboratory tests, or other measures to be taken in minimizing risk and monitoring the effects of the drug in human subjects.

Chemistry, Manufacturing, and Controls Information   Because the IND proposes that an experimental drug be administered to human subjects, the sponsor must establish in the application that it can manufacture the drug while preserving the product's identity, quality, purity, strength, and stability. Therefore, the FDA requires that the IND's chemistry, manufacturing, and controls section consist of five components:

Drug Substance. A description of the drug substance that provides at least five types of information: (1) the drug substance's physical, chemical, or biological characteristics; (2) the name and address of its manufacturer; (3) the general method of preparation of the drug substance; (4) the acceptable limits and analytical methods used to ensure the identity, strength, quality, and purity of the drug substance; and (5) information sufficient to support the stability of the drug substance during toxicological studies and the planned clinical studies. Reference to the current edition of the *U.S. Pharmacopeia* or *National Formulary* may satisfy relevant requirements in this paragraph.

In manufacturing and packaging their products, applicants often utilize components (e.g., drug substances, nonstandard excipients, containers) manufactured by other firms (i.e., contract manufacturers). In such cases, the contract manufacturer is likely to want to preserve the confidentiality of its manufacturing processes. Since an IND must provide information on these processes, contract manufacturers often submit this information to the FDA in a drug master file (DMF). This allows drug sponsors using the company's products to meet submission requirements by incorporating by reference information provided in the master file. Because the drug sponsor never sees the information in the DMF, the confidentiality of the contract facility's manufacturing processes is maintained. In the IND (or other submission), an incorporation by reference should be made in the section of the application in which the referenced information would normally appear if provided by the applicant. The incorporation by reference must identify the DMF's name and reference number, and must provide the relevant volume and page numbers to allow reviewers to locate the referenced information (i.e., the FDA stores DMFs and reviews information in the file only when referenced in a pending drug application). When the applicant is cross-referencing a DMF submitted by another firm (e.g., a bulk drug manufacturer), the IND must provide a letter of authorization from the DMF's owner in addition to the information specified above. A more detailed discussion of CDER's requirements for, and use of, DMFs can be found in the center's *Guideline for Drug Master Files* (September 1989).

Drug Product. A list of all components, which may include reasonable alternatives for inactive compounds, used in the manufacture of the investigational drug product and those which may not appear but which are used in the manufacturing process and, where applicable, the quantitative composition of the investigational drug product, including any reasonable variation which may be expected during the investigational stage; the name and address of the drug product manufacturer; a brief general description of the manufacturing and packaging procedures for the product; the acceptable limits and analytical methods used to ensure the identity, quality, purity, and strength of the drug product; and information sufficient to ensure the product's stability during the planned clinical studies. Reference to the current edition of the *U.S. Pharmacopeia* or *National Formulary* may satisfy certain requirements for this section.

A Brief General Description of the Composition, Manufacture, and Control of any Placebo Used in a Controlled Clinical Trial. This requirement is designed to ensure that the failure of a placebo to mimic the odor, taste, texture, or other physical characteristics of an investigational drug does not compromise a blinded study. However, the FDA does not require that a placebo be identical to an investigational drug in all respects.

Labeling. A copy of all labels and labeling to be provided to each investigator. Federal regulations specify the following requirements for the labeling of investigational new drugs: "(a) The immediate package of an investigational new drug intended for human use shall bear a label with the statement 'Caution: New Drug-Limited by Federal (or United States) law to investigational use.' [and] (b) The label or labeling of an investigational new drug shall not bear any statement that is false or misleading in any particular and shall not represent that the investigational new drug is safe or effective for the purposes for which it is being investigated."

Environmental Analysis (EA) Requirements. This section should provide either an environmental assessment, or a claim for a categorical exclusion from the requirement for an environmental assessment. In July 1991, the U.S. Pharmaceutical Manufacturers Association released a handbook entitled *Interim Guidance to the Pharmaceutical Industry for Environmental Assessment Compliance Requirements for the FDA.* This document, which addresses EA issues relative to INDs, NDAs, NDA supplements/amendments, and drug master files, supplements the FDA's environmental assessment regulations and a more general agency document entitled *Environmental Assessment Technical Assistance Document.*

The FDA emphasizes throughout its regulations that the amount and detail of information needed in the chemistry, manufacturing, and controls section depends on several factors, including the scope and phase of the proposed clinical investigation, the proposed duration of the study, the dosage form, and the quantity of information otherwise available. "FDA recognizes that modifications to the method of preparation of the new drug substance and dosage form and changes in the dosage form itself are likely as the investigation progresses," agency regulations state. "For example, although stability data are required in all phases of the IND to demonstrate that the new drug substance and drug product are within acceptable chemical and physical limits for the planned duration of the proposed clinical investigation, if very short-term tests are proposed, the supporting stability data can be correspondingly limited."

IND stability testing requirements are also a function of a drug's stage of clinical development. INDs should include stability data to support the conditions of the bulk drug's use in toxicology studies, and the stability of the drug substance in the initial formulations proposed for use in the clinical pharmacology studies. The objective of stability studies conducted during Phase 1 and Phase 2 studies are to evaluate the stability of formulations used in clinical trials, and to demonstrate that the product would be stable for the duration of the investigation. During Phase 3 clinical trials, the objective of stability studies is to obtain data that support the formulation proposed for marketing.

FDA regulations state that "the emphasis in an initial Phase 1 submission should generally be placed on the identification and control of the raw materials and the new drug substance. Final specifications for the drug substance and drug product are not expected until the end of the investigational process." However, when final specifications are not established until just prior to Phase 3 studies, comparability with preceding studies may be necessary. Stability testing should support the duration of use for the proposed clinical studies.

The FDA does require that sponsors comply with Current Good Manufacturing Practices (CGMP) during clinical trials. According to the FDA's *Guideline on the Preparation of Investigational New Drug Products (Human and Animal)* (March 1991): "FDA recognizes that manufacturing procedures and specifications will change as clinical trials advance. However, as research nears completion, procedures and controls are expected to be more specific because they will have been based upon a growing body of scientific data and documentation.... When drug development reaches a stage where the drugs are produced for clinical trials in humans...then compliance with the CGMP regulations is required. For example, the drug product must be produced in a qualified facility, using laboratory and other equipment that has been qualified, and processes must be validated. There must be written procedures for sanitation, calibration, and maintenance of equipment, and specific instructions for the use of the equipment and procedures used to manufacture the drug. Product contamination and wide variations in potency can produce substantial levels of side effects and toxicity, and even produce wide-sweeping effects on the physiological activity of the drug. Product safety, quality, and uniformity are especially significant in the case of investigational products. Such factors may affect the outcome of a clinical investigation that will, in large part, determine whether or not the product will be approved for wider distribution to the public."

As the testing and drug development process advances, sponsors must submit IND information amendments to the chemistry, manufacturing, and control section of the IND (see discussion below). Most importantly, these amendments must describe the effects of the transition from pilot scale production used for early clinical studies to the larger-scale production methods used for expanded clinical investigations.

In addition to the documents referenced above, the agency has published several guidelines that provide direction on the submission of chemistry, manufacturing, and controls information in both INDs and NDAs. These include the following: *Guideline for Submitting Documentation for the Manufacture of and Controls for Drug Products* (February 1987), *Guideline for Submitting Supporting Documentation in Drug Applications for the Manufacture of Drug Substances* (February 1987), *Guideline for Submitting Documentation for Packaging for Human Drugs and Biologics* (February 1987), and *Guideline for Submitting Documentation for the Stability of Human Drugs and Biologics* (February 1987).

Animal Pharmacology and Toxicology Information   In the absence of data derived from previous clinical testing or marketing use, data from animal studies serve as the basis for concluding that a drug is sufficiently safe for initial administration to humans. The IND must include information from the preclinical pharmacology and toxicology studies (animal and *in vitro*) sufficient to establish that the proposed clinical studies will not expose human subjects to unreasonable risks. Similar to that in the IND's other technical sections, the data and information necessary in the pharmacology and toxicology component depends on several factors, including the nature of the product and the nature and duration of the clinical studies proposed in the IND.

FDA regulations state that this section of the IND should consist of three elements:

Pharmacology and Drug Disposition. "A section describing the pharmacological effects and mechanism(s) of action of the drug in animals, and information on the absorption, distribution, metabolism, and excretion of the drug, if known."

Toxicology. "(a) An integrated summary of the toxicological effects of the drug in animals and *in vitro*. Depending on the nature of the drug and the phase of the investigation, the description is to include the results of acute, subacute, and chronic toxicity tests; tests of the drug's effects on reproduction and the developing fetus; any special toxicity test related to the drug's particular mode of administration or conditions of use (e.g., inhalation, dermal, or ocular toxicology); and any *in vitro* studies intended to evaluate drug toxicity; [and] (b) for each toxicology study that is intended primarily to support the safety of the proposed clinical investigation, a full tabulation of data suitable for detailed review." Although these data may be adequate to support initial drug administration, data from longer-term animal studies (e.g., carcinogenicity and mutagenicity studies) may be necessary to support later clinical studies. This information is submitted in updates to the IND (see discussion below).

Statement of Regulatory Compliance. For each nonclinical laboratory study subject to good laboratory practice (GLP) standards (e.g., "definitive" safety studies), either: (1) a statement confirming that the relevant studies complied with GLP; or (2) a brief statement explaining why GLP standards were not followed.

FDA recommendations for compiling and presenting data in this section are available through the agency's *Guideline for the Format and Content of the Nonclinical Pharmacology/Toxicology Section of an Application* (February 1987). Although the guideline is designed for NDA submissions, the FDA has stated that the guideline should also shape the organization and format of IND submissions.

Previous Human Experience With the Investigational Drug

If an investigational drug, or any of its active ingredients, has been marketed or tested in humans previously, the sponsor must provide specific information about any such use that may be relevant to the FDA's evaluation of the safety of either the drug or the proposed investigation. If the drug has been marketed outside the United States, the IND must provide a list of the countries in which the drug has been marketed or withdrawn.

Additional Information

INDs for radioactive drugs or for drugs containing ingredients with a potential for abuse or dependence must provide any supplementary information relevant to the safety or design of the proposed clinical trials.

Relevant Information   The FDA may request other information that it believes is necessary in reviewing the IND.

Additional IND Requirements

The FDA requires sponsors to submit an original and two copies of all IND-related filings, including the original application and all amendments and reports. The sponsor must provide an accurate and complete English translation for any information originally written in a foreign language. In addition, the applicant must submit the original foreign language document or literature article on which the translation is based.

Maintaining the IND

Even after submission, the IND is, in many respects, a "living document." Following the initial filing, a sponsor continually must update the IND with information that allows the agency to reassess the safety of ongoing and future clinical trials. Federal regulations require sponsors of active INDs to file four types of documents that update their original INDs: protocol amendments, IND safety reports, annual reports, and information amendments.

Protocol Amendments   Protocol amendments are necessary when a sponsor wants to change a previously submitted protocol or to add a study protocol not submitted in the original IND. New protocols and most protocol changes must have been submitted to the FDA and have received IRB approval before being initiated. However, some sponsors may choose to obtain FDA comments before implementing new protocols for pivotal studies.

Protocol amendments that introduce a new protocol must contain the protocol itself along with a brief description of the most clinically significant differences between the new and previous protocols. In explaining this requirement, the FDA writes that "...a detailed and undiscriminating enumeration of the differences would defeat the purpose of this requirement, which is to identify the most important differences between the old and new protocols and to alert FDA reviewers to major changes that may require additional supporting data, such as changes in dose, route of administration, or indication."

Amendments that specify changes to previously submitted protocols are required when a sponsor seeks: (1) to modify a Phase 1 protocol in a manner that significantly affects the safety of clinical subjects; or (2) to modify a Phase 2 or Phase 3 protocol in a manner that significantly affects the safety of the subjects, the scope of the investigation, or the scientific quality of the study. Federal regulations provide the following examples of protocol changes requiring amendments:

- any increase in drug dosage or the duration of individual subject exposure to the drug beyond that in the current protocol, or any significant increase in the number of study subjects;

- any significant change in the design of a protocol, such as the addition or deletion of a control group;

- the addition of a new test or procedure that is intended to improve monitoring for, or reduce the risk of, a side effect or adverse effect, or the elimination of a test intended to monitor safety;

- the elimination of an apparent, immediate hazard to subjects (such a change may be implemented prior to an amendment submission, provided that the FDA is subsequently notified through a protocol amendment and that the IRB is properly notified); and

- the addition of a new investigator to carry out a previously submitted protocol (the investigational drug may be shipped to the investigator and the investigator may participate in the study prior to the submission of the amendment, provided the sponsor notifies the FDA within 30 days of the investigator's first participation in the study).

Amendments for changes to existing protocols must provide a "brief description of the change and reference (date and number) to the submission that contained the protocol." Amendments for a new investigator must include "the investigator's name, qualifications to conduct the investigation, reference to the previously submitted protocol, and all additional information as is required [for other investigators]."

For certain protocol amendments, the FDA requires sponsors to reference the specific technical information that supports the new protocol or protocol change. According to FDA regulations, a protocol amendment must contain a "Reference, if necessary, to specific technical information in the IND or in a concurrently submitted information amendment to the IND that the sponsor relies on to support any clinically significant change in the new or amended protocol. If the reference is made to supporting information already in the IND, the sponsor shall identify by name, reference number, volume, and page number the location of the information." The FDA has written that "the intent of the provision...is to elicit reference to technical information supporting the clinically significant aspects of the proposed change. Thus, if a sponsor intends to change the dosage form of the investigational drug, appropriate animal tests that would support this increased human exposure are required. To the extent that FDA is apprised of the basis for a change in a protocol, it can move quickly and comprehensively to review the change. Of course, if the change is one that plainly does not require specific technical support, the sponsor would not be expected to reference any supporting technical information."

The FDA requires that protocol amendments be prominently identified in one of three ways: "Protocol Amendment: New Protocol," "Protocol Amendment: Change in Protocol," or "Protocol Amendment: New Investigator." Although amendment submissions must be submitted as required, the FDA states that "when several submissions of new protocols or protocol changes are anticipated during a short period, the sponsor is encouraged, to the extent feasible, to include these all in a single submission." The FDA encourages sponsors to batch protocol amendments and to submit the batches at 30-day intervals.

IND Safety Reports The FDA has extremely specific requirements for the processing and reporting of clinical and nonclinical adverse drug experiences. The agency's goal is to "ensure timely communication of the most important new information about experiences with the investigational drug."

FDA regulations require sponsors to review all information that might represent a possible adverse experience: "Sponsors must promptly review all information relevant to the safety of the drug from any source, foreign or domestic, including information derived from clinical investigations, animal investigations, commercial marketing experience, reports in the scientific literature, and unpublished scientific papers." Once a sponsor's employee has knowledge of safety-related data, the sponsor is considered to have received that information. Therefore, sponsors must develop efficient mechanisms to ensure that such information is communicated internally (e.g., from subsidiaries and departments).

The reporting requirements applicable to an adverse experience are based on the nature, severity, probable cause, and frequency of the experience. In determining reporting requirements, three definitions are important:

Serious Adverse Experience. A serious adverse experience is any experience that suggests a significant hazard, contraindiction, side effect, or precaution. Current FDA regulations define a serious clinical AE as "any experience that is fatal or life-threatening, is permanently disabling, requires inpatient hospitalization, or is a congenital anomaly, cancer, or overdose." As part of its international harmonization initiative, the FDA introduced a revised definition for a serious clinical AE under its MedWatch Program: "an adverse experience occuring at any dose that is fatal or life-threatening, results in persistent or significant disability/incapacity, requires or prolongs inpatient hospitalization, necessitates medical or surgical intervention to preclude impairment of a body function or permanent damage to a body structure, or a congenital anomaly." An FDA regulation formally proposing the use of this revised definition for both clinical trial and postmarketing AE reporting was expected in early 1994. The agency cannot require the use of the definition until it is published in a final regulation, however. It is also worth noting that the ICH initiative has produced a draft consensus document entitled *Clinical Safety Data Management: Definitions and Standards for Expedited Reporting* (June 1993), which attempts to harmonize international standards for the collection and reporting of clinical trial AEs. As of this writing, the parties involved in the ICH initiative (i.e., the United States, European Community, and Japan) were reviewing that document.

Regarding AEs found in animal testing, a serious adverse drug experience includes any experience suggesting "a significant risk for human subjects, including any finding of mutagenicity, teratogenicity, or carcinogenicity."

Unexpected Adverse Experience. An unexpected adverse event is "any adverse experience that is not identified in nature, severity, or frequency in the current investigator's brochure." If an investigator's brochure is not required for the study, this requirement would apply to any adverse experience that is not identified in nature, severity, or frequency in the risk information provided in the general investigational plan or elsewhere in the IND or its amendments.

Associated with the Use of the Drug. The phrase "associated with the use of the drug" is interpreted by the regulations to mean that there is a reasonable possibility that the experience may have been caused by the drug. For each unexpected fatal or life-threatening experience associated with a drug's use during clinical trials, the sponsor is required to notify the FDA initially through a telephone report made within three working days after the sponsor receives information on the reaction.

Written IND safety reports are required for any clinical or nonclinical "adverse experience associated with the use of the drug that is both serious and unexpected." These reports must be submitted to the FDA no later than ten working days after the sponsor's initial receipt of the information. Also, the reports must identify all safety reports previously filed with the IND concerning a similar adverse experience, and must provide an analysis of the adverse experience's significance in light of the previous, similar reports. Adverse reactions that require the three-day telephone alert must also be the subject of a written safety report.

In cases in which ten working days are not sufficient to determine conclusively whether an adverse event should be reported, the agency advises that sponsors submit preliminary information within ten days. Sponsors should then supplement this initial report with whatever more definitive information they obtain after the original report.

Successive cases of serious and unexpected adverse reactions must be discussed in written reports until the risk posed by the experience is sufficiently well understood to be described in the investigator's brochure, or until an equally satisfactory resolution of the issue is reached (e.g., a determination that the experience is not product related).

Sponsors should remember that a safety report to an IND does not necessarily represent a concession that there is a relationship between the product and the adverse experience. In fact, the sponsor may state this fact explicitly in the safety report.

The agency may request that a sponsor submit IND safety reports in a particular format or at a frequency different than that required by regulations. The sponsor is also free to adopt its own reporting format or frequency, provided that CDER agrees to this in advance.

The FDA does not specify a format for IND safety reports. However, the agency has written that Form FDA 1639, a form used to report adverse reactions involving marketed drugs, "is clearly inappropriate for reporting in a safety report about animal tests..." and "...is also in most cases not an appropriate means of transmitting information about human clinical experience during a clinical investigation, as more extensive information on individual adverse experiences is needed than can ordinarily be included in a one-page report." Although the agency does not encourage the use of Form FDA 1639, it has been willing to discuss with sponsors the form's utility in reporting clinical experiences during Phase 3 studies.

In addition to those brought by the MedWatch Program, other changes to the FDA's IND safety reporting requirements are expected soon. In response to a fialuridine (FIAU) clinical trial in which 5 of 15 subjects died from toxicities associated with the drug, an internal FDA task force recommended a series of major changes to IND safety reporting requirements and industry approaches in analyzing and reporting clinical trial adverse experiences. Based on the FIAU experience, the task force concluded "that current IND requirements may not be adequate to protect against events such as those that occurred in the [FIAU] study, and that certain modifications to the way clinical investigations are conducted and reported may help to ensure that drug toxicity is detected as early as possible in drug development."

In a lengthy report released in November 1993, the task force recommended the following changes to address the regulatory inadequacies:

- The FDA should revise current regulations to require a new semi-annual IND safety report in which sponsors must report all expected and unexpected deaths, serious AEs, and safety-related discontinuations. The report should present data in both a "periodic and cumulative manner, and be accompanied by a reasonable analysis by the sponsor."

- The FDA should require that some sponsors submit "summaries," or "overviews," of all safety data generated during the IND process.

- The FDA should require that sponsors submit either a final or summary study report when such a filing would provide useful information not otherwise available from the semi-annual reports and safety overviews.

- Sponsors should strongly consider using a control group, even in early Phase 1 trials, when a drug's toxicity is likely to produce AEs that might be confused with the underlying disease process.

- Sponsors should develop "appropriate" trial stopping rules based on an estimate of the expected incidence of death and serious adverse experiences in the study population arising from the underlying disease or from medications used to treat the underlying disease.

- The FDA should require that sponsors describe in INDs their safety monitoring and evaluation programs, and in cases in which a program is inadequate, require that the company develop "extra-mural resources."

FDA Commissioner David Kessler, M.D., promised in late 1993 that the agency would address these recommendations in proposed regulations expected in early 1994.

Annual Reports   Within 60 days of the anniversary date on which the initial IND "went into effect," the sponsor must submit an overview of information collected on the subject product during the previous year. Described by regulations as "a brief report of the progress of the investigation," the annual report should provide the following:

Information on Individual Studies. The FDA wants "a brief summary of the status of each study in progress and each study completed during the previous year. The summary must include the following information on each study: (1) the title of the study (with any appropriate study identifiers such as protocol number), its purposes, a brief statement identifying the patient population and a statement as to whether the study is completed"; "(2) the total number of subjects initially planned for inclusion in the study, the number entered into the study to date, the number whose participation in the study was completed and planned, and the number who dropped out of the study for any reason"; and "(3) if the study has been completed or if the interim results are known, a brief description of any available study results."

Summary Information. This section should include all additional product-related information collected during the previous year, as well as summary data from all clinical studies:

- a narrative or tabular summary showing the most frequent and most serious adverse experiences by body system;

- a summary of all IND safety reports submitted during the past year;

- a list of subjects who died while participating in the investigation, with the cause of death for each subject (this list must identify all deaths, including those persons whose cause of death is not believed to be product related);

- a brief description of any information that is pertinent to an understanding of the drug's actions (e.g., information from controlled trials and information about bioavailability);

- a list of the preclinical studies (including animal studies) completed or in progress during the past year, and a summary of the major preclinical findings; and

- a summary of any significant manufacturing or microbiological changes made during the past year.

General Investigational Plan. A brief description of the general investigational plan for the coming year must be provided. This plan should be as descriptive as that submitted in the original IND. If the plans are not yet formulated, the sponsor must indicate this fact in the report.

Investigator's Brochure Revisions. When the investigator's brochure has been revised, the sponsor must include a description of the revision and a copy of the new brochure.

Phase 1 Modifications. The sponsor must describe any significant Phase 1 protocol modifications that were made during the previous year and that were not reported previously to the FDA through a protocol amendment.

Foreign Marketing Developments. According to the IND regulations, this section should provide a "brief summary of significant foreign marketing developments with the drug during the past year, such as approval of marketing in any country or withdrawal or suspension from marketing in any country."

Request for an FDA Response. If the sponsor requests an FDA meeting, reply, or comment, a log of any relevant outstanding business with respect to the IND must be included.

Information Amendments   IND information amendments are used to report to the FDA new information that would not ordinarily be included in a protocol amendment or IND safety report, and information whose importance dictates that it must be reported before the next IND annual report. Information amendments commonly include new data from animal studies, changes or additions to the IND's chemistry, manufacturing, and controls section, and reports on discontinued clinical trials. Such information is more immediately critical than that included in the annual report. Information amendments should be submitted as necessary, but preferably not more frequently than every 30 days.

The principal content requirements for information amendments are: (1) a statement of the nature and purpose of the amendment; (2) an organized submission of the data in a format appropriate for scientific review; and (3) a request for FDA comment on the information amendment (i.e., if the sponsor wishes to obtain such comment).

Chapter 5:

CDER and the IND Review Process

Although many analyses focus on the FDA's authority to decide which new drugs reach the U.S. market, the agency plays a gatekeeper role at another key point in the drug development process. In reviewing INDs, the FDA also determines which new drugs advance from the preclinical to the clinical development phase.

When a drug sponsor submits an IND, the FDA assumes an important role in the development of a new product. From this point forward, the sponsor can do little without submitting documents to, and possibly waiting for a review and approval from, the FDA.

In fact, most sponsor activities beyond the preclinical development phase are subject to some form of federal regulation. This reality is emphasized in the following statement that a sponsor must sign in the IND: "I agree not to begin clinical investigations until 30 days after FDA's receipt of the IND unless I receive earlier notification by FDA that the studies may begin. I also agree not to begin or continue clinical investigations covered by the IND if those studies are placed on clinical hold. I agree that an Institutional Review Board (IRB) that complies with [federal regulations] will be responsible for the initial and continuing review and approval of each of the studies in the proposed clinical investigation. I agree to conduct the investigation in accordance with all other applicable regulatory requirements."

The FDA's Center for Drug Evaluation and Research (CDER) is the regulatory and scientific unit that oversees the development and marketing of all new drugs. Therefore, before outlining the IND review process, it is appropriate to profile CDER, one of the FDA's five primary program centers.

The FDA's Center for Drug Evaluation and Research (CDER)

Although it has functioned in many forms and under several titles previously, CDER was created in late 1987 as part of an FDA reorganization initiative. The reorganization split the FDA's Center for Drugs and Biologics into two separate centers: CDER and the Center for Biologics Evaluation and Research (CBER).

CDER's roughly 900 employees (as of fiscal year 1992) are responsible for the 12 principal functions that federal regulations set out for the center:

- to review INDs and NDAs;

- to develop FDA policy with regard to the safety, effectiveness, and labeling of all drug products for human use;

- to develop and implement standards for the safety and effectiveness of all over-the-counter (OTC) drugs;

- to monitor the quality of marketed drug products through product testing, surveillance, and compliance programs;

- to coordinate with CBER on the review of biological drug products;

- to develop and promulgate guidelines on Current Good Manufacturing Practice (CGMP) for use by the drug industry;

- to develop and disseminate information and educational materials concerning drug products to the medical community and the public;

- to conduct research and develop scientific standards on the composition, quality, safety, and effectiveness of human drugs;

- to collect and evaluate information on the effects and trends of the use of marketed drug products;

- to monitor prescription drug advertising and promotional labeling to ensure their accuracy and integrity;

- to analyze data on accidental poisoning and to disseminate toxicity and treatment information on household products and medicines; and

- to cooperate with other FDA offices, other federal and international agencies, volunteer health organizations, universities, individual scientists, nongovernmental laboratories, and manufacturers of drug products in carrying out these functions.

To fulfill these responsibilities, CDER has more than two dozen divisions, which function under nine principal offices (see chart below):

Office of Drug Evaluation I (ODE I) and Office of Drug Evaluation II (ODE II). These two offices house the ten divisions that review all INDs, NDAs, and other applications associated with new drugs.

Office of Generic Drugs (OGD). OGD regulates generic drugs and reviews abbreviated new drug applications (ANDA) submitted for such products.

Office of OTC Drug Evaluation. This office regulates, and sets policies for, over-the-counter (OTC) medicines. Among this group's goals is to become more involved in the review of NDAs proposing prescription-to-OTC drug switches, applications traditionally reviewed by ODE I and ODE II.

Office of Epidemiology and Biostatistics. This unit provides statistical expertise for CDER's drug reviews, and is responsible for the center's postmarketing adverse experience (AE) surveillance program.

Office of Compliance. This office monitors industry compliance with a variety of regulatory standards, including CGMP, good laboratory practice (GLP), good clinical practices (GCP), and labeling requirements.

Office of Drug Standards. This unit's responsibilities include monitoring the drug industry's marketing, advertising, and promotional efforts.

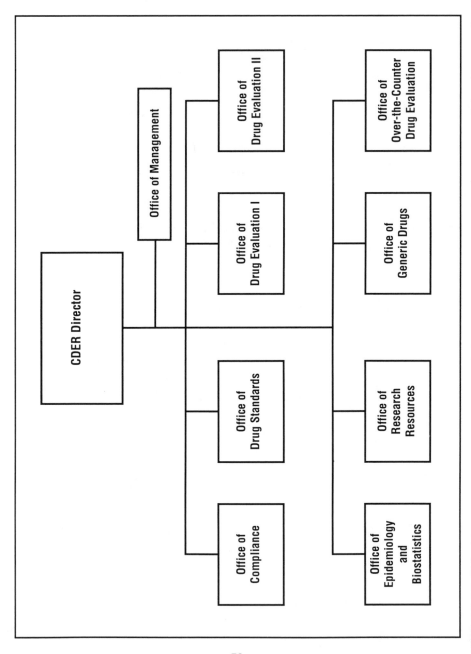

Office of Management. This office spearheads CDER's planning, budgeting, training, and information management activities.

Office of Research Resources. This unit provides research support services in several areas, including clinical pharmacology, drug analysis, and biopharmaceutics.

CDER's Drug Review Divisions

Although the offices profiled above each play an essential role in drug regulation, this chapter focuses on the structure and responsibilities of ODE I and ODE II. These two CDER offices house the ten drug review divisions that process and evaluate INDs and NDAs, and that decide which drugs can be tested in clinical trials and, ultimately, marketed in the United States.

Since their decisions determine the fates of therapeutically and commercially significant new drugs, these divisions are certainly among the most closely monitored and highly pressured offices within the FDA. With the advent of user fees—fees paid by industry to support and accelerate the drug review process—the industry, congressional, and public scrutiny under which these divisions traditionally have operated is expected to intensify during the mid-1990s.

As the division titles (cardio-renal, antiviral, etc.) indicate, the reviewing responsibilities are apportioned to CDER's ten drug review divisions by therapeutic area. Each unit has its own areas of expertise, and reviews all new drugs proposed for use in these areas. As one would expect, this separation of responsibility creates a disparity in the workloads facing each division (see table below), and fundamental differences in the scientific and medical issues that each division must address in reviewing new drugs.

CDER's ten drug review divisions differ in other ways. Although the groups function under the same legal and regulatory framework, each division has considerable autonomy to establish its own policies and procedures within this framework. The divisions have their own distinctive personalities, approaches to the new drug review process, and style of interacting with sponsors.

These divisions will see fundamental change over the next several years. Under the Prescription Drug User Fee Act of 1992, CDER will absorb about

Breakdown of Drug Divisions' Review Workload
(Pending as of December 31, 1992)

Division	Active INDs (# Commercial)	Pending NDAs	Pending Supplements (# Manufacturing)
Pilot Drug Evaluation Staff	1002 (399)	12	599 (157)
Cardio-Renal Drug Products	776 (379)	14	87 (24)
Neuropharmacological Drug Products	1446 (373)	18	554 (174)
Oncology and Pulmonary Drug Products	1109 (471)	16	209 (101)
Medical Imaging, Surgical and Dental Drug Products	1181 (273)	31	189 (147)
Gastrointestinal and Coagulation Drug Products	481 (172)	14	68 (27)
Metabolism and Endocrine Drug Products	2256 (423)	17	219 (117)
Anti-Infective Drug Products	1000 (464)	32	452 (173)
Antiviral Drug Products	1106 (195)	8	83 (30)
TOTAL	10357 (3149)	162	2460 (950)

300 new staffers by fiscal year (FY) 1997, most of them within the ten drug review divisions. The divisions will also have to cope with the demanding new NDA review time lines that the agency has agreed to meet under the provisions of the statute (see Chapter 9).

The following sections provide brief profiles of CDER's drug review divisions, with particular emphasis on the therapeutic categories of drugs that each unit regulates.

Division of Anti-Infective Drug Products   By several measures, CDER's Division of Anti-Infective Drug Products was the busiest of the center's drug review divisions through the early 1990s. According to CDER's *Offices of Drug Evaluation Statistical Report-1992*, the unit:

- had the most NDAs—32—under review at year-end 1992;

- received the plurality of new NDA submissions in 1992—in fact, fully 27 of the 100 submitted to CDER during the year; and

- received the plurality of commercial INDs during 1992.

At least two other factors made this unit's workload particularly unenviable. Because many of the drugs regulated by the unit are studied for multiple indications (e.g., broad-spectrum antibiotics), the NDAs that it reviews are among the largest within CDER. Secondly, the division's reviewing responsibilities were expanded somewhat in 1993. Specifically, the unit reinherited responsibility for ophthalmic drugs from the Division of Medical Imaging, Surgical, and Dental Drug Products. At this writing, however, this shift seem to be temporary, as CDER was in the process of creating the Division of Topical Drug Products (see discussion below), which was to assume responsibility for most dermatological and ophthalmic drugs from the Division of Anti-Infective Drug Products.

In the past several years, the division has looked to innovative review approaches to cope with its large and growing workload. Under the leadership of its former director and current CDER Deputy Director for Review Management Murray Lumpkin, M.D., the division has, quite successfully, used new review methodologies to speed reviews and significantly reduce its application backlog in recent years.

From January 1989 through July 1993, for example, the Division of Anti-Infective Drug Products had accepted 28 computer-assisted new drug applications (CANDA), virtually one-third of all CANDAs submitted to the agency during that period, according to FDA statistics. In other efforts to expedite drug reviews, the division has assigned a team of medical reviewers (as opposed to one, which is conventional) to an NDA, apportioning the application's clinical studies among several physician-reviewers.

Following the transfer of dermatologic and ophthalmic drugs to the Division of Topical Drug Products, the Division of Anti-Infective Drug Products' responsibilities can be divided into three broad therapeutic categories:

Systemic Antimicrobial Drugs. Aminoglycosides, antimalarials, antisepsis immunomodulators, cephalosporins, macrolides, penem

81

antibiotics, penicillins, quinolones, sulfonamides, tetracyclines, and other antiparasitic and systemic antimicrobial drugs.

Topical Anti-Infectives. Topical antimicrobials, anti-acne drugs (antimicrobials only), topical sulfonamides, topical macrolides, topical clindamycines, and topical tetracyclines.

Topical Vaginal Drugs. Topical antifungal vaginal drugs.

Division of Topical Drug Products CDER created the Division of Topical Drug Products in March 1994 largely to lessen the workload in what had become the center's busiest review division. To head the new unit, the center hired Jonathan Wilkins, M.D., formerly a member of CDER's Dermatologic Drug Products Advisory Committee. When its formation was announced, the division was to have review responsibilities in at least two therapeutic areas:

Ophthalmics. Alpha adrenergic agonist/blockers, antibiotics, antiprotozoals, antivirals, beta adrenergic blockers, corticosteroids, and nonsteroidal anti-inflammatory agents.

Dermatological Drugs. Anti-acne drugs (except antimicrobials), topical antimicrobial burn preparations, antiperspirants, topical antipruritics, topical astringents, topical aural drugs, topical corticosteroids, pediculocides, miscellaneous topical and systemic immunosuppressants.

Division of Medical Imaging, Surgical and Dental Drug Products Since mid-1991, the Division of Medical Imaging, Surgical and Dental Drug Products has had three different division directors. Most recently, in August 1993, former Pilot Drug Evaluation Staff Medical Officer Patricia Love, M.D., was appointed as the unit's director.

Although the division had the fewest IND submissions in 1992, it had the second highest number—15—of NDA submissions during the year. The group also had the second highest number of pending NDAs at year-end 1992.

Currently, one division priority is establishing more specific and relevant clinical endpoints for studies involving medical imaging agents. In what

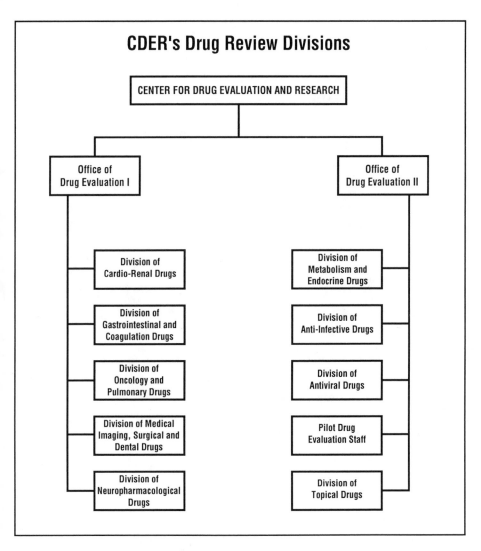

CDER's Drug Review Divisions

CENTER FOR DRUG EVALUATION AND RESEARCH

Office of
Drug Evaluation I

Office of
Drug Evaluation II

Division of
Cardio-Renal Drugs

Division of
Metabolism and
Endocrine Drugs

Division of
Gastrointestinal and
Coagulation Drugs

Division of
Anti-Infective Drugs

Division of
Oncology and
Pulmonary Drugs

Division of
Antiviral Drugs

Division of Medical
Imaging, Surgical and
Dental Drugs

Pilot Drug
Evaluation Staff

Division of
Neuropharmacological
Drugs

Division of
Topical Drugs

division officials say is a "refining" of clinical effectiveness endpoints, the division is asking that sponsors provide more detailed information on the disease/condition associated with the subject image, the conditions under which the imaging agent will be used, how the agent alters or improves diagnoses, and plans for assessing the agent's sensitivity and/or specificity.

The division's responsibilities can be divided into three general therapeutic classes:

Radiopharmaceutical Drugs. Magnetic resonance image enhancement agents, radioactive diagnostic agents, radioactive therapeutic agents, radiopaque contrast agents, ultrasound agents, and adjuvants used with the above agents (e.g., potassium perchlorate).

Surgical Drugs. Burn treatment agents, peritoneal dialysis solutions, osmotic diuretics, injectable surgical adjunct enzymes, topical enzymes, irrigating fluids, large volume parenterals, sclerosing agents, and urological products.

Dental Drugs. Anticaries preparations, antiplaque agents, mouthwashes, and periodontal treatments.

Pilot Drug Evaluation Staff CDER established the Pilot Drug Evaluation Staff in 1989, and provided the unit with broad powers to experiment with innovative drug review approaches. The goal of this effort was to help identify new approaches that could reduce drug review times. The division is, in effect, a "living laboratory" responsible for reviewing neurological, anti-inflammatory, anesthetic, and abusable drugs.

The Pilot Drug Evaluation Staff was the brainchild of John Harter, M.D., the division's first director. Although CDER announced in early 1994 that Harter would be leaving the division to assume another position within CDER, center officials maintained that this change would not affect the nature of the unit.

When it was established, the division was set outside the authorities of ODE I and ODE II. To encourage innovation and minimize some of the traditional bureaucratic pressures facing any division of a large organization, the unit reported directly to the office of then-CDER Director Carl Peck, M.D. As part of a limited CDER reorganization in late 1993, the Pilot Drug Evaluation Staff was placed within ODE II. However, this administrative change is not intended to affect the division's experimentation with innovative review approaches, which include:

Computerized Submissions. As the Pilot Drug Evaluation Staff's first director, Harter was one of the most vocal advocates of CANDA use. The division is active in using computers in not only NDA reviews, but IND-stage reviews as well. In some projects, the division is also said to be accepting and reviewing computerized clinical data as it becomes available during clinical trials.

NDA Days. Pioneered by the division in 1988, the NDA Day (see Chapter 19) brings together key FDA and drug sponsor personnel for an intensive one- or two-day meeting during which drug labeling and other late-stage NDA review issues are addressed. Division staff credit NDA Days with condensing a process that would ordinarily consume weeks or months into a few days of intensified face-to-face meetings. The division has also incorporated both CANDA-type reviews and advisory committee meetings into NDA Day sessions.

Rotation of Key Staff. To provide its key managers with insights into the full range of drug review issues, the division periodically rotates its medical officers into various management positions, including the division director post.

The division's product review responsibilities can be divided into four therapeutic areas:

Abusable Drugs. Drugs to treat alcoholism, enkephalin analgesics, hallucinogenic agents, methadone and other addictives, narcotic antagonist/agonists/analgesics, narcotics in addiction research, and drugs to treat nicotine addiction.

Anesthetic Drugs. Epidural and intrathecal analgesics, lidocaine for cardiac arrhythmia, neuromuscular blocking agents, preanesthetic sedatives, and general, local, and regional anesthetic agents.

Anti-Inflammatory Drugs. Inhalant corticosteroids, systemic corticosteroids, nonsteroidal anti-inflammatory agents, anti-gout drugs, and immunomodulators for rheumatic diseases.

Neurological Drugs. Non-narcotic analgesics, antipyretics, and muscle relaxants.

Division of Metabolism and Endocrine Drug Products   The Division of Metabolism and Endocrine Drug Products reviews INDs and NDAs for fertility, maternal health, metabolic, and endocrine drug products. Already responsible for evaluating some drugs for weight-loss indications, the division inherited responsibilities for other weight-loss products from the Division of Neuropharmacological Drug Products in mid-1993.

The division's responsibilities can be divided into two broad therapeutic categories:

Metabolic and Endocrine Drugs. Adrenal/ACTH, androgens/anabolic steroids, bone calcium and phosphorus metabolism, drugs for diabetes (miscellaneous), dopamine agonists, gonadotropins, growth hormone and analogs, hyperglycemic agents, oral hyperglycemic agents, insulin, lipid-altering agents, metabolic agents, nutrients/amino acids, somatostatin, thyroid agents, vasopressin, and vitamins (other than vitamin D).

Fertility and Antifertility Drugs. Contraceptives (not oral), oral contraceptives, estrogens, oxytocics, progestins, uterine-acting agents.

The Division of Oncology and Pulmonary Drug Products   For administrative purposes, CDER's oncology and pulmonary drug groups are part of a single division—the Division of Oncology and Pulmonary Drug Products. In many other respects, including physical location, the groups are separate divisions.

In May 1993, the division's oncology reviewers relocated to take office space adjacent to CBER's Oncology Products Group. The long-term objective of this pooling of oncology reviewers is to form a single oncology review group, with drug and biologic applications being assigned to CBER and CDER medical reviewers regardless of their center affiliations. In the "pilot" experiments for the group, which were initiated in mid-1993, a biological IND was assigned to a CDER medical reviewer and a drug IND was assigned to a CBER medical reviewer.

The division's responsibilities can be split into the oncology and pulmonary therapeutic areas:

Oncology Drugs. Drugs to treat AIDS patients with Kaposi's sarcoma, biological response modifiers for cancer treatment, cancer chemotherapy agents, drugs to treat graft-versus-host disease, and immunomodulators.

Pulmonary-Antiallergic Drugs. Antiasthmatics (nonsteroidal), bronchoconstrictors, bronchodilators, cough-cold-allergy preparations (antihistamines, antitussives, decongestants, etc.), mucolytic agents, and pulmonary surfactants.

Division of Antiviral Drug Products   Since it was founded in 1983, the Division of Antiviral Drug Products has labored with a nation peering over its shoulder. As the division that reviews therapies to treat AIDS, the unit has responded to public pressure for new AIDS therapies by working pro-actively with product sponsors early in drug development, and by working closely with other government agencies such as the National Institute of Allergies and Infectious Diseases (NIAID).

Due to the nature of its primary mission, the division was isolated from reviewing responsibilities as diverse as those found in most other divisions. Currently, the Division of Antiviral Drug Products reviews systemic antifungals, antiparasitic agents, antiretrovirals, antivirals, immunomodulators, drugs to prevent the rejection of transplanted organs, and some systemic antimicrobial drugs.

As one might expect given its relatively narrow therapeutic responsibilities, the division's workload is smaller than those of its sister divisions. As of year-end 1992, the division had only eight pending NDAs, easily the lowest within CDER. On the other hand, the division also received the most IND submissions during 1992, the vast majority of which were research and emergency INDs.

The Division of Antiviral Drug Products is also unique in that it has a formal Pre-IND Program, the only such program within CDER. Managed by a full-time coordinator, the division's Pre-IND Program is designed to facilitate early-stage sponsor/FDA communications and to assist sponsors in developing the data necessary to support the IND filing and the initiation of clinical studies. Although the program was originally intended to support the development of AIDS and AIDS-related therapies, it was recently expanded to include other drugs regulated by the division. Under the Pre-IND Program, the division reviews pre-IND submissions; provides guidance on development plans, study designs, and data requirements; and identifies other government resources available to sponsors. To further support early-stage development efforts for AIDS therapies, the division also published several guidance documents, including: *Points to Consider in the Preparation of IND Applications for New Drugs Intended for the Treatment of HIV-Infected Individuals* (December 1993); *Points to Consider in the Preclinical Development of Antiviral Drugs*; *Points to Consider in the Preclinical Development of Immunomodulatory Drugs for the Treatment of HIV Infection and Associated Disorders* (September 1992); and *Points to Consider in the Immunotoxicology Evaluation of New Drugs Intended for the Treatment of HIV Infection and Related Disorders.*

Division of Cardio-Renal Drug Products Like the Division of Antiviral Drug Products, the Division of Cardio-Renal Drug Products has rel-atively homogeneous drug review authorities. The unit's review authorities can be divided into two broad categories:

Antihypertensive Renal Drugs. ACE inhibitors, agents used in hypotension and shock, antihypertensive agents, diuretics and renal tubule inhibitors, and potassium salts.

Cardiac Drugs. Angiographic diagnostic adjuncts, antianginal agents, antiarrhythmics, beta blocking agents, calcium channel blockers, central alpha-2 agonists, coronary vasodilators, and peripheral vasodilators.

Although the division's existing IND and NDA workload is roughly com-parable to CDER averages, the unit has been one of the more enthusiastic about CANDA projects. Having pioneered the use of CANDAs in the early and mid-1980s, the division remains active in recruiting new CANDA pro-jects (see Chapter 19).

The Division of Gastrointestinal and Coagulation Drug Products
Stephen Fredd, M.D., the director of the Division of Gastrointestinal and Coagulation Drug Products, credits his division's focus on internal reviewing efficiencies and its consistency in applying agency policies, such as CDER's refuse-to-file (RTF) policy for deficient applications, for the lack of an IND or NDA backlog within the group. During the early 1990s, the division has consistently recorded one of CDER's best average approval times for new drugs.

The division's efficiency is one reason why it has not looked to such innovative approaches as NDA Days to accelerate drug reviews, say division staffers. Although the division is among the least-experienced with CANDAs, the unit does encourage computer submissions, particularly for coagulation drugs.

The division's review responsibilities can be broken down into two principal therapeutic areas:

Coagulation Drugs. Anticoagulants, antifibrinolytics, antiplatelet agents, chelating agents, coagulants, fibrinolytics, hematologics, prostaglandins, postoperative thromboembolic agents, and thromboxane antagonists.

Gastrointestinal Drugs. Antacids, anticholinergics, anticolitis and anti-ileitis agents, antiemetics, antiflatulents, gastrointestinal anti-motility and antispasmodics, antiulcer agents, cholecystokinetic agents, choleretics and hydrocholeretics, gastrointestinal diagnostics, gallstone solvents, hemorrhoidal preparations, laxatives, liver agents, motility stimulants, pancreatic agents, and gastrointestinal prostaglandins.

The Division of Neuropharmacological Drug Products   Over the past two years, the Division of Neuropharmacological Drug Products has faced a handful of priorities that have diverted considerable resources from normal division activities. Concern over the sleep aid Halcion and the antidepressant Prozac and the growing effort to find effective treatments for Alzheimer's disease have been the principal culprits.

Such priorities have resulted in an increase in the number of INDs and NDAs pending at the division. The number of pending NDAs doubled from 9 in 1991 to 18 at the end of 1992. During May 1993, that workload decreased somewhat as the division transferred responsibilities for reviewing anti-obesity drugs to the Division of Metabolism and Endocrine Drug Products.

The division's current responsibilities can be divided into two general therapeutic categories:

> *Neurology Drugs.* Anticonvulsants, antiemetics, antinauseants, anti-Parkinson agents, antispasticity agents, cerebral stimulants, vascular agents, drugs to assist memory (Alzheimer's/senility/dementia), and drugs to treat migraine, movement disorders, multiple sclerosis, narcolepsy/sleep apnea, stroke, and tardive dyskinesia.

> *Psychiatric Drugs.* Anorexigenic agents/CNS stimulants, antianxiety agents/anxiolytics, antidepressants, antimanics, antipsychotics, hypnotics, sedatives, and drugs to treat schizophrenia, eating disorders, learning disorders (dyslexia), minimal brain dysfunction, obsessive compulsive disorder, and panic.

Inside the FDA's Drug Review Divisions

Although CDER's ten review divisions differ in many ways, they are similar in nature and structure. Each unit is lead by a division director who is generally a physician. Most divisions have deputy directors as well.

At the core of each division is a three- or four-discipline review structure. IND, NDA, and other drug application reviews are conducted by individuals from each of three or four technical disciplines: medical/clinical; nonclinical pharmacology/toxicology; chemistry, and microbiology (i.e., for anti-infective drugs).

Medical/Clinical Discipline   Often called medical officers, medical/clinical reviewers are almost exclusively physicians. In rare instances, such as in the review of some psychiatric drugs, non-physicians are used as medical officers to evaluate drug efficacy.

Medical reviewers are responsible for evaluating the clinical sections of submissions, such as the safety of the clinical protocols in an IND or the results of this testing as submitted in the NDA. Within most divisions, clinical reviewers take the lead role in the IND or NDA review, and are responsible for synthesizing the results of the chemistry, pharmacology, and clinical reviews to formulate the basis upon which a drug will be approved or used in early clinical testing.

A division's medical reviewers often are assigned to one of two or more drug groups. Each of these groups is headed by a medical supervisor, and is staffed by physicians who possess expertise in a specific drug category/disease state for which the division is responsible.

Chemistry Discipline   Each review division employs a team of chemists responsible for reviewing the chemistry, manufacturing, and control sections of drug applications. In general terms, chemistry reviewers address issues related to drug identity, manufacturing and control, and analysis.

Pharmacology Discipline   The pharmacology review team is staffed by pharmacologists and toxicologists who evaluate the results of animal testing in attempting to relate nonclinical drug effects to potential effects in humans.

Microbiology Discipline   Within the Division of Anti-Infective Drug Products and the Division of Antiviral Drug Products, there is a fourth technical review discipline—microbiology. Since antimicrobial and antiviral drug products are designed to affect microbial or viral, rather than human, physiology, the groups employ microbiologists to evaluate the products' effects on viruses or other microorganisms.

Consumer Safety Officers   There is at least one other group of individuals who are critical to the application review process—consumer safety officers (CSO). CSOs serve as a drug sponsor's primary contact with a division during the product development and application review processes. As is a professional from each of the primary technical disciplines, a CSO is assigned to each IND and NDA upon its submission.

Since most CSOs have scientific backgrounds (i.e., primarily in pharmacy), they can provide informed reports of technical issues that arise during the drug review process. Their real expertise, however, is their knowledge of the drug review process, and of the policies, procedures, and idiosyncracies of their respective divisions.

The IND Review Process

The IND review process is unique among the FDA's application review processes. In many respects, that process and the FDA's treatment of INDs is a curious balance between the federal government's responsibility to protect patients from unnecessary risks and its desire to avoid becoming an impediment to the advance of medical research. Given these dual goals, the FDA must perform a safety review of an IND, but is given only 30 days in which to reach an initial decision on the application.

The FDA's principal goals during the IND review are: (1) to determine if the preclinical test data show that the drug is reasonably safe for administration to humans; and (2) to determine if the protocol for the proposed clinical studies will expose clinical subjects to unnecessary risks (assuming the protocol proposes only Phase 1 studies).

Initial Processing of the IND   The FDA's early processing of the IND depends on the manner in which the application is shipped to the agency. INDs arriving by regular mail, for example, are forwarded to the general FDA mail room, while applications shipped by courier are sent directly to CDER's Central Document Room.

Once within CDER's Central Document Room, the IND is stamped with the date of receipt, an extremely important event since it starts the 30-day review clock. Staffers within this office assign an identification number to the IND, and then log information about the filing into a computer database—the sponsor's name, the drug's name, and the application's identification number. Finally, before sending the application to a review division, staffers package the application (e.g., in review jackets if necessary).

Given the tight IND review time frame, this initial processing occurs extremely quickly. INDs arriving in the CDER's Central Document Room during the morning will be forwarded to the review division within the same day in most cases. For treatment INDs, the staffers attempt to forward the application within an hour of its receipt.

The IND within the Review Division   Once within the review division, the IND is sent to a file or document room where a staffer creates a history card containing the applicant's name, the IND's date of receipt and identification number, and other information. The division then develops and sends an "acknowledgement letter," which tells the applicant that the FDA has received the IND. The letter also specifies the IND's identification number and receipt date, and provides the name of the CSO who will act as the FDA contact person on matters involving the application.

The assigned CSO will then act as the unofficial coordinator of the review, seeing that the application is forwarded to the relevant individuals. At this stage, the CSO may choose to review the contents of the IND to identify any deficiencies.

As previously discussed, an IND faces reviews by the three or four technical review disciplines within a division—medical/clinical, pharmacology, chemistry, and, in two divisions, microbiology. The first copy of the IND will usually be forwarded to a supervisory medical officer, sometimes called a "group leader," who has expertise in the subject drug's therapeutic category. In some review divisions, it is the group leader who analyzes the results of the medical, pharmacology, and chemistry reviews, and recommends whether or not the contents of the IND are adequate to allow the initiation of clinical trials.

Obviously, each review discipline has its own concerns:

Pharmacology Review. The reviewing pharmacologist focuses on the results of animal pharmacology and toxicology testing, and attempts to relate these test results to human pharmacology.

Chemistry Review. The reviewing chemist evaluates the manufacturing and processing procedures for a drug to ensure that the compound is adequately reproducible and stable in its pure form. If the drug is either unstable or not reproducible, then the validity of any clinical testing would be undermined and, more importantly, the studies may pose significant risks.

Clinical Review. The medical reviewer evaluates the clinical trial protocol to determine: (1) if the subjects will be protected from unnecessary risks; and (2) if the study design will provide data relevant to the safety and effectiveness of the drug. Under federal regulations, proposed Phase 1 studies are evaluated almost exclusively for safety reasons. Since the late 1980s, FDA reviewers have been instructed to provide drug sponsors with greater freedom during

Phase 1, as long as the investigations do not expose subjects to undue risks. In evaluating Phase 2 and 3 investigations, however, FDA reviewers also must ensure that these studies are of sufficient scientific quality, and that they are capable of yielding data that can support marketing approval.

Microbiology Review. The microbiologist evaluates data on the drug's *in vivo* and *in vitro* effects on the physiology of the target virus or other microorganism.

During the drug evaluation process, reviews in the three or four technical areas are supplemented by what are called "consultative reviews" in biostatistics and biopharmaceutics. At the IND review stage, agency biostatisticians may evaluate animal data to determine the statistical significance of drug effects in animals, including tumor rates and dose-response relationships. And, while FDA biopharmaceutics staffers may not become directly involved in the IND review (except for AIDS drugs and other critical therapies), these staffers can review biopharmaceutics and pharmacokinetic data (i.e., drug concentrations in blood and urine) from initial clinical studies to provide advice on dosing, dosing intervals, and other drug administration issues for later trials.

When the reviewers complete their evaluations, they each submit a report summarizing their findings to the group leader, who is left to synthesize these findings and to make a final recommendation to the division director. Recommendations made by group leaders are rarely overturned by the division director.

While a division must complete a safety evaluation within the 30-day period, reviewers may continue to evaluate the IND after the period expires. If new safety concerns arise from this continuing review, the FDA may order that ongoing clinical trials be discontinued until these concerns are addressed and resolved.

The 30-Day Review Clock   The FDA has no uniform procedures for informing applicants about the results of IND reviews. Most drug review divisions, for instance, do not contact the sponsor if no problems are found with drug safety and the proposed clinical trials. Rather, the divisions just allow the 30-day review period to expire, thereby permitting the sponsor to initiate clinical studies immediately. In this way, INDs are never formally approved, but are "passively" approved when the FDA chooses not to contact the sponsor to delay clinical plans. Although it is not required, sponsors should contact the agency before initiating clinical trials.

CDER staffers caution, however, that a firm that has not received an acknowledgement letter should not initiate trials, no matter how long the company believes that an IND has been at the agency. Because INDs can be lost during shipment or misplaced at the agency, applicants should contact the FDA if they have not received an acknowledgement letter.

When deficiencies are found in an IND, the FDA may take one of two actions. If the review division decides that an IND deficiency is not serious enough to justify delaying clinical studies, the division may either telephone or forward a deficiency letter to the sponsor. In either case, the division informs the sponsor that it may proceed with the planned clinical trials, but that additional information is necessary to complete or correct the IND file.

The Clinical Hold

When CDER discovers serious deficiencies that cannot be addressed before or during the IND review process, the center will contact the sponsor within the 30-day review period to delay the clinical trial. The clinical hold is the mechanism that CDER uses to accomplish this.

Through this order, the agency may either delay the initiation of an early-phase trial on the basis of information submitted in the IND, or discontinue an ongoing study based on either a re-review of the original IND or a review of newly submitted clinical protocols, safety reports, protocol amendments, or other information. When a clinical hold is issued, a sponsor must address the issue that is the basis of the hold before the order is removed.

The FDA's authority regarding clinical holds is outlined in federal regulations. The regulations specify the clinical hold criteria that the FDA applies to the various phases of clinical testing.

Clinical Holds and Phase 1 Trials　One of the principal goals of the FDA's 1987 IND regulations was to give sponsors "greater freedom" during the initial stages of clinical research. Therefore, the regulation states that the

95

FDA should not place a clinical hold on a Phase 1 study "unless it presents an unreasonable and significant risk to test subjects." In the regulation's preamble, the FDA states that it will "defer to sponsors on matters of Phase 1 study design," and will not consider a Phase 1 trial's scientific merit in deciding whether it should be allowed to proceed.

The regulation specifies four situations in which the FDA can either delay a Phase 1 study proposed in an IND or discontinue an ongoing Phase 1 trial:

- if human subjects are or would be exposed to an unreasonable and significant risk of illness or injury;

- if the clinical investigators named in the IND are not qualified by reason of their scientific training and experience to conduct the investigation described in the IND;

- if the investigator's brochure (i.e., material supplying drug-related safety and effectiveness information to clinical investigators) is misleading, erroneous, or materially incomplete; or

- if the IND does not contain sufficient information as required under federal regulations to assess the risks that the proposed studies present to subjects.

According to the estimates of FDA staffers, 5 to 20 percent of Phase 1 protocols are placed on clinical hold at the IND review stage. Hold rates, however, probably vary considerably between review divisions, and are influenced by factors such as the nature of the drugs a division reviews.

Clinical Holds and Phase 2 and 3 Studies   The FDA has greater discretionary powers to delay and discontinue Phase 2 or Phase 3 trials. Current regulations allow the agency to place a clinical hold on a Phase 2 or 3 trial if: (1) any of the four Phase 1 clinical hold criteria outlined above are met; or (2) the "plan or protocol for the investigation is clearly deficient in design to meet its stated objectives."

The second criterion has been somewhat controversial. The FDA had never before held the authority to stop a trial due to design or scientific deficiencies unrelated to patient safety. Some industry officials, particularly those at more experienced firms, believe that companies should be allowed to experiment and establish their own scientific and medical arguments, and that FDA involvement should be limited to issues pertaining to patient safety.

How Clinical Holds Work   The FDA acknowledges that the imposition of a clinical hold is a relatively informal and flexible process. Given the nature of product development, the agency has resisted suggestions that it formalize the clinical hold process.

Current regulations state that the process will, in many cases, begin with an FDA-sponsor discussion: "Whenever FDA concludes that a deficiency exists in a clinical investigation that may be grounds for the imposition of a clinical hold, FDA will, unless patients are exposed to immediate and serious risk, attempt to discuss and satisfactorily resolve the matter with the sponsor before issuing the clinical hold order."

In certain situations, a division may ask sponsors, on an informal basis, to voluntarily agree to an extension of the 30-day review to avoid a clinical hold order. For example, if a reviewing pharmacologist is unable to complete a review of an IND's preclinical data within the 30-day limit, the division may ask the sponsor to delay its clinical studies for a brief time so a more thorough review can be completed. Called an "informal clinical hold," this mechanism allows the FDA and the sponsor alike to avoid complications associated with formal clinical hold orders (e.g., paperwork). In such cases, the division typically promises to contact the sponsor as soon as a decision is reached.

Federal regulations make clear, however, that the FDA is not obligated to initiate a dialogue or to pursue alternative means before issuing a hold: "While the agency is committed to making a good faith attempt to discuss and satisfactorily resolve deficiencies in an IND before considering the need to impose a clinical hold, it does not believe that it is obligated to establish procedural...[requirements obligating the agency to take such action]. The nature of the agency contact with sponsors will depend on the imminence of hazard to human subjects, on the availability of key agency and sponsor personnel, and on a variety of other factors. For similar reasons, FDA believes that it cannot in the abstract specify the extent of notice that can approximately be given before making a hold effective."

CDER may issue a clinical hold order by letter, telephone, or some other method of rapid communication. This order "will identify the studies under the IND to which the hold applies, and will briefly explain the basis for the action." A full written explanation from CDER will follow as "soon as possible, and no more than 30 days after imposition of the clinical hold." The sponsor may appeal the FDA's decision.

When the hold order is issued, identified studies must be delayed or discontinued immediately. If the study has not yet begun, no subjects may be administered the investigational drug. Ongoing studies placed on clinical holds must be discontinued immediately, and no new subjects may be recruited to the study or placed on the treatment. CDER may, however, permit subjects already on the treatment to continue receiving the experimental drug.

Under the terms of some clinical hold orders, sponsors may be allowed to begin or to continue the affected investigations when the required modification is instituted and without the prior notification of CDER. In many other cases, the investigation may proceed only after the sponsor has notified CDER, and after the company has received the center's authorization to begin or resume the clinical program.

At various times, the FDA has been concerned about the consistency of clinical hold decisions. In mid-1993, for example, CDER established a permanent committee, comprised largely of senior CDER officials, to periodically review clinical hold orders.

IND Status

Once the FDA's 30-day review period expires and clinical investigations are initiated, an IND may be classified into any one of five status categories:

Active Status. Generally, an active IND is one under which clinical investigations are being conducted. In other words, the FDA has decided not to delay or suspend the clinical studies proposed under the initial IND or subsequent protocol amendments. However, an IND may remain on active status for extended periods even though no trials are being conducted under the application. In such cases, clinical studies may be initiated under the IND without further notification to the FDA.

Inactive Status. An IND on inactive status is one under which clinical investigations are not being conducted. There are two ways through which an IND can be put on inactive status. First, the IND sponsor may ask the FDA to place the application on inactive status, thereby eliminating the IND updating and submission requirements applicable to the sponsor. Also, the FDA may put the application on inactive status if the agency finds either: (1) that no subjects are entered into an IND's clinical studies for a period of two years or more, or (2) that all investigations under an application remain on clinical hold for one year or more.

Clinical Hold. As previously discussed, a clinical hold is an FDA order to delay a proposed investigation or to suspend an ongoing investigation. If all investigations covered by an IND remain on clinical hold for one year or more, the FDA may place the IND on inactive status.

Withdrawn Status. The sponsor of an IND can withdraw an IND at any time and for any reason. When the sponsor withdraws an IND, all clinical investigations under the IND must be ended, all investigators notified, and all stocks of the drug returned to the sponsor or otherwise disposed of at the request of the sponsor.

IND Termination. The FDA will seek to terminate an IND if the agency is unable to resolve deficiencies in an IND or in the conduct of an investigation through a clinical hold order or through a more informal alternative. Except when continuing an investigation will present an immediate danger to clinical subjects, the FDA will issue a proposal to terminate and will offer the sponsor an opportunity to respond before finalizing a termination.

Chapter 6:

The Clinical
Development of New
Drugs

by Eric L. Hurden, M.Sc., Ph.D.
Independent Management and Training Consultant
and
Mark Mathieu
PAREXEL International Corporation

Virtually all preclinical work—animal pharmacology/toxicology testing and the development of the IND—is undertaken to obtain the FDA's permission to initiate clinical trials, the ultimate premarketing testing ground for unapproved drugs. During these trials, an investigational compound is administered to human subjects and is evaluated for its safety and efficacy in treating, preventing, or diagnosing a specific disease or condition. The results of this testing will comprise the single most important factor in the FDA's approval/disapproval of a new drug.

While the goal of clinical trials is to obtain safety and efficacy data, there is an overriding consideration in these studies: the safety of clinical subjects. Because human subjects are involved, the FDA becomes a concerned and interested regulator during clinical trials. Under the FDA's watchful eyes, drug sponsors must see that clinical trials are designed and conducted in ways that do not expose clinical subjects to unnecessary risks.

The clinical development program is the most complex and costly element in the development process. At a minimum, it requires a sponsor willing to assume the financial, legal, and regulatory responsibilities associated with the program; the commitment and expertise of physicians, nurses, and other health-care professionals; and patients willing to take the chance that an experimental drug will do more for them than existing therapies. Actually, there are at least six key entities involved in every clinical development program:

- *Sponsor.* According to federal regulations, the sponsor is "the person or agency who assumes the responsibility for an investigation of a new drug, including responsibility for compliance with applicable provisions of the act and regulations. The 'sponsor' may be an individual, partnership, corporation, or government agency, and may be a manufacturer, scientific institution, or investigator regularly and lawfully engaged in the investigation of new drugs." The sponsor generally assumes most, if not all, of the financial and legal responsibility for the conduct of a clinical trial.

- *Investigators.* Investigators are typically physicians who agree to supervise the use of an investigational drug in clinical subjects. Their responsibilities include administering the experimental drug, observing and testing clinical subjects, and recording the data essential in assessing a drug's safety and effectiveness. Above all, however, the investigator is responsible for the welfare of clinical subjects.

- *Monitors.* Monitors are individuals responsible for monitoring a clinical trial's progress, and for ensuring that investigators are conducting the research within the framework of the clinical protocol and federal regulations. Clinical monitors, who may be employees of the sponsor or independent consultants hired by the sponsor, fulfill many of their responsibilities through visits to investigational sites (e.g. hospitals, clinics).

- *Institutional Review Board (IRB).* The IRB, or ethical review committee, is a panel found in most medical institutions that conduct clinical investigations. The board reviews proposed protocols to

102

ensure that the rights and welfare of human subjects are protected. The reviews are also designed to ensure that clinical studies do not conflict with the institution's philosophies or local and state laws. IRBs possess the authority to order revisions in clinical protocols.

- *Subjects.* Clinical subjects are those persons who volunteer to participate in a clinical trial.

- *The FDA.* As the government agency that regulates the clinical testing of new drugs, the FDA is a key figure in the clinical testing process. A more complete discussion of the FDA's role is provided below.

Role of the FDA

The FDA plays at least three major roles in the clinical testing of a drug. As it does for animal studies, the FDA sets general standards for clinical studies to ensure that data derived from clinical trials are accurate. This is done essentially through a set of loosely related guidelines and regulations called Good Clinical Practices, or GCP (see Chapter 7). These documents define the responsibilities of the key figures involved in the clinical trial.

The FDA's second role is to protect, as much as possible, the human subjects participating in the clinical trial. Obviously, since such testing involves the administration of pharmacologically active drugs to humans, the agency cannot guarantee the safety of clinical subjects. The FDA's role, then, is to ensure: (1) that clinical subjects are not exposed to any unnecessary risks; (2) that clinical subjects are exposed to the least possible risk given the benefit anticipated from the use of the drug; and (3) that all clinical subjects give their informed consent before entering a trial. The FDA does this not only through regulations, but also by reviewing all proposed clinical protocols and all proposed changes to the protocols that may affect the safety of the subjects.

Lastly, by deciding the nature and quantity of clinical data necessary to establish a drug's safety and effectiveness, the FDA determines what testing is necessary in a clinical development program. Because the scientific and medical issues differ so significantly between drugs and medical conditions, the agency reaches such determinations on a case-by-case basis.

FDA Clinical Guidelines To help drug sponsors design clinical trials that are based upon sound scientific principles and that provide for the protection of clinical subjects, the FDA has developed a guideline entitled *General Considerations for the Clinical Evaluation of Drugs*. First released in September 1977, this guideline outlines the major elements of the clinical testing process, details acceptable approaches to meet FDA requirements, and discusses study planning and design. In addition to the *General Considerations* document, the FDA has published numerous guidelines on the clinical evaluation of specific types of drugs. These include the following:

- *General Considerations for the Clinical Evaluation of Drugs in Infants and Children;*

- *Guidelines for the Clinical Evaluation of Antidepressant Drugs;*

- *Guidelines for the Clinical Evaluation of Antianxiety Drugs;*

- *Guidelines for the Clinical Evaluation of Radiopharmaceutical Drugs;*

- *Guidelines for the Clinical Evaluation of Anti-Infective Drugs (Systemic);*

- *Draft Guideline for the Clinical Evaluation of Anti-Anginal Drugs;*

- *Draft Guideline for the Clinical Evaluation of Anti-Arrhythmic Drugs;*

- *Guidelines for the Clinical Evaluation of Antidiarrheal Drugs;*

- *Guidelines for the Clinical Evaluation of Gastric Secretory Depressant (GSD) Drugs;*

- *Guidelines for the Clinical Evaluation of Hypnotic Drugs;*

- *Guidelines for the Clinical Evaluation of General Anesthetics;*

- *Guidelines for the Clinical Evaluation of Local Anesthetics;*

- *Guidelines for the Clinical Evaluation of Anti-Inflammatory Drugs (Adults and Children);*

- *Guidelines for the Clinical Evaluation of Psychoactive Drugs in Infants and Children;*

- *Guidelines for the Clinical Evaluation of Antacid Drugs;*

- *Guidelines for the Clinical Evaluation of G.I. Motility-Modifying Drugs;*

- *Guidelines for the Clinical Evaluation of Laxative Drugs;*

- *Guidelines for the Clinical Evaluation of Bronchodilator Drugs;*

- *Guidelines for the Clinical Evaluation of Drugs to Prevent, Control, and/or Treat Periodontal Disease;*

- *Guidelines for the Clinical Evaluation of Drugs to Prevent Dental Caries;*

- *Guidelines for the Clinical Evaluation of Analgesic Drugs;*

- *Guidelines for the Clinical Evaluation of Drugs Used in the Treatment of Osteoporosis;*

- *Guidelines for the Clinical Evaluation of Lipid-Altering Agents in Adults and Children;*

- *Guidelines for the Clinical Evaluation of Antiepileptic Drugs (Adults and Children);*

- *Guidelines for the Clinical Evaluation of Antineoplastic Drugs; and*

- *Guidelines for the Study and Evaluation of Gender Differences in the Clinical Evaluation of Drugs.*

The Structure of Clinical Trials

Like that of an animal study, the design of a clinical trial will differ significantly from one drug and disease state to another. The nature of a drug, the product's proposed use, the results of the preclinical testing, and other pertinent information are all considered when designing a clinical trial.

Although clinical trials for different drugs can vary greatly in design, they are often similar in structure. Prior to clinical investigations, researchers still know relatively little about a new drug. Although the preclinical testing results provide initial indications of a drug's toxicity and pharmacological activity, the drug's potential effects in humans are still largely unknown. For this reason, each phase of clinical development is carefully designed to use and build upon the information obtained from the research stage preceding it.

Clinical programs for most new drugs begin with the cautious use of the investigational compound in small, carefully selected population groups, and proceed into larger, more relevant, and more diverse patient pools. In its October 1988 Plan for Accelerated Approval of Drugs to Treat Life-Threatening and Severely Debilitating Illnesses, the FDA discusses the structure of clinical trials and the basis for this structure: The clinical "...drug development process is generally thought of, in simplified terms, as consisting of three phases of human testing to determine if a drug is safe and effective: Phase 1 with 10 to 50 patients to study how the drug is tolerated, metabolized, and excreted; phase 2 with 50 to 200 patients in which the safety and efficacy of the drug are first evaluated in controlled trials; and phase 3 with 200 to 1,000 or more patients to confirm and expand upon the safety and efficacy data obtained from the first two phases.... The three phases describe the usual process of drug development, but they are not statutory requirements. The basis for marketing approval is the adequacy of the data available; progression through the particular phases is simply the usual means the sponsor uses to collect the data needed for approval. The statute itself focuses on the standard of evidence needed for approval, as derived from adequate and well-controlled clinical investigations, with no mention of phases 1, 2, and 3."

Phase 1 Clinical Trials

The earliest Phase 1 clinical trials, sometimes called "clinical pharmacology studies," represent the first introduction of a new drug into human subjects.

The focus at this stage is the assessment of clinical safety. Except for extrapolations based on the safety profile obtained from animal studies, investigators know little about the drug's possible clinical effects.

Phase 1 clinical trials provide an initial clinical indication of whether a drug is sufficiently safe to be used in further human testing. According to FDA regulations, "Phase 1 includes the initial introduction of an investigational new drug into humans. Phase 1 studies are typically closely monitored and may be conducted in patients or normal volunteer subjects. These studies are designed to determine the metabolism and pharmacologic actions of the drug in humans, the side effects associated with increasing doses, and, if possible, to gain early evidence on effectiveness. During Phase 1, sufficient information about the drug's pharmacokinetics and pharmacological effects should be obtained to permit the design of well-controlled, scientifically valid Phase 2 studies. The total number of subjects and patients included in Phase 1 studies varies with the drug, but is generally in the range of 20 to 80.

"Phase 1 studies also include studies of drug metabolism, structure-activity relationships, and mechanism of action in humans, as well as studies in which investigational drugs are used as research tools to explore biological phenomena or disease processes." These studies can also provide basic pharmacokinetic information, which allows for the comparison of human drug disposition to that of animals so that nonclinical findings can be correlated and verified.

It is worth noting that the term Phase 1 can refer not only to a stage of development (i.e., earliest human exposure), but also to a type of study (i.e. generally any clinical pharmacology study). The latter type of study may occur at various times throughout the clinical testing of a particular drug.

Phase 1 testing of a new drug is considered highly exploratory because there are often no human safety data available. For this reason, these studies are entered into very cautiously, with the drug being used in small numbers of subjects, each of whom must submit to close clinical observation for drug effects. Healthy adults whose schedules permit short hospitalization stays are ideal subjects, as are hospital employees and students who are accessible for comprehensive clinical monitoring.

However, testing certain drugs in healthy adults is not considered ethical. Because of the known toxicities of certain classes of drugs, such as those used in treating AIDS and cancer, Phase 1 studies are conducted with patients who have the condition for which the drug is being studied. Nevertheless, the studies remain focused on safety issues.

In its guideline on *General Considerations for the Clinical Evaluation of Drugs*, the FDA makes several recommendations for subject selection in Phase 1, including the following:

- in most cases, Phase 1 tests should involve "normal" volunteers (i.e., individuals free from abnormalities that would complicate the interpretation of the experiment or that might increase the subjects' sensitivity to the drug's toxic potential);

- individuals with mild but stable illnesses may be considered for inclusion in the initial study of a drug (e.g., patients with mild, uncomplicated hypertension or arthritis);

- it is permissible and is sometimes desirable to include subjects with certain abnormalities for which the drug is indicated;

- in most cases, children and patients with a serious primary disease and serious unrelated problems (e.g., cardiac, hepatic, renal, hematologic abnormalities) should be excluded from Phase 1 studies;

- generally, patients receiving concomitant drug therapy should be excluded, except when concomitant therapy is considered mandatory or routine;

- even when concomitant therapy is considered routine, every effort should be made to design and execute trials excluding concomitant therapy, provided this is consistent with ethical principles of patient care;

- generally, outpatients should not be utilized as initial recipients of an investigational drug;

- because of their close proximity to the investigator and their advanced medical knowledge, hospital employees or adult students (volunteers) may, in some cases, be used as initial recipients of a drug;

- pretreatment physical exams and the following laboratory tests should be performed to screen out individuals with medically significant abnormalities: complete blood count (including platelet estimate); fasting blood sugar (or two-hour postprandial blood sugar); an electrocardiogram; blood urine nitrogen (or serum creatinine); liver function studies; and any other tests specifically indicated for the drug under study; and

- a glucose-6-phosphatase deficiency screen should be performed on individuals likely to be involved in repeated drug testing.

This guideline also reflects the FDA's previous policy that women of childbearing potential be excluded from Phase 1 studies. Because this policy was seen by some as paternalistic and because it denied women the right to make their own health-related decisions, the FDA changed this policy in 1993. The agency's *Guideline for the Study and Evaluation of Gender Differences in the Clinical Evaluation of Drugs* states that "the strict limitation on the participation of women of childbearing potential in Phase 1 and early Phase 2 trials that was imposed...has been eliminated." The guideline emphasizes the need to include both genders in clinical studies to "reflect the population that will receive the drug when it is marketed." Data should be analyzed to assess gender-based differences in individual studies and in the overall integrated analyses of safety and effectiveness.

PK/PD and Phase 1 Trials   Based on the FDA's reviewing experience, the selection of the starting dose for clinical trials continues to be a weakness of many clinical programs. Traditional dose-based comparisons between animals and humans are inadequate largely because of major differences between species in the disposition and metabolism of drugs. Thus, calculations based on animal half-lives and dosing intervals often lead to errors in selecting the starting dose for Phase 1 trials.

Under former CDER Director Carl Peck, M.D., the FDA advocated the greater use of pharmacokinetic/pharmacodynamic-based methods for the calculation of the starting dose. One such approach, which is supported by National Institutes of Health (NIH) studies of oncologic agents, reduces the number of dose levels required to reach a drug's maximum tolerated dose

(MTD), thereby decreasing the number of patients needed for such tests. Termed "pharmacologically guided dose escalation," the technique uses target plasma levels based on preclinical studies to determine the size of doses to be administered during Phase 1 studies.

Peck also advocated the incorporation of pharmacokinetic/pharmacodynamic (PK/PD) studies in the first dose-tolerance trials. He maintained that these trials offer a unique, and possibly the only, opportunity to evaluate drug concentration-acute toxic effect relationships of poorly tolerated doses that will be avoided in subsequent trials.

Phase 1 Investigator Selection   Sponsors usually select the investigators to conduct their Phase 1 studies before the IND submission so that the names and qualifications of these physicians may be provided in the IND (additional investigators may be added at any time). The investigators responsible for conducting Phase 1 tests must meet specific qualification criteria; obviously, the scientific training and expertise of the clinical investigators must qualify them as suitable experts to investigate the safety of the drug.

The FDA advises that investigators performing Phase 1 tests involving "normal" volunteers should be skilled in the "initial evaluation of a variety of compounds for safety and pharmacological effect." In those rare cases in which diseased patients are being studied under a Phase 1 protocol, investigators should be experts in the particular disease categories to be treated and/or experts in the evaluation of drug effects on the disease process.

Recording Phase 1 Data   Phase 1 studies are relatively straightforward experiments. Before the administration of a drug, investigators obtain baseline data (i.e., information on a patient's existing medical condition and personal characteristics). By defining the patient's condition before the study, baseline data give investigators a basis on which to measure a drug's short-term effects after administration.

Investigators monitor drug-related changes found in several measurable parameters. Factors such as the drug's purpose and the adverse effects found in preclinical studies will determine which clinical parameters investigators will monitor most closely during clinical trials. Blood pressure, for example, would be a key parameter when the drug under study is either a hypertensive or was found to have adverse effects on the cardiovascular systems of laboratory animals during preclinical testing.

Important baseline and drug effects information is recorded on case report forms throughout clinical testing. Designed specifically for the clinical study of a particular drug, case report forms should allow for the collection of accurate and comprehensive data under a clinical protocol, and should promote the development of logical and usable data bases. These forms generally provide for the collection of objective data such as age and sex, measurements of important parameters such as blood pressure and white blood cell count, and depending on the nature of the study, subjective clinical assessments such as disease ratings and patient assessments on pain.

It is the principal investigator's responsibility to record and verify the accuracy of data included on case report forms. When completed, the forms must be signed by the investigator and forwarded to the sponsor for tabulation and analysis (copies are retained at the site). Federal regulations contain provisions regarding the storage and submission of case report forms and the source documents that support them, and specify that FDA inspectors must be given access to the forms during agency audits of key clinical studies.

FDA-Sponsor Communication During Clinical Trials   Although clinical studies become the focus of a drug's development once Phase 1 trials begin, other activities continue to support these trials. As clinical trials progress, FDA reviewers continually reassess the safety of such testing. Because the FDA wants these assessments to be based on the latest available data and information, the agency requires that sponsors submit periodic reports on completed and upcoming research. During clinical trials, at least four important types of data and information flow regularly from the sponsor to the FDA:

- *New Animal Data.* As mentioned previously, animal testing continues during clinical development. Submitted in the form of information amendments, additional toxicology and pharmacokinetic data may be needed from animal studies to support the safety of new and/or modified clinical studies. For example, longer term toxicology studies are required as the duration of treatment in humans is extended.

111

- *Protocols and Protocol Amendments.* Because protocols for Phase 2 and Phase 3 trials are not normally included in the IND, protocols for these studies must be forwarded to the FDA for evaluation. Also, whenever sponsors want to make changes to previously submitted protocols, they must submit protocol amendments (see Chapter 4).

- *Annual Reports.* Current regulations require sponsors to submit brief annual reports on the progress of the investigation. These reports must include information on individual studies, provide a summary of the clinical experience with the drug, and provide information on the general investigational plan for the upcoming year, changes in the investigator's brochure, and foreign regulatory and marketing developments (see Chapter 4).

- *IND Safety Reports.* Drug sponsors must notify the FDA and all participating investigators about information that the sponsor receives from any source indicating or suggesting any significant hazards, contraindications, side effects, or precautions that are associated with the use of the drug. All significant safety findings must be reported (see Chapter 4).

Phase 2 Clinical Trials

Phase 2 clinical trials represent a shift away from testing designed almost entirely for safety to testing designed to evaluate efficacy as well. In Phase 2 studies, a drug, generally for the first time, is used in patients who suffer from the disease or condition that the drug is intended to prevent, diagnose, or treat.

In the Phase 2 trial of an antiemetic, for instance, efficacy may be measured by the incidence of chemotherapy patients' vomiting, nausea, and related symptoms (see discussion on clinical endpoints below). Generally, Phase 2 study objectives also include the determination of the minimum dose that is maximally effective, or that is sufficiently effective without undue toxicity.

Since a drug's short-term side effects are still concerns during Phase 2 investigations, the compound is administered to a limited number of subjects—generally between 100 to 200—who are closely monitored by the investigators. The subjects are generally not monitored continuously as they are in Phase 1. They should, however, be able to comply with treatment and monitoring activities indicated for the disease and the drug under study. Generally, the frequency of a subjects' clinic visits and laboratory tests progress from a weekly to a biweekly to a monthly schedule.

FDA regulations describe Phase 2 trials as follows: "Phase 2 includes the controlled clinical studies conducted to evaluate the effectiveness of the drug for a particular indication or indications in patients with the disease or condition under study and to determine the common or short-term side effects and risks associated with the drug. Phase 2 studies are typically well-controlled, closely monitored, and conducted in a relatively small number of patients, usually involving no more than several hundred subjects."

When it is both possible and useful, Phase 2 studies should be "controlled" investigations. In other words, the studies should involve the comparison of the experimental drug against a placebo and/or standard therapy. Generally, the experimental drug is administered to one group of subjects, while the placebo or standard therapy is administered to a similar group. The safety and effectiveness of the two therapies can then be compared.

Specific FDA recommendations for Phase 2 studies, as taken from the agency's *General Considerations for the Clinical Evaluation of Drugs*, include the following (many of these same recommendations apply equally to Phase 3):

- Phase 2 studies should be performed by investigators who are considered experts in the particular disease categories to be treated and/or in the evaluation of drug effects on the disease process;

- patients selected for early Phase 2 studies ordinarily should be free of hematologic, hepatic, renal, cardiac, or other serious diseases;

- to avoid possible interference with the assessment of safety and effectiveness of the investigational drug, patients should, in most cases, be receiving no concomitant therapy;

- patients with concomitant diseases and therapy may be included in late Phase 2 studies, since they are representative of certain segments of the population that would use the investigational drug if it gained marketing approval;

• the frequency of visits and of laboratory tests for Phase 2 will vary depending on the nature and safety of the drug (including its intended use);

• specialized "safety" and pharmacological laboratory tests should be performed as required by the nature of the drug;

• routine "safety" laboratory tests should be performed at frequent intervals (CBC should include platelet estimates);

• when an investigational drug or another active compound is altered significantly during manufacturing or through the use of excipients to accommodate a single or double-blinded trial, blood-level studies (or urinary excretion studies if blood levels are not feasible) should be performed to indicate that the alteration has not materially affected its absorption or excretory process;

• any significant change in the formulation or manufacture of the investigational drug during the course of late Phase 2 clinical trials will require bioavailability studies so that meaningful comparisons can be made among the clinical trials performed with the various formulations;

• for chronically administered drugs that are known to be absorbed, complete ophthalmologic examinations (pre- and post-drug) should be performed on a representative number of patients followed for six months or preferably longer on the drug; and

• for drugs administered for shorter periods in clinical trials, eye examinations should be performed at the end of drug administration (however, the possibility of delayed effects on the eye should be considered).

Because many regulatory agencies have concluded that sponsors often fail to take adequate steps to definitively and accurately define the dose-response of new compounds, the importance of well-designed Phase 2 studies has increased in recent years. The participants in the International Conferences on Harmonization (ICH) have noted that, in many cases, drugs have been initially marketed at what were later recognized as excessive doses, sometimes with adverse consequences (e.g., thiazide-type diuretics in hypertension).

Since sponsors want to avoid prolonging the duration of Phase 2 studies unnecessarily, they often do not devote additional time to explore fully the entire dose range and dose intervals. Frequently, an effect is seen at a certain dose that is then subjected to wider exposure in Phase 3 studies without a further definition of the relationships involved. Dose-finding should be viewed as an integral component of the drug development process, and as an essential step in establishing a drug's safety and effectiveness. Ultimately, conducting adequate dose-ranging studies at an early stage of clinical development may reduce the number of failed Phase 3 trials, speeding the development process and conserving resources.

End-of-Phase 2 Meetings   Traditionally, the FDA has reserved end-of-Phase 2 conferences for sponsors of either new molecular entities (NME) or important new uses of already-marketed drugs. And although the agency still points out that these meetings are "designed primarily" for sponsors of such products, the FDA has made the conferences available to all new drug sponsors, regardless of the classification of their products.

FDA regulations state that the purpose of end-of-Phase 2 meetings "…is to determine the safety of proceeding to Phase 3, to evaluate the Phase 3 plan and protocols, and to identify any additional information necessary to support a marketing application for the uses under investigation." The ultimate goal of such a meeting is for the sponsor and the FDA to reach agreement on plans for the conduct and design of Phase 3 trials.

As the name implies, end-of-Phase 2 meetings take place after the completion of Phase 2 clinical trials and before the initiation of Phase 3 studies. Since FDA recommendations may bring about significant revisions to a sponsor's Phase 3 trial plans, the agency suggests that these meetings be held before "major commitments of effort and resources to specific Phase 3 tests are made." The FDA adds, however, that such meetings are not intended to delay the transition from Phase 2 to Phase 3 studies.

The FDA considers the sponsor's preparation for an end-of-Phase 2 conference to be of critical importance in determining the meeting's ultimate utility. According to the new regulations, "At least 1 month in advance of an end-of-Phase 2 meeting, the sponsor should submit background information on the sponsor's plan for Phase 3, including summaries of the Phase 1 and 2 investigations, the specific protocols for Phase 3 clinical studies, plans for any additional nonclinical studies, and, if available, tentative labeling for the drug." FDA staffers advise that the sponsor be prepared to discuss any remaining issues regarding manufacturing and controls, since the drug formulation used in Phase 3 should correspond closely to the product that is ultimately approved and marketed.

At the conference, to which both the FDA and the sponsor may bring outside consultants, agency attendees may number a dozen or more, and may include the reviewing chemist, medical officer, and pharmacologist (and possibly their supervisors), the division director and deputy director, the reviewing biostatistician, a biopharmaceutics reviewer, and the consumer safety officer (CSO) assigned to the IND. The focus "...should be directed primarily at establishing agreements between FDA and the sponsor of the overall plan for Phase 3 and the objectives and design of particular studies. The adequacy of technical information to support Phase 3 studies and/or a marketing application may also be discussed." Ideally, end-of-Phase 2 conferences result in FDA-sponsor agreements in each of these areas.

As they should during all communication with the FDA, sponsors should try to obtain from FDA reviewers and officials specific recommendations during the meeting. FDA staffers advise that sponsors develop highly specific questions, and that they focus these questions not only on safety issues regarding Phase 3 protocols, but on what studies and data will be necessary for the ultimate approval of the drug as well.

According to FDA regulations, "Agreements reached at the meetings on these matters will be recorded in minutes of the conference that will be taken by FDA...and provided to the sponsor. The minutes along with any other written material provided to the sponsor will serve as a permanent record of any agreements reached." The regulations add that, "Barring a significant scientific development that requires otherwise, studies conducted in accordance with the agreement shall be presumed to be sufficient in objective and design for the purpose of obtaining marketing approval for the drug."

How useful are end-of-Phase 2 conferences? CDER's 1992 *New Drug Evaluation Statistical Report* suggests that the conferences can help to accelerate drug review times. In a study of NMEs approved from 1987 through 1992, those drugs for which end-of-Phase 2 conferences were held had an average review time of 29.7 months, while NMEs for which no conferences were held took an average of 31.5 months to review.

Phase 3 Clinical Trials

In Phase 3 investigations, a drug is tested under conditions more closely resembling those under which the drug would be used if approved for marketing. During this phase, an investigational compound is administered to a significantly larger patient population (i.e., from several hundred to several thousand subjects) to, in the FDA's terms, "gather additional information about effectiveness and safety that is needed to evaluate the overall benefit-risk relationship of the drug and to provide an adequate basis for physician labeling."

The larger patient pool and the genetic, lifestyle, and physiological diversity that it brings allow the investigators to identify potential adverse drug reactions and to determine the appropriate dosage of the drug for the more diverse general population. Patient population criteria for Phase 3 trials may also be expanded to include those with concomitant therapies and conditions.

Depending on the drug and the seriousness of the disease/condition under study, Phase 3 trials may be conducted on an outpatient basis. Since a drug's safety has already been established in smaller groups, Phase 3 subjects often are monitored less rigorously. An outpatient setting requires extensive coordination, including the screening, scheduling, treatment, and evaluation of the larger patient population.

The Pivotal Clinical Study Phase 3 testing may produce data from controlled and uncontrolled trials conducted at several hospitals, clinics, or other "sites" outlined in the protocol. But the clinical data that the FDA will review most closely and upon which the agency will base its approval/disapproval decision are those derived from tests specified in federal regulations as "adequate and well-controlled studies." These are sometimes called "pivotal" studies.

No factor plays a greater role in determining the regulatory fate of new drugs than the results of these "adequate and well-controlled" clinical trials. The FDA clearly states in federal regulations that, "Reports of 'adequate and well-controlled' investigations provide the primary basis for determining whether there is 'substantial evidence' to support the claims of effectiveness for new drugs and antibiotics."

The focus on pivotal clinical studies as the primary criterion for approving new drugs is rooted in the Federal Food, Drug and Cosmetic Act, which states that, "The term 'substantial evidence' means evidence consisting of adequate and well-controlled investigations...on the basis of which it could fairly and responsibly be concluded by...experts that the drug will have the effect it purports or is represented to have under the conditions of use prescribed, recommended, or suggested in the labeling or proposed labeling thereof."

The concept of substantial evidence has a second important component. With rare exceptions, at least two adequate and well-controlled studies are necessary to obtain FDA approval for a new drug. According to the FDA's *Guideline for the Content and Format of the Clinical and Statistical Sections of an Application*: "The requirement for well-controlled clinical investigations has been interpreted to mean that the effectiveness of a drug should be supported by more than one well-controlled trial and carried out by independent investigators. This interpretation is consistent with the general scientific demand for replicability. Ordinarily, therefore, the clinical trials submitted in an application will not be regarded as adequate support of a claim unless they include studies by more than one independent investigator who maintains adequate case histories of an adequate number of subjects."

Because of their importance to the FDA's approval decision, pivotal studies must meet particularly high scientific standards: "The purpose of conducting clinical investigations of a drug is to distinguish the effect of a drug from other influences, such as spontaneous change in the course of the disease, placebo effect, or biased observation." Adequate and well-controlled trials, then, are designed so that the drug's effects are isolated from extraneous factors that might otherwise undermine the validity of the trials' results.

Generally, a study must meet four criteria to be considered pivotal:

1. A pivotal study must be a controlled trial. As previously discussed, a controlled trial compares a group of patients treated with a placebo

or standard therapy against a group of subjects treated with the investigational drug.

2. A pivotal study must have a blinded design when such a design is practical and ethical. Double-blinded trials are those in which patients and investigators are kept from knowing which subjects are receiving the experimental drug and which are receiving the placebo/standard therapy. In trials employing a single blind, only the subjects are kept from knowing whether they are receiving placebo/standard therapy. Blinding provides greater assurance that treatment evaluations are as objective as possible.

3. A pivotal study must be randomized. This means that clinical subjects are assigned randomly to the investigational drug and the placebo/standard. Therefore, each patient has an equal chance of being in the control or the experimental group. Randomization prevents the investigator from influencing the outcome by assigning patients with a better prognosis to the preferred treatment.

4. A pivotal study must be of adequate size. The study must involve enough patients to provide statistically significant evidence that a new drug offers a therapeutic or safety advantage over existing therapies. Sample size calculations require many assumptions about the results to be obtained with the treatment and population being studied. Because considerable clinical judgement is employed in making these assumptions, FDA officials warn that faulty presumptions frequently result in studies of inadequate statistical power. In fact, trial sample size is said to be the most common clinical design flaw.

These criteria also are included in FDA regulations, which state that the "characteristics" of adequate and well-controlled studies are:

- a clear statement of the objectives of the study;

- a design that permits a valid comparison with a control to provide a quantitative assessment of the drug effect;

- a method of subject selection that provides adequate assurance that subjects have the disease or condition being studied, or that they show evidence of susceptibility and exposure to the condition against which prophylaxis is directed;

- a method of assigning patients to treatment and control groups that minimizes bias and that is intended to assure comparability of the groups with respect to pertinent variables such as age, sex, severity of disease, duration of disease, and the use of drugs or therapy other than test drugs;

- adequate measures to minimize bias by the subjects, observers, and analysts of the data;

- well-defined and reliable methods of assessing subjects' responses; and

- an adequate analysis of the study results to assess the effects of the drug.

About this listing, the FDA wrote in 1987 that it "has long considered the characteristics listed in the regulation as the essentials of an adequate and well-controlled study.... In general, the regulation on adequate and well-controlled studies has two overall objectives: (1) To allow the agency to assess methods for minimizing bias; and (2) to assure a sufficiently detailed description of the study to allow scientific assessment and interpretation of it."

It is worth noting that federal regulations do not provide a comprehensive discussion of the testing conditions necessary for pivotal trials. Mentions of other standards that the FDA sees as necessary are scattered throughout agency guidelines. According to the FDA's *General Considerations for the Clinical Evaluation of Drugs*, for instance, pivotal studies must be of suitable size, that size being dependent upon: (1) the degree of response one wishes to detect; (2) the desired assurance against a false positive finding; and (3) the acceptable risk of failure to demonstrate the response when it is present in the population. Other FDA guidelines point out that studies for which patient case report forms are unavailable will not be viewed as critical well-controlled studies.

There are, of course, many factors that influence the ultimate design of a trial, and the FDA does not apply its requirements inflexibly. For example, federal regulations list five different methods through which pivotal studies may be controlled. The preamble to a 1987 regulation stated that "FDA recognizes...that ethical and practical considerations will play a central role in the type of study selected, a decision that will ordinarily depend upon the type and seriousness of the disease being treated, availability of alternative therapies, and the nature of the drug and the patient population. In each case, applicants must choose the particular type of study they will use based on ethical, scientific, and practical reasons. So long as these judgements are justifiable, and the studies are properly designed, the approvability of an application will not be affected."

Regardless of how closely the FDA works with sponsors on trial design issues, experienced researchers and agency staffers know that any of several complicating factors can contribute to the possibility that a trial's design will be questioned. These include the following:

Limits on the Trial Design Issues That Can Be Resolved in Advance. Trial size is a typical example of the design issues that are difficult to resolve entirely in advance, according to FDA staffers.

Sponsor-FDA Disagreements. Meetings are not always successful in resolving different viewpoints.

Changes in Technology and Medical Knowledge. In the several years needed to test a new drug in humans, it is possible—in some situations likely—that new technology, medical knowledge, and competing therapies will somehow change the standards by which a drug will be evaluated. Such advances will sometimes undermine the principles (e.g., the value of clinical endpoints) on which a study's design is based.

Clinical Testing in Special Populations During recent years, the FDA has taken steps to emphasize the importance of including special patient populations in clinical studies. In the span of several months in late 1992 and early 1993, the agency introduced four unrelated initiatives that had implications for clinical testing in special populations.

Drug Effectiveness and Clinical Endpoints

Clinical effectiveness endpoints were the focus of considerable contro-
versy during the 1980s, and have been the subject of widespread discussion and debate in the early 1990s. Endpoints are generally clinical
events (e.g., death, loss of vision, myocardial infarction, etc.) or measurements (e.g., blood pressure or antibody count) used to help assess a
drug's effectiveness. In the context of a clinical trial, the assessment of
a drug's effectiveness will consist of the product's ability to prevent an
adverse clinical event such as death or illness, or to otherwise modify a
clinical endpoint in a manner that has clear clinical benefits for the
patient.

Typically, effectiveness endpoints are grouped into two categories:
primary endpoints and surrogate endpoints. Primary endpoints include
death, serious morbidity, and other events whose presence or absence
have a clear and definite clinical effect on a patient. Because primary
endpoints have obvious clinical relevance and are comparatively easy
to observe and measure, they are ideal for the objective study of drug
efficacy.

A secondary measure, or "surrogate" endpoint, is generally an event
or measure that is thought to be related to, and to be likely to predict,
the drug's effect on a more clinically relevant, or primary, endpoint.
The FDA does have a history of basing its approval on surrogate endpoints when there exists substantial evidence that drug effects on the
surrogate marker would lead to, or are associated with, the desired
effects on morbidity and mortality. For example, the agency has
approved drugs for hypertension based on their effects on blood pressure rather than on survival or stroke rate. Likewise, the FDA has
approved drugs for hypercholesterolemia based on effects on serum
cholesterol rather than on coronary artery disease (i.e., angina, heart
attacks). More recently, the agency has approved certain AIDS products based on surrogate endpoints (i.e., increases in CD4 cell counts).

In December 1992, the FDA established, for the first time, specific
policies under which it would approve drugs based on surrogate end-

---

points that are "not so well established as the surrogates ordinarily used as bases for approval in the past." Under this accelerated drug approval regulation, the agency stated that, when appropriate, it would base the approvals of drugs for serious and life-threatening conditions on surrogate endpoints, but that it would require that the sponsor conduct postmarketing studies to verify the relationship between the surrogate and the ultimate clinical benefit (see Chapter 17).

In discussing its plan, the FDA acknowledged both the benefits and drawbacks of surrogate endpoints: "Approval of a drug on the basis of a well-documented effect on a surrogate endpoint can allow a drug to be marketed earlier, sometimes much earlier, than it could if a demonstrated clinical benefit were required.... Reliance on a surrogate endpoint almost always introduces some uncertainty into the risk/benefit assessment, because clinical benefit is not measured directly and the quantitative relation of the effect on the surrogate to the clinical effect is rarely known. The expected risk/benefit relationship may fail to emerge because: (1) The identified surrogate may not in fact be causally related to clinical outcome (even though it was thought to be) or (2) the drug may have a smaller than expected benefit and a larger than expected adverse effect that could not be recognized without large-scale clinical trials of long duration. Reliance on surrogate markers therefore requires an additional measure of judgement, not only weighing benefit versus risk, as always, but also deciding what the therapeutic benefit is based upon the drug effect on the surrogate."

The complexities of assessing the true relationships between surrogate endpoints and clinical benefits has led researchers to seek alternative methods of confirmation. The most notable is the so-called "large, simple trial." By conducting very large studies (i.e., several thousands of patients) with a relatively straightforward design, researchers can assess the small-to-moderate, but real, drug effects on tangible endpoints, such as major morbidity and mortality, in a reasonably short time. Although many of these studies have been conducted on a postmarketing basis, the implication is that future large, simple trials could be conducted during Phase 3.

Two of these initiatives involved clinical testing in population groups at opposite ends of the age spectrum. Under an October 1992 proposed regulation, the FDA encouraged industry to conduct more studies in children to support more informative labeling regarding pediatric drug uses. In the proposal, the FDA stated that it "recognizes an alternative way (rather than by reliance on adequate and well-controlled studies in children) to conclude that there is substantial evidence of effectiveness in children for drugs already approved for the same use in adults." The initiative would allow sponsors to include in drug labeling a "pediatric use statement" when such a statement is "based on adequate and well-controlled studies in adults, provided that there is additional information [e.g., pediatric pharmacokinetic data] to show that the course of the disease and the drug effects are sufficiently similar in children and adults to permit extrapolation from the adult data to children."

In the past, the FDA has provided guidelines on drug testing in geriatric populations. More recently, the FDA's standards in this area were highlighted in a 1993 ICH guideline entitled *Studies in Support of Special Populations: Geriatrics.* This document confirms the arbitrary definition of the geriatric population as individuals over 65 years of age, but also stresses the importance of seeking patients in the older age range, 75 years and above. The guideline states that geriatric patients should be included in the Phase 3 data base (and in Phase 2, at the sponsor's option) in meaningful numbers. For drugs used in diseases that are present in, but are not unique to, the elderly, the guideline states that a minimum of 100 patients would suffice. For diseases that are characteristically associated with aging (e.g., Alzheimer's disease), geriatric patients should constitute the major portion of the clinical data base.

Since the most "recognized important differences between younger and older patients have been pharmacokinetic differences," the guideline states that "it is important to determine whether or not the pharmacokinetic behavior of the drug in elderly subjects or patients is different from that in younger adults and to characterize the effects of influences, such as abnormal renal or hepatic function, that are more common in the elderly...." Sponsors most often opt to conduct formal pharmacokinetic studies in the elderly in Phase 1, although one alternative approach is the use of a pharmacokinetic screen during Phase 2 or Phase 3 trials. Special studies in renally or hepatically impaired patients or studies designed to examine specific drug-to-drug interactions should be included as results dictate.

Another ICH guideline entitled *The Extent of Population Exposure to Assess Clinical Safety* focuses on the principles of the safety evaluation of drugs intended for the long-term treatment (greater than six months) of non-life-threatening diseases. Since current information indicates that most adverse experiences (AE) first occur within a few months of initial drug treatment, the guideline suggests that a minimum of 300 to 600 patients treated for 6 months at the dose intended for clinical use will produce data sufficient to support approval. Additionally, a minimum of 100 patients should be treated with the drug for 12 months in an attempt to characterize the uncommon AEs that may increase in frequency or severity with time or that may occur later than 6 months after initial treatment. The guideline, which is expected in final form in 1994, notes that these numbers may not be sufficient for assessing drug efficacy.

In 1994, the ICH also expects to publish a draft guideline entitled *Ethnic Factors in the Acceptability of Foreign Data.* Current evidence suggests that inter-ethnic differences are no greater than intra-ethnic differences, at least in terms of AUC or C_{max} measures.

Completing a Drug's Clinical Study

It is in the best interest of the sponsor, the clinical subjects, and, in many cases, the general public that a drug's clinical study be completed and an NDA be submitted as soon as sufficient safety and efficacy data are obtained. If a drug is found during the trial to be unsafe or ineffective, then continuing a trial only exposes more clinical subjects to a dangerous or useless compound, and in some cases, keeps study subjects from using better or safer therapies. On the other hand, if the drug is clearly shown to be safer or more effective than existing therapies, then delaying the submission of an NDA to gain excess data needlessly prolongs the approval process.

A clinical trial may be discontinued before its scheduled date of completion for any one of several reasons:

- a dangerous adverse effect is found;

- a drug lacks significant effects or has an effect less advantageous than that of an existing therapy;

- a drug has a significant effect, but that effect does not justify the risks associated with its use; and

- a drug shows clear evidence of being safe and effective.

While it is often self-evident when a clinical trial should be discontinued because of inadequate effectiveness or dangerous adverse effects, it is more difficult to determine the exact quantity of the data needed to prove a new drug's safety and efficacy to the FDA. Actually, this decision is often made before clinical trials even begin. When designing the trial, statisticians will establish what are called "stopping rules." These are rigorous statistical criteria or goals that, if met at some point during the study of a drug, will signal the end of the clinical trial.

The periodic analysis of accrued data is undertaken during the clinical trial to determine if any of the stopping criteria have been met. Generally, to justify discontinuing the trial, the data must meet stringent standards to show that the drug's effects are: (1) statistically significant (i.e., that the drug was tested in a large enough patient population to ensure that observed effects were not due to chance); and (2) clinically significant (i.e., that the test results are sufficient to show that there is a perceptible difference in the clinical effect between the investigational drug and the placebo and/or a standard therapy).

Phase 4 Clinical Studies

In a very real sense, the clinical development process continues long after a product's approval. The continuing collection and analysis of adverse experience information and other data provide the sponsor and the FDA with a flow of information so that a drug's safety and effectiveness periodically can be reassessed in light of the latest data.

Phase 4 clinical trials, which are studies initiated after a drug's marketing approval, have become an increasingly important and common method through which sponsors obtain new information about their marketed drugs. A drug manufacturer may undertake postmarketing clinical studies for any one of several reasons, including the following:

- To satisfy an FDA request made prior to an NDA's approval that Phase 4 trials be conducted following approval. For example, the

126

FDA may want the sponsor to better characterize the drug's safety and/or effectiveness in patient groups that may not have been widely represented in pivotal trials (e.g., children, persons using concomitant medications, etc.). Agency data suggest that the FDA is requesting such studies more frequently.

- To develop pharmacoeconomic, or cost-effectiveness, data that can be used to support marketing claims highlighting the advantages of a drug over competing therapies. Some experts claim that growing numbers of companies are now incorporating the study of pharmacoeconomic parameters in their premarketing studies. According to some estimates, 75 percent of NDAs now include such data.

Aside from the fact that they are conducted after approval, Phase 4 studies may differ in a number of important respects from Phase 1, 2, and 3 trials. Phase 4 studies are often of a larger scale than are premarketing studies. Also, they may be less rigorously controlled than key preapproval studies, although the FDA is taking steps to ensure the scientific integrity of these studies. In 1993, for example, agency officials announced their plans to look more closely at the issue of pharmacoeconomic research and expressed their desire to recruit an expert who could help establish standards for pharmacoeconomic studies.

Since the FDA's powers to require Phase 4 studies had not been outlined in federal laws or regulations, some have criticized agency requests for such trials. In practice, however, an FDA request to an applicant anxious to obtain marketing approval probably takes on the effective force of a regulatory requirement. Furthermore, under an accelerated drug approval program unveiled in December 1992, the FDA defended its authority to require Phase 4 studies (see Chapter 17).

Chapter 7:

Good Clinical Practices (GCP)

The FDA's authorities regarding clinical research extend beyond simply its role in deciding what clinical studies are necessary to support a new drug's approval. Because these trials involve human subjects, and because the FDA bases regulatory decisions on data produced from these studies, the agency sets minimum standards for conducting clinical research as well.

The agency does this through a set of regulations generally referred to as "good clinical practices," or GCP. By defining the responsibilities of the key entities involved in clinical trials, the FDA's GCP regulations seek:

(1) to establish standards and procedures that will ensure the quality and integrity of the data obtained from clinical testing, and to ensure that the FDA's decisions based upon these data are informed and responsible; and

(2) to protect the rights and, to the degree possible, the safety of clinical subjects.

In reality, GCP is a term of convenience used by those in government, clinical research, and the pharmaceutical industry to identify a collection of loosely related regulations and guidelines that, when taken together, define the responsibilities of the key figures involved in a clinical trial—the sponsor, the investigator, the monitor, and the institutional review board (IRB). GCP is comprised primarily of the following regulations and guidelines:

• a 1981 final regulation on the informed consent of clinical subjects;

- a 1981 final regulation on the responsibilities of IRBs;

- the 1987 IND Rewrite regulations, which define the responsibilities of the investigator and the sponsor;

- a 1988 *Guideline for the Monitoring of Clinical Investigations*, which outlines the monitor's responsibilities; and

- a 1991 regulation that standardizes the IRB and informed consent requirements for all federal agencies engaged in regulating clinical research.

While these documents form the core of GCP, several other FDA guidance documents provide detailed GCP-related information as well. Among these is a series of *Clinical Investigator Information Sheets (see listing below)*, and several FDA compliance policy guidance manuals that specify how FDA inspectors ensure that clinical sponsors, monitors, investigators, and IRBs are complying with GCP (see Chapter 16).

Responsibilities of the Drug Sponsor

Federal regulations define "sponsor" as "...a person who takes responsibility for and initiates a clinical investigation. The sponsor may be an individual or pharmaceutical company, governmental agency, academic institution, private organization, or other organization."

In practice, drug sponsors are generally, although not exclusively, drug manufacturers that have developed a pharmaceutical substance and that have the principal financial interest in the product. A sponsor may also be a physician, commonly called a "sponsor-investigator," who federal regulations describe as "an individual who both initiates and conducts an investigation and under whose immediate direction the investigational drug is administered or dispensed."

Sponsor responsibilities are defined in federal regulations, which state that "Sponsors are responsible for selecting qualified investigators, providing them with the information they need to conduct an investigation properly, ensuring proper monitoring of the investigation(s), ensuring that the investi-

---

FDA Clinical Investigator Information Sheets

- Acceptance of Foreign Data and IRB and Informed Consent Requirements
- Advertising for Study Subjects
- Payment to Research Subjects
- Clinical Investigator Regulatory Sanctions
- Clinical Investigators Unaffiliated with an Institution with an IRB
- Continuing Review
- Cooperative Research
- Emergency Use of an Investigational Drug
- FDA Inspections of Clinical Investigators
- FDA Institutional Review Board Inspections
- Guidance for the Emergency Use of Unapproved Medical Devices
- Guidance on Significant and Nonsignificant Risk Device Studies
- Informed Consent and the Clinical Investigation
- Investigational Drug Use in Patients Entering a Second Institution
- Investigational Use of Marketed Products
- IRBs and Medical Devices
- Non-Local IRB Review
- Placebo-Controlled and Active Controlled Drug Study Designs
- Required Recordkeeping in Clinical Investigations
- Sponsor-Clinical Investigator-IRB Interrelationship
- Treatment Use of Investigational Drugs
- Waiver of IRB Requirements

Source: FDA

---

gation(s) is conducted in accordance with the general investigational plan and protocols contained in the IND, maintaining an effective IND with respect to the investigations, and ensuring that FDA and all participating investigators are promptly informed of significant new adverse effects or risks with respect to the drug." Sponsor responsibilities can be grouped into the following general areas:

- selecting investigators and monitors;

- informing investigators;

- reviewing ongoing investigations;

- recordkeeping and record retention; and

- ensuring the disposition of unused drug supplies.

Selecting Investigators and Monitors *Investigator Selection.* The sponsor must select investigators—individuals (usually physicians) contracted by the sponsor to conduct the clinical study—who are qualified by training and experience as appropriate experts to investigate the drug. Experimental drugs can be shipped by the sponsor only to these investigators.

To compile evidence that an investigator is qualified to conduct a particular study, a sponsor must obtain certain information from the investigator:

- Completed and Signed Investigator Statement (Form FDA-1572). This form contains information about the investigator, the site of the investigation, and the subinvestigators—research fellows and residents—who assist the investigator in conducting the investigation. By signing the form, the investigator also pledges: (1) to conduct the study in accordance with the clinical protocol(s) and to take proper actions should deviations be needed; (2) to comply with all requirements regarding the obligations of clinical investigators and other relevant requirements; (3) to personally conduct or supervise the described investigation; (4) to inform patients, or any persons used as controls, that the drugs are being used for investigational purposes and to ensure that the requirements related to informed consent and IRB review and approval are met; (5) to report to the sponsor adverse experiences that occur in the course of the investigation in accordance with regulatory requirements; (6) to read and understand the information in the investigator's brochure, including the potential risks and side effects of the drug; and (7) to ensure that all associates, colleagues, and employees who assist in conducting the studies are informed about their obligations in fulfilling the commitments specified above. Through the form, the investigator pledges that an IRB that meets regulatory requirements will be responsible for the initial and continuing review and approval of the clinical investigation. The investigator also pledges to report to the IRB all unanticipated problems involving risks to human subjects, and not to make any changes in the research activity without IRB approval, except where necessary to eliminate apparent and immediate hazards to human subjects.

- Curriculum Vitae. A curriculum vitae or other statement of qualifications of the principal investigator must show the education, training, and experience that qualifies the investigator as an expert in the clinical investigation of the drug.

- Clinical Protocol. For Phase 1 investigations, the sponsor must obtain from the investigator a general outline of the planned investigation, including the estimated duration of the study and the maximum number of subjects that will be involved. For Phase 2 or 3 investigations, the sponsor must obtain "an outline of the study protocol including an approximation of the number of subjects to be treated with the drug and the number to be employed as controls, if any; the clinical uses to be investigated; characteristics of subjects by age, sex, and condition; the kind of clinical observations and laboratory tests to be conducted; the estimated duration of the study and copies or a description of case report forms to be used." Despite this regulatory passage, the FDA recognizes that, in most cases, sponsors now develop clinical protocols either on their own or in consultation with investigators.

133

Selecting Monitors. Drug sponsors are required to monitor clinical investigations to ensure: (1) the quality and integrity of the clinical data derived from clinical trials; and (2) that the rights and safety of human subjects involved in a clinical study are preserved. The monitoring function may be performed by the sponsor or its employees, or may be delegated to a contract research organization (CRO).

Specific FDA recommendations on proper monitoring duties and procedures are found in the agency's *Guideline for the Monitoring of Clinical Investigations* (January 1988). In this document, the FDA identifies six principal monitoring responsibilities:

Selection of a Monitor. A sponsor may designate one or more appropriately trained and qualified individuals to monitor the progress of a clinical investigation. Physicians, clinical research associates, paramedical personnel, nurses, and engineers may be considered qualified monitors, depending on the type of product involved in the study.

Written Monitoring Procedures. A sponsor should establish written procedures for monitoring clinical investigations to ensure the quality of the study, and to ensure that each person involved in the monitoring process carries out his or her duties.

Preinvestigation Visits. Through personal contact between the monitor and each investigator, a sponsor must assure that the investigator, among other things, clearly understands and accepts the obligations involved in undertaking a clinical study. The sponsor must also determine whether the investigator's facilities are adequate for conducting the investigation, and whether the investigator has sufficient time to fulfill his or her responsibilities in the trial.

Periodic Visits. A sponsor must ensure, throughout the clinical investigation, that the investigator's obligations are being fulfilled, and that the facilities used in the clinical investigation continue to be acceptable. The monitor must visit the clinical site frequently enough to provide such assurances.

Review of Subject Records. A sponsor must ensure that safety and efficacy data to be submitted to the FDA are accurate and complete. The FDA recommends that the monitor review individual subject records and other supporting documentation, and compare those records with the reports prepared by the investigator for submission to the sponsor.

Record of On-site Visits. The monitor or sponsor should maintain a record of the findings, conclusions, and actions taken to correct deficiencies for each on-site visit to an investigator.

Informing Investigators   The sponsor is responsible for keeping all investigators involved in the clinical testing of its drug fully informed about the investigational drug and new research findings. Before initiating a study, a sponsor must provide participating clinical investigators with an investigator's brochure (see Chapter 4), which provides a description of the drug and summaries of its known pharmacological, pharmacokinetic, biological, and potential adverse effects identified during animal tests and, if available, clinical use. Once clinical trials begin, regulations require sponsors to "keep each participating investigator informed of new observations discovered by or reported to the sponsor on the drug, particularly with respect to adverse effects and safe use." This information may be distributed through periodically revised investigator's brochures, reprints of published studies, reports or letters to clinical investigators, or other appropriate means. Important safety information must be relayed to investigators and the FDA through written and/or telephone IND safety reports (see Chapter 4).

Review of Ongoing Investigations   There are several reasons why the FDA requires a sponsor to closely monitor the conduct and progress of its clinical trials. Investigator non-compliance and significant drug risks are two of the most important reasons.

Should a sponsor discover that an investigator is not complying with his or her research commitments (i.e., as made in Form FDA-1572), the general investigational plan, or other relevant regulatory requirements, the firm must either secure compliance or discontinue both drug shipments to the investigator and the investigator's participation in the study. If the sponsor takes the latter course, it must require that the investigator dispose of or return the drug in accordance with applicable requirements, and must report this to the FDA (see discussion below).

The sponsor must review and evaluate safety and efficacy evidence as it is supplied by the investigator. In addition to providing important safety information through IND safety reports, the sponsor must supply to the FDA annual reports on the progress of the investigation. The FDA was expected to propose additional AE analysis and reporting requirements in early 1994 (see Chapter 4).

When a sponsor discovers that its drug presents unreasonable and significant risks to subjects, the firm must: (1) discontinue those investigations that present the risks; (2) notify the FDA, all IRBs, and all investigators who have at any time participated in the investigation being discontinued: (3) ensure the disposition of all outstanding stocks of the drug; and (4) furnish the FDA with a full report of its actions.

Recordkeeping and Record Retention A sponsor must maintain adequate records showing the receipt, shipment, or other disposition of the investigational drug. The records must include, as appropriate, the name of the investigator to whom the drug is shipped, and the date, quantity, and batch or code mark of each such shipment. Regulations require sponsors to "retain [these] records and reports for 2 years after a marketing application is approved for the drug; or, if an application is not approved for the drug, until 2 years after shipment and delivery of the drug for investigational use is discontinued and FDA has been so notified."

Ensuring the Disposition of Unused Drug Supplies The sponsor must ensure the return of all unused supplies of the drug from each investigator whose participation is discontinued or eliminated. The sponsor may authorize alternative plans, provided these do not expose humans to risks from the drug. Any disposition of unused drug supplies must be thoroughly documented.

Responsibilities of Investigators

A clinical investigator is the individual who actually conducts, or who is the responsible leader of a team of individuals that conducts, a clinical investigation. It is under the immediate direction of this individual that the drug is administered or dispensed to a clinical subject. Federal regulations state that an "…investigator is responsible for ensuring that an investigation is conducted according to the signed investigator statement, the investigational plan, and applicable regulations; for protecting the rights, safety, and welfare of subjects under the investigator's care; and for the control of drugs under investigation." As part of the investigator's role in protecting the rights of clinical subjects, he or she must obtain the informed consent of all human subjects to whom the drug is administered. Specific investigator responsibilities detailed in the provisions of GCP include:

Control of the Drug   The investigator can administer the drug only to subjects under his or her personal supervision or under the supervision of a subinvestigator. Regulations do not allow the investigator to supply the drug to persons not authorized to receive it.

Recordkeeping and Record Retention   The investigator must keep adequate records regarding the disposition of the drug, and subject case histories recording all observations and data pertinent to the investigation. These records must be maintained "for a period of 2 years following the date a marketing application is approved for the drug for the indication for which it is being investigated; or, if no application is to be filed or if the application is not approved for such indication, until 2 years after the investigation is discontinued and FDA is notified." Upon its request, the FDA must be given access to these records.

Investigator Reports   The investigator must provide to the sponsor: (1) annual reports on the progress of the clinical investigations; (2) safety reports on all adverse effects that may reasonably be regarded as caused by, or probably caused by, the drug; and (3) a final report shortly after completion of the investigator's participation—FDA officials indicate that completed case report forms on all subjects will suffice.

Assurance of IRB Review   The investigator must assure that an IRB complying with regulatory requirements will be responsible for the initial and continuing review and approval of the proposed clinical study. He or she must also promptly report to the IRB all changes in the research activity and all unanticipated problems involving risks to human subjects, and must not make any changes in the research without IRB approval, except when necessary to eliminate apparent immediate hazards to human subjects.

Handling of Controlled Substances   If the investigational drug is subject to the Controlled Substances Act, the investigator must take adequate precautions to prevent the theft or diversion of the substance.

Results of FDA Routine Data Audits of Clinical Investigators

From June 1, 1977, through January 24, 1994, CDER has reviewed 3,092 routine, or surveillance, inspections of clinical investigators. While 19 percent of these investigators were found to be in full compliance, the remainder were cited for one or more GCP-related deficiencies. The table below identifies the most common deficiencies.

Type of Deficiency	Percent of Investigators Found Deficient
Inadequate Patient Consent Form	56%
Failure to Adhere to Protocol	29%
Inadequate and Inaccurate Records	23%
Inadequate Drug Accountability	22%
Failure to Keep IRB Informed of Changes, Progress	9%
Problems With Records Availability	3%
Unapproved Concomitant Therapy	3%
Failure to Obtain IRB Approval When Necessary	3%
Failure to List Additional Investigators	3%

Source: CDER's Division of Scientific Investigations

Informed Consent

Informed consent is a concept designed to ensure that patients do not participate in a clinical trial either against their will or without an adequate understanding of their medical situation or the implications of the clinical study itself. Federal regulations dictate that, except under special circumstances, "...no investigator may involve a human being as a subject in research unless the investigator has obtained the legally effective informed consent of the subject or the subject's legally authorized representative. An investigator shall seek such consent only under circumstances that provide the prospective subject or the representative sufficient opportunity to consider whether or not to participate and that minimize the possibility of coercion or undue influence. The information that is given to the subject or the representative shall be in language understandable to the subject or the representative."

Clearly, informed consent implies an informed patient. Any subject volunteering for the study must be fully aware of his or her medical condition, alternative treatments, and the purpose of, and risks involved in, the clinical study. Federal regulations state that, at the minimum, the following information must be provided to clinical subjects before involving them in the trial:

- a statement that the study involves research, an explanation of the purposes of the research and the expected duration of the subject's participation, a description of the procedures to be followed, and the identification of any procedures that are experimental;

- a description of any reasonably foreseeable risks or discomforts to the subject;

- a description of any benefits that the subjects or others may reasonably expect from the research;

- a disclosure of appropriate alternative procedures or courses of treatment, if any, that might be advantageous to the subject;

- a statement that describes the extent, if any, to which confidentiality of records identifying the subject will be maintained, and that notes the possibility that the FDA may inspect the records;

- for research involving more than minimal risk, an explanation as to whether any compensation or medical treatments are available if injury occurs, and, if so, what the treatments and/or compensation consist of, or where further information may be obtained;

- an explanation of whom to contact for answers to pertinent questions about the research and research subjects' rights, and whom to contact in the event of a research-related injury to the subject; and

- a statement that participation is voluntary, that refusal to participate will involve no penalty or loss of benefits to which the subject is otherwise entitled, and that the subject may discontinue participation at any time without penalty or loss of benefits to which the subject is otherwise entitled.

When appropriate, one or more of the following must also be provided to subjects:

- a statement that a particular treatment or procedure may involve risks to the subject (or to the embryo or fetus, if the subject is or may become pregnant) that are currently unforeseeable;

- anticipated circumstances under which the subject's participation may be terminated by the investigator without regard to the subject's consent;

- any additional costs to the subject that may result from participation in the research;

- the consequences of a subject's decision to withdraw from the research, and procedures for ordering the termination of the subject's participation;

- a statement that significant new findings developed during the course of the research that may relate to the subject's willingness to continue in the study will be provided to the subject; and

- the approximate number of subjects involved in the study.

In most cases, informed consent must be obtained by having the subject or the subject's representative sign a written consent form that has been approved by the IRB. Unless the IRB waives the informed consent requirements due to an absence of risk, the consent form may take either one of two forms: (1) a written consent document that embodies the basic elements of informed consent and that may be read to the subject or the subject's representative, who is then given adequate opportunity to read it before signing; or (2) a "short form" written consent document stating that the basic elements of informed consent have been presented orally to the subject or the subject's representative. If the short form is used, there are several other requirements—there must be a witness to the oral presentation; the IRB must approve a written summary of what will be said to the subject or the subject's representative; the witness must sign both the short form and a copy of the summary; the person actually obtaining the consent must sign a copy of the summary; and the subject must be given both the summary and a copy of the consent form.

While the investigator is most directly responsible for obtaining a subject's informed consent and seeing that the subject is truly informed, the IRB and the sponsor/monitor also play roles in ensuring that informed consent requirements are met.

The Institutional Review Board (IRB)

To ensure that ethical concerns are addressed before and during clinical studies, federal regulations assign certain responsibilities to the IRBs found within virtually every hospital, medical center, and research institution that conduct clinical trials. Sometimes called an institutional review committee, an IRB is a board, committee, or other group designated by a medical institution to review proposed and ongoing clinical trials and ensure that the rights and welfare of human subjects are protected. The board also ensures that a proposed study is not in conflict with the institution's research policies, philosophies, or existing commitments or abilities.

The IRB's function is to see that risks to clinical subjects are minimized, and that the subjects are adequately informed about the clinical trial and its implications for their treatment. In doing so, the IRB's authority goes beyond just reviewing proposed clinical protocols and ongoing trials. Although the board's main concern is not the adequacy of study design, the board can order that a trial be modified for safety or other reasons.

The IRB itself must consist of at least five persons, each of whom is chosen by the institution. Board members must be judged to have the professional competence necessary to review specific research activities, and to have the ability to assess the acceptability of proposed research in terms of institutional commitments and regulations, applicable law, and standards and practice.

IRB members are often physicians, pharmacologists, and administrative managers from the parent institution. However, at least one board member must have a primary interest in a nonscientific area such as law, ethics, or religion. Federal regulations also include several other requirements that are designed to preserve the independence of the board and to guard against conflicts of interest.

Generally, drug sponsors have little, if any, direct contact with an IRB. In fact, the FDA openly discourages drug sponsors from communicating directly with IRBs. The investigator heading the study at a particular institution will usually act as a liaison, and will present the study plans for IRB consideration and approval. Through past experience, the investigator will be familiar with the particular concerns and priorities of an IRB, and will be better prepared to deal with its members.

Aside from safety concerns, an IRB may consider a number of additional issues in evaluating a certain study, including specific standards of the institution, state, and locality. Any research program that the board does approve, however, must meet several criteria specified in federal regulations:

- risks to subjects must be minimized;

- risks to subjects must be reasonable in relation to the anticipated benefits and the importance of the knowledge that may be expected to be gained;

- subject selection must be equitable;

- informed consent must be sought from each prospective subject or the subject's legally authorized representative;

- informed consent must be appropriately documented;

- when appropriate, the research plan must make adequate provision for monitoring the data collected to ensure the safety of subjects; and

- when appropriate, there must be adequate provisions to protect the privacy of subjects and to maintain the confidentiality of data.

As are sponsors, monitors, and investigators, IRBs are subject to reporting and recordkeeping requirements. The board must retain minutes of meetings, copies of all research proposals reviewed, sample consent documents, correspondence with investigators, board procedures, and other documents. These records must be retained for at least three years after the completion of the research. IRB meetings and records are subject to FDA inspections, and an institution can be disqualified from conducting clinical studies if an FDA inspector finds that an IRB is violating GCP requirements.

Chapter 8:

The New Drug Application (NDA)

The new drug application (NDA) is the vehicle through which drug sponsors formally propose that the FDA approve a new pharmaceutical for sale and marketing in the United States. To obtain this government authorization, a drug manufacturer submits in an NDA thousands of pages of nonclinical and clinical test data and analyses, drug chemistry information, and descriptions of manufacturing procedures.

The NDA is the largest and most complex premarketing application that the FDA reviews. According to some estimates, an NDA will consist of between 50,000 and 250,000 pages. An FDA study of applications submitted and approved in 1992 revealed that NDAs for new molecular entities (NME) consisted of 214 volumes of information on average.

An NDA must provide sufficient information, data, and analyses to permit FDA reviewers to reach several key decisions, including:

1. Whether the drug is safe and effective in its proposed use(s), and whether the benefits of the drug outweigh the risks.

2. Whether the drug's proposed labeling is appropriate, and, if not, what the drug's labeling should contain.

3. Whether the methods used in manufacturing the drug and the controls used to maintain the drug's quality are adequate to preserve the drug's identity, strength, quality, and purity.

A Short History of the NDA

For decades, the regulation and control of new drugs in the United States has been based on the NDA. Since 1938, each new drug must have been the subject of an NDA before it could be, for commercial purposes, sold in, imported to, or exported from the United States. The Drug Exports Amendments Act of 1986 allows some unapproved drugs to be exported from the United States under limited circumstances.

The NDA has evolved considerably during its history. When the Food, Drug and Cosmetic Act (FD&C Act) was passed in 1938, NDAs were required only to contain information pertaining to the investigational drug's safety. In 1962, the historic Harris-Kefauver Amendments to the FD&C Act required NDAs to contain evidence that a new drug was effective in its intended use as well. Perhaps more importantly, these amendments required, for the first time, that NDAs be approved before a drug could be marketed.

The NDA was again the subject of change in 1985, when the FDA completed a comprehensive revision of the regulations pertaining to NDAs. While this revision, commonly called the NDA Rewrite, modified content requirements, it was mainly intended to restructure the ways in which information and data are organized and presented in the NDA to expedite FDA reviews.

More recent initiatives have brought many subtle changes to, and some further clarification of, NDA requirements:

- NDAs must include certifications that the sponsor did not and will not use in any capacity the services of any FDA-debarred person in connection with the application. Under the Generic Drug Enforcement Act of 1992, the FDA is authorized to debar individuals convicted of crimes relating to the development, approval, or regulation of drugs.

- A U.S.-based drug sponsor must submit a "field" copy of the NDA to its "home" FDA district office, and must certify in the NDA that it has done so. Foreign sponsors must submit the field copy with the NDA to FDA headquarters.

- Applicants must now include certain information about the batches of the drug product used to conduct the "pivotal" bioavailability and bioequivalence studies and the "primary" drug stability studies.

- As part of an initiative begun in early 1993, CDER reviewers were instructed to ensure that all NDAs submitted to the agency included analyses of drug effects in key "demographic subsets, including gender, age, and racial subsets...." The FDA stated that the request for the subset analyses already exists in its 1988 *Guideline for the Format and Content of the Clinical and Statistical Sections of New Drug Applications*, and that, in most clinical studies, there is sufficient data to analyze differences based on gender, age, and race.

- Companies must now forward one-half of the total user fee applicable to an NDA when the submission is sent to the FDA. Although the payment must be mailed separately and is not part of the NDA submission per se, an NDA will no longer be "filed" for review purposes without such a payment. The remaining portion of the fee is due when the FDA acts on the submission.

- During the early 1990s, the presentation medium for NDAs continued to migrate from paper to computers. From January 1989 to June 1993, for example, 71 computer-assisted new drug applications (CANDA) were submitted to the FDA. And although annual CANDA submissions have declined since reaching a high of 27 in 1991, the FDA plans to make computer submissions a requirement by 1995. In addition, new FDA regulations planned for release in proposal form during early 1994 will permit the agency to accept computer submissions as official documentation. Currently, only paper-based submissions may serve as official submissions.

- Under its user-fee program, the FDA has established new policies that delineate when sponsors can "bundle" data for different forms (e.g., indications, dosage forms, routes of administration) of the same drug under a single application (see Chapter 18).

147

NDA Content and Format Requirements

With the possible exception of clinical testing, FDA regulations and guidelines collectively provide more guidance on NDA content and format requirements than any other aspect of the drug development process. Although the exact requirements are a function of the nature of a specific drug, the NDA must, in each case, provide all relevant data and information that a sponsor has collected during the product's research and development.

FDA regulations provide the most fundamental description of NDA content and format requirements: "Applications...are required to be submitted in the form and contain the information, as appropriate for the particular submission.... An application for a new chemical entity will generally contain an application form, an index, a summary, five or six technical sections, case report tabulations of patient data, case report forms, drug samples, and labeling. Other applications will generally contain only some of those items and information will be limited to that needed to support the particular submission.... The application is required to contain reports of all investigations of the drug product sponsored by the applicant, and all other information about the drug pertinent to an evaluation of the application that is received or otherwise obtained by the applicant from any source. The Food and Drug Administration will maintain guidelines on the format and content of applications to assist applicants in their preparation."

In fact, the agency has more than a dozen separate guidelines that relate to NDA content and format issues. These documents include the following guidelines:

- *Guideline for the Format and Content of the Summary for New Drug and Antibiotic Applications* (February 1987);

- *Guideline for the Format and Content of the Nonclinical Pharmacology/Toxicology Section of an Application* (February 1987);

- *Guideline for the Format and Content of the Clinical and Statistical Sections of New Drug Applications* (July 1988);

- *Guideline for the Format and Content of the Chemistry, Manufacturing, and Controls Section of an Application* (February 1987);

- *Guideline for the Format and Content of the Human Pharmacokinetics and Bioavailability Section of an Application* (February 1987);

- *Guideline for the Format and Content of the Microbiology Section of an Application* (February 1987);

- *Guideline for the Submission in Microfiche of the Archival Copy of an Application* (February 1987);

- *Guideline on Formatting, Assembling, and Submitting New Drug and Antibiotic Applications* (February 1987);

- *Guideline for Submitting Supporting Documentation in Drug Applications for the Manufacture of Drug Substances* (February 1987);

- *Guideline for Submitting Documentation for the Manufacture of and Controls for Drug Products* (February 1987);

- *Guideline for Submitting Documentation for Packaging for Human Drugs and Biologics* (February 1987);

- *Guideline for Submitting Documentation for the Stability of Human Drugs and Biologics* (February 1987); and

- *Guideline for Submitting Samples and Analytical Data for Methods Validation* (February 1987).

The Fundamentals of NDA Submissions

Although the quantity of information and data submitted in NDAs can vary considerably, the component parts of NDAs are somewhat more uniform. According to Form FDA-356h, the *Application To Market A New Drug For Human Use Or As An Antibiotic Drug For Human Use*, NDAs can consist of as many as 15 different sections in addition to the form itself:

- Index;

149

New Drug Development: A Regulatory Overview

- Summary;

- Chemistry, Manufacturing, and Control Section;

- Samples, Methods Validation Package, and Labeling Section;

- Nonclinical Pharmacology and Toxicology Section;

- Human Pharmacokinetics and Bioavailability Section;

- Microbiology Section (for anti-infective drugs only);

- Clinical Data Section;

- Safety Update Report Section (typically submitted 120 days after the NDA's submission);

- Statistical Section;

- Case Report Tabulations;

- Case Report Forms;

- Patent Information;

- Patent Certification; and

- Other Information.

The components of any NDA are, in part, a function of the nature of the subject drug and the information available to the applicant at the time of submission. The safety update report section is not submitted in the original NDA, but is forwarded 120 days after the NDA submission (see discussion below). Each of the NDA sections is discussed further below.

The Archival, Review, and Field Copies of the NDA   Since October 8, 1993, drug sponsors have been required to submit three different copies of an NDA to the agency. The review and archival copies of the NDA have been regulatory requirements for years, while the field copy of the application is the newest NDA requirement.

The FDA provides specific guidance on content requirements for the archival and review copies of the NDA in its *Guideline on Formatting, Assembling, and Submitting New Drug and Antibiotic Applications* (February 1987). The role and content of these versions of the NDA differ (see exhibit below). The archival copy, which is stored by the FDA as a reference document, must contain all the relevant sections identified above. It must also include cover letters confirming FDA-applicant agreements, identifying company contact persons, or providing other information relevant to the NDA review. The purpose of the archival copy is to permit individual reviewers to refer to information not included in their review copies, to give other agency personnel access to the complete application for official business, and to maintain in a single file a complete copy of the entire NDA.

The review copy is a less comprehensive version of the NDA. It consists of the NDA's five or six technical sections—clinical, pharmacology, chemistry, statistics, biopharmaceutics, and, for anti-infective drugs, microbiology as well. Each of these technical sections is packaged for distribution to, and evaluation by, reviewers in the corresponding technical disciplines. Therefore, these sections must be bound separately, and be accompanied by a table of contents and a copy of the NDA's application form, index, and summary.

Under a final regulation that became effective on October 8, 1993, NDA sponsors must also submit a "field" copy of the NDA. To be used by FDA inspectors during preapproval manufacturing inspections, the field copy consists of an NDA's chemistry, manufacturing, and controls section, the NDA application form (Form FDA-356h), and the NDA summary. In addition, the field copy must include a certification that it provides an exact copy of the chemistry, manufacturing, and control section "contained in the archival and review copies of the application."

U.S.-based applicants must submit the field copy directly to their respective "home" FDA district offices. Only foreign applicants should submit field copies to FDA headquarters along with their archival and review copies.

Contents of the NDA's Archival and Review Copies

Elements of NDA (Color of Binder)	Archival (Blue)	Chemistry (Red)	Pharmacology (Yellow)	Pharmacokinetics (Orange)	Microbiology (White)	Clinical (Light-Brown)	Statistics (Green)
Application Form (Form 356h)	X	X	X	X	X	X	X
-cover letter	X	X	X	X	X	X	X
-patent information	X	X	X	X	X	X	X
-letter of authorization (if applicable)	X	X	X	X	X	X	X
1. Index to application	X	X	X	X	X	X	X
index to section [a]	⋮	X	X	X	X	X	X
2. Summary	X	X	X	X	X	X	X
3. Chemistry Manufacturing Controls	X	X	⋮	⋮	⋮	⋮	⋮
4. Samples [b]	⋮	⋮	⋮	⋮	⋮	⋮	⋮
Methods Validation [c]	X	X	⋮	⋮	⋮	⋮	⋮
Labeling: [d] -draft labeling (4 copies) or	X	X	X	⋮	⋮	X	⋮
-FPL (12 copies)	X	⋮	⋮	⋮	⋮	⋮	⋮
5. Nonclinical Pharmacology Toxicology	X	⋮	X	⋮	⋮	⋮	⋮
6. Human Pharmacokinetics Bioavailability	X	⋮	⋮	X	⋮	⋮	⋮
7. Microbiology (if required)	X	⋮	⋮	⋮	X	⋮	⋮
8. Clinical Data	X	⋮	⋮	⋮	⋮	X	⋮

Contents of Application (continued)

Elements of NDA (Color of Binder)	Archival (Blue)	Sections of the Review Copy					
		Chemistry (Red)	Pharmacology (Yellow)	Pharmacokinetics (Orange)	Microbiology (White)	Clinical (Light-Brown)	Statistics (Green)
9. Safety Update	X	:	:	:	:	X	:
10. Statistical Data	X	:	:	:	:	:	X
11. Case Report Tabulations	X	:	:	:	:	:	:
12. Case Report Forms	X	:	:	:	:	:	X
13. Patent Information	[attached to application form]	X	X	X	X	X	X
14. Patent Certification	X	X	X	X	X	X	X
15. Other (if applicable)	X	X	X	X	X	X	X

a Review Sections should contain a copy of the index to the entire application in addition to the index for the specific section.

b Samples should be submitted upon request.

c One copy of methods validation should be submitted in the archival copy; three copies should be submitted in the chemistry section of the review copy.

d The applicant should submit 4 copies of draft labeling or 12 copies of FPL (if available). The archival copy should contain 1 copy of all proposed labeling for the product (draft labeling or FPL and carton labeling, if available).

153

Application Form All three versions of the NDA must contain an NDA application form, Form FDA-356h (see exhibit below). This form, which ultimately serves as the NDA's cover sheet, provides a comprehensive checklist of the elements that each application should include.

In completing the form, the sponsor also provides basic information about itself (e.g., name and address), the investigational drug (e.g., chemical name, dosage form, and proposed indication), and the NDA (e.g., whether it is an original submission, amendment, or supplement).

The application form, copies of which are available from the FDA, must be completed and signed by the applicant, or the applicant's attorney, agent, or other authorized official. If the sponsor does not have a residence or place of business within the United States, the application form must contain the name and address of, and be countersigned by, an attorney, agent, or other authorized official who resides or maintains a place of business in the United States.

By signing this form, the sponsor also agrees to comply with a variety of legal and regulatory requirements, including current good manufacturing practice (CGMP) standards, safety update reporting requirements, and local, state, and federal environmental impact laws.

The Index The archival copy of the NDA must provide a comprehensive index "by volume number and page number" to the NDA summary, each of the five or six technical sections, and the case report forms and tabulations section. FDA guidelines state that the index should serve as a detailed table of contents for the entire archival NDA.

Each of the separately bound technical sections comprising the review copies must include a copy of the NDA index as well. In addition, each section should include its own individual table of contents based upon the portions of the larger NDA index relevant to that technical section.

The NDA Summary In many respects, the NDA summary is an abridged version of the entire application. It explains the application's intent—to prove the drug's safety and effectiveness for a specific use—and highlights the data and analyses that support the product's use.

Given that all reviewers receive a copy of the summary, its importance cannot be overstated. A well-prepared summary, which should include an

DEPARTMENT OF HEALTH AND HUMAN SERVICES PUBLIC HEALTH SERVICE FOOD AND DRUG ADMINISTRATION	Form Approved: OMB No. 0910-0001 Expiration Date: December 31, 1992 See OMB Statement on Page 3.	
	FOR FDA USE ONLY	
APPLICATION TO MARKET A NEW DRUG FOR HUMAN USE	DATE RECEIVED	DATE FILED
OR AN ANTIBIOTIC DRUG FOR HUMAN USE *(Title, Code of Federal Regulation, 314)*	DIVISION ASSIGNED	NDA/ANDA NO. ASS.

NOTE: No application may be filed unless a completed application form has been received (21 CFR Part 314).

NAME OF APPLICANT	DATE OF SUBMISSION
	TELEPHONE NO. *(Include Area Code)*
ADDRESS *(Number, Street, City, State and Zip Code)*	NEW DRUG OR ANTIBIOTIC APPLICATION NUMBER *(if previously issued)*

DRUG PRODUCT

ESTABLISHED NAME *(e.g., USP/USAN)*	PROPRIETARY NAME *(If any)*	
CODE NAME *(If any)*	CHEMICAL NAME	
DOSAGE FORM	ROUTE OF ADMINISTRATION	STRENGTH(S)

PROPOSED INDICATIONS FOR USE

LIST NUMBERS OF ALL INVESTIGATIONAL NEW DRUG APPLICATIONS *(21CFR Part 312)*, NEW DRUG OR ANTIBIOTIC APPLICATIONS *(21 CFR Part 314)*, AND DRUG MASTER FILES *(21 CFR 314.420)* REFERRED TO IN THIS APPLICATION:

INFORMATION ON APPLICATION

TYPE OF APPLICATION *(Check one)*

☐ THIS SUBMISSION IS A FULL APPLICATION (21 CFR 314.50)　　☐ THIS SUBMISSION IS AN ABBREVIATED APPLICATION (ANDA) (21 CFR 314.55)

IF AN ANDA, IDENTIFY DRUG PRODUCT THAT IS THE BASIS FOR THE SUBMISSION

NAME OF DRUG	HOLDER OF APPROVED APPLICATION

TYPE SUBMISSION *(Check one)*

☐ PRESUBMISSION　　☐ AN ADMENDMENT TO A PENDING APPLICATION　　☐ SUPPLEMENTAL APPLICATION

☐ ORIGINAL APPLICATION　　☐ RESUBMISSION

SPECIFIC REGULATION(S) TO SUPPORT CHANGE OF APPLICATION *(e.g., Part 314.70(b)(2)(iv)*

PROPOSED MARKETING STATUS *(Check one)*

☐ APPLICATION FOR A PRESCRIPTION DRUG PRODUCT *(Rx)*　　☐ APPLICATION FOR AN OVER-THE-COUNTER PRODUCT *(OTC)*

FORM 356h (6/92)　　PREVIOUS EDITION IS OBSOLETE　　Page 1

155

CONTENTS OF APPLICATION
This application contains the following items: *(Check all that apply)*
1. Index
2. Summary (21 CFR 314.50(c))
3. Chemistry, manufacturing, and control section (21 CFR 314.50 (d) (1))
4. a. Samples (21CFR 314.50 (e) (1)) (Submit only upon FDA's request)
b. Methods Validation Package (21 CFR 314.50 (e) (2) (i))
c. Labeling (21 CFR 314.50 (e) (2) (ii))
i. draft labeling (4 copies)
ii. final printed labeling (12 copies)
5. Nonclinical pharmacology and toxicology section (21 CFR 314.50 (d) (2))
6. Human pharmacokinetics and bioavailability section (21 CFR 314.50 (d) (3))
7. Microbiology section (21 CFR 314.50 (d) (4))
8. Clinical data section (21 CFR 314.50 (d) (5))
9. Safety update report (21 CFR 314.50 (d) (5) (vi) (b))
10. Statistical section (21 CFR 314.50 (d) (6))
11. Case report tabulations (21 CFR 314.50 (f) (1))
12. Case report forms (21 CFR 314.50 (f) (1))
13. Patent information on any patent which claims the drug (21 U.S.C. 355 (b) or(c))
14. A patent certification with respect to any patent which claims the drug (21 U.S.C. 355 (b) (2) or (j) (2) (A))
15. OTHER (Specify)

I agree to update this application with new safety information about the drug that may reasonably affect the statement of contraindications, warnings, precautions, or adverse reactions in the draft labeling. I agree to submit these safety update reports as follows: (1) 4 months after the initial submission, (2) following receipt of an appovable letter and (3) at other times as requested by FDA. If this application is approved, I agree to comply with all laws and regulations that apply to approved applications, including the following:

1. Good manufacturing practice regulations in 21 CFR 210 and 211.
2. Labeling regulations in 21 CFR 201.
3. In the case of a prescription drug product, prescription drug advertising regulations in 21 CFR 202.
4. Regulations on making changes in application in 21 CFR 314.70, 314.71, and 314.72.
5. Regulations on reports in 21 CFR 314.80 and 314.81.
6. Local, state, and Federal environmental impact laws.

If this application applies to a drug product that FDA has proposed for scheduling under the controlled substances Act , I agree not to market the product until the Drug Enforcement Administration makes a final scheduling decision.

NAME OF RESPONSIBLE OFFICIAL OR AGENT	SIGNATURE OF RESPONSIBLE OFFICIAL OR AGENT	DATE

ADDRESS *(Street, City, State, Zip Code)*	TELEPHONE NO. *(Include Area Code)*

(**WARNING:** A willfully false statement is a criminal offense. U.S.C. Title 18, Sec. 1001.)

unbiased presentation and analysis of a drug's beneficial and adverse effects, can build a reviewer's confidence in the applicant, in the validity and completeness of the information in the NDA, and in the drug itself.

As evidence of the importance that is placed on the NDA summary, the FDA published a February 1987 guideline entitled *Guideline for the Format and Content of the Summary for New Drug and Antibiotic Applications.* According to this guideline, "Each full application is required...to contain a summary, ordinarily 50 to 200 pages in length, that integrates all of the information in the application and provides reviewers in each review area, and other agency officials, with a good general understanding of the drug product and of the application. The summary should discuss all aspects of the application and should be written in approximately the same level of detail required for publication in, and meet the editorial standards generally applied by, refereed scientific and medical journals.... To the extent possible, data in the summary should be presented in tabular and graphic forms.... The summary should comprehensively present the most important information about the drug product and the conclusions to be drawn from this information. The summary should avoid any editorial promotion of the drug product, i.e., it should be a factual summary of safety and effectiveness data and a neutral analysis of these data. The summary should include an annotated copy of the proposed labeling, a discussion of the product's benefits and risks, a description of the foreign marketing history of the drug (if any), and a summary of each technical section."

Specifically, federal regulations require the NDA summary to provide the following:

- the proposed text of the labeling for the drug, with annotations to the information in the summary and technical sections of the application that support the inclusion of each statement in the labeling, and, if the application is for a prescription drug, statements describing the reasons for omitting a section or subsection of the labeling format;

- a statement identifying the pharmacologic class of the drug and a discussion of the scientific rationale for the drug, its intended use, and the potential clinical benefits of the drug product;

- a brief description of the marketing history, if any, of the drug outside the United States, including a list of the countries in which the drug has been marketed, a list of any countries in which the drug has been withdrawn from marketing for any reason related to safety or effectiveness, and a list of countries in which applications for marketing are pending (the section must describe marketing by the applicant and, if known, the marketing history of other persons);

- a summary of the chemistry, manufacturing, and control section of the application;

- a summary of the nonclinical pharmacology and toxicology section of the application;

- a summary of the human pharmacokinetics and bioavailability section of the application;

- a summary of the microbiology section of the application (for anti-infectives only);

- a summary of the clinical data section of the application, including the results of statistical analyses of the clinical trials; and

- a concluding discussion that presents the benefit and risk considerations related to the drug, including a discussion of any proposed additional studies or surveillance the applicant intends to conduct following approval.

Chemistry, Manufacturing, and Control Section The chemistry, manufacturing, and controls section is the first of the NDA's technical components. In this section, the sponsor describes, and provides data on, the composition, manufacture, and specifications of both the drug substance (i.e., the active ingredient) and the final drug product, including their physical and chemical characteristics and stability.

Historically, deficiencies have been more common in this portion of the NDA than in other sections of the application. This is probably due to several factors, including the fact that sponsors cannot develop final product formulations and commercial-scale manufacturing processes until late in the drug development process.

Recognizing this, the FDA released, in the mid-1980s, a spate of guidelines that provide agency advice on preparing chemistry, manufacturing, and controls sections for NDAs and other applications, including the following: *Guideline for the Format and Content of the Chemistry, Manufacturing, and Controls Section of an Application* (February 1987); *Guideline for Submitting Documentation for the Manufacture of and Controls for Drug Products* (February 1987); *Guideline for Submitting Documentation for Packaging for Human Drugs and Biologics* (February 1987); *Guideline for Submitting Documentation for the Stability of Human Drugs and Biologics* (February 1987); and *Guideline for Submitting Supporting Documentation in Drug Applications for the Manufacture of Drug Substances* (February 1987). More recently, the FDA has published two documents that might also prove relevant: *Draft Guidelines for Submitting Supporting Chemistry Documentation in Radiopharmaceutical Drug Applications* (November 1991) and *Guideline for Drug Master Files* (September 1989).

According to FDA regulations, an NDA's chemistry, manufacturing, and control section should consist of four principal elements: (1) a description of the drug substance; (2) a description of the drug product; (3) an environmental impact analysis report (or request for a waiver); and (4) a field copy certification.

A Description of the Drug Substance. The sponsor's description of the drug substance should include the following:

The Substance's Stability and Physical and Chemical Characteristics. Provide the substance's chemical name and related names (if available and appropriate), structural formula, physicochemical characteristics, the physical and chemical data necessary to elucidate and confirm the substance's chemical structure, and a description of the studies (including results) on the substance's stability.

The Name and Address of the Manufacturer. Provide the name and address of each facility (i.e., besides those of the applicant) that participates in manufacturing the drug substance (e.g., performs the synthesis, isolation, purification, testing, packaging, or labeling), and describe the operation(s) that each facility performs.

Method(s) of Manufacture and Packaging. Provide a full description of the materials and method(s) used in the synthesis, isolation, and purification of the drug substance, including a list of starting materials, reagents, solvents, and auxiliary materials. Also, describe the process controls used at various stages of the manufacture, processing, and packaging of the drug substance, and information on the characteristics of, and the test methods used for, the container-closure system. In addition, the original application should provide a full description of the preparation of any reference standard substance used, including a description of the purification steps.

Specifications and Analytical Methods for the Drug Substance. Provide a full description of the acceptance specifications and test methods used to assure the identity, strength, quality, and purity of the drug substance and the bioavailability of drug products made from the drug substance, including specifications relating to stability, sterility, particle size, and crystalline form. It is also typical to include data from the validation of these studies in this section as well.

Solid State Drug Substance Forms and Their Relationship to Bioavailability. Provide appropriate specifications characterizing the drug substance (e.g., particle size) to assure the bioavailability of the drug product.

The sponsor may provide for the use of alternatives in meeting any of the applicable requirements, including alternative sources, process controls, methods, and specifications. In some cases, reference to the current edition of the *U.S. Pharmacopeia* and the *National Formulary* may satisfy the above content requirements.

Often, applicants utilize components (e.g., drug substances, nonstandard excipients, containers) manufactured by other firms. In such cases, the contract manufacturer is likely to want to preserve the confidentiality of its manufacturing processes. Since an NDA must provide information on these

160

processes, contract manufacturers will often submit this information directly to the FDA in a drug master file (DMF). This allows drug sponsors using the company's products to meet submission requirements by incorporating by reference information provided in the DMF. Because the drug sponsor never sees the information in the DMF, the confidentiality of the contract facility's manufacturing processes is maintained.

An incorporation by reference should be made in the section of the NDA in which the referenced information would normally appear. The incorporation by reference must identify specifically where the agency can find the information in the DMF (or other referenced document), and must identify the file by name, reference number, volume, and page number (i.e., the FDA stores DMFs and reviews the information in the file only when referenced in a pending drug application). When the applicant cross-references a DMF submitted by another firm (e.g., a bulk drug manufacturer), the NDA must include a letter of authorization from the DMF's owner in addition to the information specified above. For more information on DMFs, refer to CDER's *Guideline for Drug Master Files* (September 1989).

Drug Product. In many ways similar to the drug substance section, this section should include the following:

A List of Components. Provide a list of all components used in the manufacture of the drug product (regardless of whether they appear in the final drug product).

A Statement of Drug Product Composition. Provide a statement of the product's quantitative composition, indicating the weight or measure for each substance used in the manufacture of the dosage form. Also, provide the batch formula to be used in the product's manufacture.

Specifications and Analytical Methods for Inactive Components. Provide a full description of the acceptance specifications and test methods used to assure the identity, quality, and purity of each inactive ingredient.

Name and Address of Manufacturer(s). Provide the name and address of each facility involved in manufacturing the drug product (e.g., the drug processing, packaging, labeling, or control applications), and describe the operations that each will perform.

Method(s) of Manufacture and Packaging. Provide a copy of the master/batch production and control records or a comparably detailed description of the production process (a schematic diagram of the production process is often helpful). Also, provide complete information on the characteristics of, and test methods used for, the container-closure system or other component parts of the drug product package to assure their suitability for packaging the drug product.

Specifications and Analytical Methods for the Drug Product. Provide a full description of the specifications and analytical methods necessary to assure the product's identity, strength, quality, purity, homogeneity, and bioavailability throughout its shelf life. The methods and standards of acceptance should be sufficiently detailed to permit FDA laboratories to duplicate them. It is typical to include data on the validation of the analytical methods in this section as well.

Stability. Provide a complete description of, and data derived from, studies of product stability, including information establishing the suitability of the analytical method(s) used.

In this section as well, the sponsor may provide alternatives for meeting relevant requirements, including alternative components, manufacturing and packaging procedures, in-process controls, methods, and specifications. Reference to the current edition of the *U.S. Pharmacopeia* and the *National Formulary* may satisfy relevant requirements.

A September 1993 final regulation modified content requirements for this portion of the chemistry, manufacturing, and controls section. The regulation mandates that applicants provide certain information about the batches of the drug product used to conduct the "pivotal" bioavailability and bioequivalence studies and the "primary" stability studies:

- the batch production record;

- the specifications and test procedures for each component and for the drug product itself;

- the names and addresses of the sources of the active and noncompendial inactive components and of the container and closure system for the drug product;

- the name and address of each contract facility involved in the manufacture, processing, packaging, or testing of the drug product, and identification of the operation performed by each contract facility; and

- the results of tests performed on the drug product and on the components used in the product's manufacture.

In addition, the 1993 regulation requires that this section provide the "proposed or actual master production record, including a description of the equipment, to be used for the manufacture of a commercial lot of the drug product or a comparably detailed description of the production process for a representative batch of the drug product."

Environmental Impact Analysis Report. In recent years, the FDA has been placing more emphasis on environmental assessments, which describe the environmental implications of releasing a drug substance and drug product into the air, water, and soil. Under current regulations, NDAs must include either an environmental assessment (EA) or a claim for a categorical exclusion from the regulations requiring the EA submission.

Although the FDA has its own environmental assessment regulations, they are not specific to drugs. In July 1991, the U.S. Pharmaceutical Manufacturers Association (PMA) released a handbook entitled *Interim Guidance to the Pharmaceutical Industry For Environmental Assessment Compliance Requirements for the FDA*. In addressing EA issues relative to INDs, NDAs, NDA supplements/amendments, and drug master files, this document supplements the FDA's more general *Environmental Assessment Technical Assistance Document*.

163

New Drug Development: A Regulatory Overview

Field Copy Certification. U.S.-based applicants must include in this section a statement "certifying that the field copy of the application has been provided to the applicant's home district office." Since foreign applicants must provide the field copy with the archival and review copies, no such certification is needed in their applications.

Given the nature and detail of the chemistry, manufacturing, and controls section, the FDA permits sponsors to submit the completed section 90 to 120 days before the anticipated submission of the entire NDA. In some cases, the agency claims, this may speed the NDA review process.

For such early submissions, both the archival and review copies of the section are required, while the field copy may be forwarded when the full NDA is submitted. The early submission should provide a cover letter, the application form, an index to facilitate the location of the information within the section, and identification of a sponsor contact person with whom the FDA may discuss the data. If any information required for the section is unavailable at the time of the advance submission, this should be noted in the cover letter.

Samples, Methods Validation Package, and Labeling Section
The archival copy of an NDA must include a labeling section and a methods validation package. When requested by the FDA, applicants must submit drug samples to the agency following the NDA submission as well.

Samples. Drug samples should not accompany the NDA submission, but should be submitted only in response to an FDA request. The FDA may request these samples to validate the adequacy of the analytical methods that the sponsor uses to identify the drug product and drug substance. Typically, the FDA requests that applicants submit samples directly to "two or more" agency laboratories that will perform the validation work.

Upon such a request, the applicant must submit "four representative samples of the following, with each sample in sufficient quantity to permit FDA to perform three times each test described in the application to determine whether the drug substance and the drug product meet the specifications given in the application:"

• the drug product proposed for marketing;

164

- the drug substance used in the drug product from which the samples of the drug product were taken; and

- reference standards and blanks (except that reference standards recognized in an official compendium need not be submitted).

Upon an FDA request, sponsors must also provide samples of the product's "finished market package." The FDA may ask for two copies of the package, although one generally suffices.

Methods Validation Package. The methods validation package provides information that allows FDA laboratories to validate all of the analytical methods for both the drug substance and drug product. It should include a listing of all samples to be submitted, including lot number, identity, package type and size, and quantity. In addition, the package will usually include descriptive information copied from pertinent sections of the NDA. FDA regulations state that "related descriptive information includes a description of each sample; the proposed regulatory specifications for the drug; a detailed description of the methods of analysis; supporting data for accuracy, specificity, precision and ruggedness; and complete results of the applicant's tests on each sample." To aid the reviewing chemist, these copies should retain the original pagination of the NDA sections from which they were copied. The FDA provides specific advice on the development of this section in its *Guideline for Submitting Samples and Analytical Data for Methods Validation* (February 1987).

Four copies of the methods validation package should be included with the initial submission. Although FDA regulations state that three of the copies should be submitted in the archival copy, agency guidelines recommend submitting one copy with the archival copy and three additional copies with the chemistry, manufacturing, and controls section of the review copy. If the applicant does the latter, the submission should include a statement indicating that this option was selected.

Labeling. The NDA's archival copy must contain copies of the label and all labeling proposed for the drug product. In the NDA, applicants must submit either 4 copies of a product's draft labeling or 12 copies of the final printed labeling (FPL).

If a sponsor submits draft labeling, one copy should be bound in the archival copy, with single copies being placed in the review copies for the clinical, chemistry, and pharmacology sections (labeling in the review sections may be bound separately in the appropriate colored jacket for the respective review sections).

When a sponsor provides FPL and carton labeling, one copy should be mounted, bound, and inserted in the archival copy. The remaining 11 copies should be mounted, bound, and submitted in a separate jacket clearly marked "Final Printed Labeling."

Nonclinical Pharmacology and Toxicology Section   Federal regulations state that this section should "describe, with the aid of graphs and tables, animal and *in vitro* studies with [the] drug." The section should include all nonclinical animal and laboratory studies involving the drug, including data from preclinical studies originally submitted in the IND; data compiled and submitted during clinical investigations (e.g., long-term testing such as carcinogenicity and reproductive testing); and, in some cases, nonclinical studies not submitted previously.

The FDA reviews these studies to evaluate their adequacy and comprehensiveness, and to ensure that there are no inconsistent or inadequately characterized toxic effects. According to federal regulations, the principal content requirements for this section are:

1. studies of the pharmacological actions of the drug in relation to its proposed therapeutic indication, and studies that otherwise define the pharmacologic properties of the drug or that are pertinent to possible adverse side effects;

2. studies of the toxicological effects of the drug as they relate to the drug's intended clinical use(s), including, as appropriate, studies assessing the drug's acute, subacute, and chronic toxicity, and studies of toxicities related to the drug's particular mode of administration or conditions of use;

3. studies, as appropriate, of the effects of the drug on reproduction and on the developing fetus;

166

4. any studies of the absorption, distribution, metabolism, and excretion of the drug in animals; and

5. for each nonclinical laboratory study, a statement that it was conducted in compliance with good laboratory practice (GLP) regulations, or if the study was not conducted in compliance with those regulations, a brief statement of the reason for the noncompliance.

The FDA is sensitive to organizational problems regarding the presentation of toxicological, pharmacological, and other data from nonclinical studies. Therefore, drug sponsors should refer to specific recommendations in the FDA's *Guideline for the Format and Content of the Nonclinical Pharmacology/Toxicology Section of an Application* (February 1987). Although it concedes that nonclinical data are collected over several years and are submitted in varying formats, the guideline recommends that the data be reorganized for the NDA submission: "The agency recognizes that most or all of the nonclinical data submitted to an application will have been developed over several years and submitted intermittently to an investigational drug application (IND). We recommend the reorganization of the studies to...the extent feasible for submission to an application even though the formats of all individual studies cannot always easily be made to conform in all details to these guideline recommendations. We anticipate that this guideline will also shape future IND submissions so that relatively little revision will be needed for the application other than to rearrange study order."

Human Pharmacokinetics and Bioavailability Section The NDA must include a section providing and analyzing data from all human pharmacokinetic and bioavailability studies (or information supporting a waiver of *in vivo* bioavailability data). The section should include data from and descriptions of any of the five general types of biopharmaceutic studies that were required for the investigational drug:

1. pilot and background studies, which are conducted to provide a preliminary assessment of absorption, distribution, metabolism and/or elimination (ADME) of a drug as a guide in the design of early clinical trials and definitive kinetic studies;

167

2. bioavailability/bioequivalence studies, including bioavailability, bioequivalence, and dosage form proportionality studies (this discussion should include a description of the analytical and statistical methods used in each study);

3. pharmacokinetic studies, descriptions of which must include a discussion of the analytical and statistical methods used in each study;

4. other *in vivo* studies using pharmacological or clinical endpoints; and

5. *in vitro* studies designed to define the release rate of a drug substance from the dosage form (obviously, such dissolution tests are not relevant for drug forms such as injectables and some others).

According to FDA regulations, this section should consist of as many as three elements:

- "A description of each of the bioavailability and pharmacokinetic studies of the drug in humans performed by or on behalf of the applicant that includes a description of the analytical and statistical methods used in each study and a statement [that it was conducted according to relevant federal regulations];"

- "If the application describes in the chemistry, manufacturing, and controls section specifications or analytical methods needed to assure the bioavailability of the drug product or drug substance, or both, a statement in this section of the rationale for establishing the specification or analytical methods, including data and information supporting this rationale."

- "A summarizing discussion and analysis of the pharmacokinetics and metabolism of the active ingredients and the bioavailability or bioequivalence, or both, of the drug product."

The FDA provides its most detailed recommendations on the development and presentation of this section in its *Guideline for the Format and Content of* the Human Pharmacokinetics and Bioavailability Section of an Application (February 1987).

Microbiology Section   This section is required only in NDAs for anti-infective drugs. Since these drugs affect microbial, rather than clinical, physiology, reports on the drug's *in vivo* and *in vitro* effects on the target microorganisms are critical for establishing product effectiveness.

Current regulations require that an NDA's anti-infective drug section include microbiology data describing: (1) the biochemical basis of the drug's action on microbial physiology; (2) the drug's antimicrobial spectra, including results of *in vitro* preclinical studies demonstrating concentrations of the drug required for effective use; (3) any known mechanisms of resistance to the drug, including results of any known epidemiologic studies demonstrating prevalence of resistance factors; and (4) clinical microbiology laboratory methods needed to evaluate the effective use of the drug. Full reports of the studies, summary tables, and a summary narrative should be included for each portion of this section.

More specific guidance on developing the microbiology component of the NDA is available from the FDA's *Guideline for the Format and Content of the Microbiology Section of an Application* (February 1987).

Clinical Data Section   Clearly, an NDA's clinical data section is the single most important element of the application. In fact, the FDA's conclusions about a new drug's safety and effectiveness are based largely on the data and analyses provided in the clinical section.

When taken together with the NDA's statistical component (see discussion below), the clinical section is also the application's most complex and voluminous. According to an FDA study of NME NDAs submitted and approved during 1992, for instance, an average of 87 percent of the submitted information in those applications was clinical in nature.

Therefore, it is not surprising that the most detailed NDA-related guideline addresses the NDA's clinical and statistical sections. The FDA's 125-page *Guideline for the Format and Content of the Clinical and Statistical Sections of an Application* (July 1988) provides recommendations on formatting and organizing these sections and on presenting the clinical and statistical information and accompanying documentation. The guideline also describes a fully integrated clinical and statistical report for documenting the results of individual studies.

As specified in the guideline, the first two elements in this section are: (1) a list of investigators supplied with the drug or known to have studied the drug, INDs under which the drug has been studied, and NDAs submitted for the same drug substance; and (2) a background/overview of the clinical investigations (i.e., the general approach and rationale used in developing clinical data). According to FDA regulations and the guideline referenced above, the NDA's clinical data section should consist of as many as 11 additional elements:

1. A description and analysis of each clinical pharmacology study of the drug, including a brief comparison of the results of the human studies with the animal pharmacology and toxicology data.

2. A description and analysis of each controlled clinical study pertinent to a proposed use of the drug, including the protocol and a description of the statistical analyses used to evaluate the study. If the study report is an interim analysis, this must be noted and a projected completion data provided. Controlled clinical studies that have not been analyzed in detail should be provided, along with a copy of the protocol and a brief description of the results and status of the study.

3. A description of each uncontrolled study, a summary of the results, and a brief statement explaining why the study is classified as uncontrolled.

4. A description and analysis of any other data or information relevant to an evaluation of the safety and effectiveness of the drug product obtained or otherwise received by the applicant from any foreign or domestic source. This might include information derived from commercial marketing experience, reports in scientific literature, unpublished scientific papers, and controlled and uncontrolled studies of uses of the drug other than those proposed in the application.

5. An integrated summary of the data demonstrating substantial evidence of effectiveness for the claimed indications. Evidence is also

required to support the dosage and administration section of the labeling, including support for the dosage and dose interval recommended, and modifications for specific subgroups of patients (e.g., pediatrics, geriatrics, patients with renal failure).

6. An integrated summary of all available information about the safety of the drug product, including pertinent animal data, demonstrated or potential adverse effects of the drug, clinically significant drug/drug interactions, and other safety considerations, such as data from epidemiological studies of related drugs. Unless provided under section (2) above, this section should also describe any statistical analyses used in analyzing the safety data.

7. For drugs that might be abused, a description and analysis of studies or information related to abuse of the drug, including a proposal for scheduling, and a description of any studies related to overdosage.

8. An integrated summary of the benefits and risks of the drug, including a discussion of why the benefits exceed the risks under the conditions stated in the labeling.

9. A statement noting that each human clinical study was conducted in compliance with the IRB regulations and with the informed consent regulations. If the study was not subject to IRB regulations, the applicant must state this fact.

10. If the sponsor transferred any of its regulatory obligations regarding the conduct of a clinical study (e.g. monitoring) to a contract research organization (CRO), a statement providing the name and address of the CRO, the identity of the clinical study, and a listing of the responsibilities transferred. When a sponsor transfers all of its obligations, the NDA may provide a "general statement of this transfer" in lieu of an itemized listing.

11. If the sponsor reviewed or audited original subject records during the course of monitoring any clinical study to verify the accuracy of the

case report forms submitted by the investigator, the NDA must provide a list identifying each clinical study so audited or reviewed.

During the early 1990s, the FDA became increasingly concerned with gen-
der-, age-, and race-related drug response differences. In March 1993, then-
CDER Director Carl Peck, M.D., undertook an initiative "to underscore
FDA's concern and to reinforce the importance of examining [in an NDA]
pertinent demographic subsets, including gender, age, and racial subsets, as
asked for in the [*1988 Guideline for the Format and Content of the Clinical
and Statistical Sections of New Drug Applications*]." The initiative was the
agency's response to a study showing that many NDAs failed to provide such
information.

In a letter to the U.S. Pharmaceutical Manufacturers Association (PMA),
Peck informed industry that CDER had taken the following steps:

"1. A memorandum...has been provided to all reviewing divisions
directing the staff to make certain that demographic analyses are
performed pursuant to the guideline. Where such analyses are
absent or inadequate, the division will request that sponsors provide
the appropriate analyses promptly. We anticipate such analyses usually could be completed promptly; if they cannot, refusal to file will
be considered.

2. Reviewers have been urged to note in their reviews the presence of
these analyses, to comment on their adequacy and findings, and to
formulate a conclusion about clinical relevance, labeling implications, and the need for further investigation."

Safety Update Report Section   As stated earlier, this section is not submitted with the original NDA, but is submitted in the form of update reports
at specific points in the application review process. In these reports, the sponsor must update its pending NDA "with new safety information learned about
the drug that may reasonably affect the statement of contraindications, warnings, precautions, and adverse reactions in the draft labeling."

The reports must include the same types of information (from clinical studies, animal studies, and other sources), and must be submitted in the same

format as the NDA's integrated safety summary. They must also include case report forms for each patient who died during a clinical study or who did not complete the study because of an adverse event (unless this requirement is waived).

Applicants must submit safety update reports four months after the NDA's submission, following the receipt of an approvable letter, and at other times requested by the FDA. Companies are encouraged to consult with the FDA on the form and content of these reports prior to the submission of the first report.

Statistical Section   As evidenced by the FDA's treatment of the NDA's clinical and statistical sections in a single guideline, the two components are closely related. In fact, the core of the statistical section is comprised of data and analyses taken directly from the application's clinical data section.

According to the agency's *Guideline for the Format and Content of the Clinical and Statistical Sections of New Drug Applications* (July 1988), the core of the statistical section should be comprised of the following sections taken verbatim from the NDA's clinical section:

• a list of investigators supplied with the drug or known to have investigated the drug, INDs under which the drug has been studied, and NDAs submitted for the same drug substance;

• a background/overview of clinical investigations;

• the controlled clinical studies section;

• the integrated summary of effectiveness data;

• the integrated summary of safety data; and

• the integrated summary of benefits and risks.

The FDA encourages applicants to meet with CDER—specifically with the assigned reviewer within CDER's Division of Biometrics—before an NDA's submission to discuss the section's format, tabulations, statistical analyses, and other important issues. In some cases, the agency permits applicants to submit for review and comment the preliminary tabulation of patient data and the materials on the statistical analyses of controlled clinical studies and/or safety data (see discussion of pre-NDA meetings below).

Case Report Tabulations Section During the FDA's most recent overhaul of its NDA regulations, the agency declared that "an efficient agency review of individual patient data should be based primarily on well-organized, concise, data tabulations...." Reviews of the "more lengthy patient case report forms" should be reserved for those instances in which a more detailed review is necessary, says the agency (see discussion below).

In its *Guideline on Formatting, Assembling, and Submitting New Drug and Antibiotic Applications* (February 1987), however, the agency advises sponsors to "meet with FDA to discuss the extent to which tabulations of patient data in clinical studies, data elements within tables, and case report forms are needed. Such discussions can also cover alternative modes of data presentation and the need for special supporting information (for example, electrocardiograms, x-rays, or pathology slides)."

According to agency regulations and guidelines, the NDA must provide data tabulations on individual patients from each of the following:

- the initial clinical pharmacology studies (Phase 1 studies);

- effectiveness data from each adequate and well-controlled study (Phase 2 and Phase 3 studies); and

- safety data from all studies.

Under current regulations, these tabulations should include "the data on each patient in each study, except that the applicant may delete those tabulations that the agency agrees, in advance, are not pertinent to a review of the drug's safety or effectiveness." The FDA is willing to discuss appropriate deletions from these tabulations at a "pre-NDA" conference (see discussion below).

Case Report Forms Section As stated above, the FDA does not require the routine submission of patient case report forms. Rather, the forms are required only for: (1) patients who died during a clinical study; and (2) patients who did not complete a study because of any adverse event, whether or not the adverse event is considered drug-related by the investigator or sponsor.

The FDA may request that the sponsor submit additional case report forms that the agency views as important to the drug's review. Typically, the agency will request all case report forms for the pivotal studies. In doing so, the review division will attempt to designate the critical studies for which case report forms are required approximately 30 days after the NDA's receipt. If a sponsor fails to submit the CRFs within 30 days of the FDA's request, the agency may view the eventual submission as a major amendment and extend the review period as appropriate.

Patent Information   Applicants must provide information on any patent(s) on the drug for which approval is sought, or on a method of using the drug.

Patent Certification   Applicants must provide a patent certification or statement regarding "any relevant patents that claim the listed drug or that claim any other drugs on which investigations relied on by the applicant for approval of the application were conducted, or that claim a use for the listed or other drug."

According to the FDA's *Guideline on Formatting, Assembling, and Submitting New Drug and Antibiotic Applications* (February 1987), the patent certification and patent information (see above) should be attached to the application form in the NDA submission.

Other Information   If necessary, the sponsor may use this portion of the application to incorporate by reference any information submitted previous to the IND filing. The sponsor must also provide an accurate and complete English translation of any foreign language document for any information originally written in a foreign language.

Pre-NDA Meetings

The NDA is perhaps the most complex and lengthy premarketing application that the FDA evaluates. Because of this complexity and because the FDA wants to avoid investing scarce resources reviewing deficient NDAs, the agency offers conferences called pre-NDA meetings to all drug sponsors.

Federal regulations state that the primary purpose of pre-NDA meetings "…is to uncover any major unresolved problems, to identify those studies that the sponsor is relying on as adequate and well-controlled to establish the drug's effectiveness, to acquaint FDA reviewers with the general information to be submitted in the marketing application (including technical information), to discuss appropriate methods for statistical analysis of the data, and to discuss the best approach to the presentation and formatting of data in the marketing application."

As is the case with end-of-Phase 2 conferences, a sponsor must request a pre-NDA meeting with the division responsible for a drug's review. Although federal regulations establish that all drug sponsors have access to such conferences, the importance of the drug, the time constraints facing the relevant drug review division, and the significance of the scientific and regulatory issues at hand will do much to determine whether the FDA grants a pre-NDA meeting to a particular applicant. The meeting can take place anytime before an NDA submission, but should not be held before Phase 3 studies near completion.

The success of a pre-NDA meeting depends largely on sponsor preparation. To help FDA staffers prepare, sponsors "…should submit to FDA's reviewing division at least 1 month in advance of the meeting the following information: (i) a brief summary of the clinical studies to be submitted in the application; (ii) a proposed format for organizing the submission, including methods for presenting the data; and (iii) any other information for discussion at the meeting."

FDA staffers stress that a particularly important element of pre-NDA meetings is that devoted to the statistical review. To make optimal use of the meeting, the sponsor should send, or have present at the meeting, sample mock-ups or computer printouts of data to provide FDA statisticians the opportunity to offer advice on data organization and presentation.

Assembling and Submitting the NDA

The FDA has extremely specific requirements for the NDA's assembly, many of which are provided in the agency's *Guideline on Formatting, Assembling, and Submitting New Drug and Antibiotic Applications* (February 1987). This

32-page document offers general guidance on such issues as content requirements, and more detailed specifications on such issues as paper size, maximum volume size, volume identification, and pagination.

Amending the NDA

Either at its own initiative or in response to an FDA request, an applicant
may seek to clarify or augment the information provided in the original NDA
during the review process. For example, the applicant may submit a new
analysis of previously submitted data, new data not available at the time of
the NDA submission, or information needed to address a deficiency in the
drug application.

Any such information provided for an unapproved application is considered an NDA amendment. The submission of a significant amendment may
trigger an extension in the FDA's time line for the application's review.

Chapter 9:

The NDA Review Process

The FDA's new drug application review process may be the single most scrutinized of all agency activities. It is probably the most harshly criticized FDA activity as well.

Most of this scrutiny and criticism is directed at the length, not the quality, of the drug review process. FDA critics argue that such factors as administrative inefficiencies and conservatism in scientific and medical decision-making are responsible for NDA reviews that averaged about 30 months through the late 1980s and early 1990s. Such lengthy reviews, critics claim, undermine the global competitiveness of the U.S. pharmaceutical industry and, worse, result in needless deaths and suffering by delaying access to emerging therapies.

There is, in fact, a body of evidence that suggests that drug development in the United States is long in relative as well as absolute terms. A 1993 study released by the Center for the Study of Drug Development at Tufts University concluded that fully 21 percent of drugs approved by the FDA from 1990 through 1992 had been approved six or more years earlier by at least one other country. Another 36 percent of these drugs were approved between one to five years earlier by at least one other country.

As FDA officials readily point out, however, the length of the drug review process is a product of many factors, including the quality of the NDA submissions, an applicant's response time to mid-review questions and issues, the importance of the therapy, and the availability of scarce FDA resources. It is also true that the FDA functions under the watchful eyes of an American public and a legislature passionately intolerant of errors in judgement, particularly those affecting the public health.

Regardless of the underlying reasons, however, it is understandable why the FDA and the drug industry have faced considerable pressure to do something—to do anything—to speed drug reviews. During the 1980s and 1990s, this pressure became so acute regarding AIDS therapies that the agency established formal procedures for expediting the development and review of drugs for serious or life-threatening conditions, and for providing desperately ill patients with early access to promising experimental-stage therapies.

But in 1992, the FDA and the drug industry took a much bolder step that had far more significant and wide-reaching implications for the drug review process. The two reached a groundbreaking accord that Senator Edward Kennedy (D-MA) called a solution to the "mismatch between accelerating pharmaceutical research and declining FDA resources." Specifically, the accord resulted in a new law, the Prescription Drug User Fee Act of 1992, that will shape the FDA's drug review process through at least the late 1990s.

Under the legislation, the FDA is collecting from the pharmaceutical industry a series of user fees. The FDA is using these newfound revenues to increase existing staffing levels—by approximately 600 staffers split roughly evenly between CDER and CBER—and to otherwise improve its new drug and biologics review processes. In exchange for these new funds, the FDA committed itself to a series of new and aggressive drug review time lines beginning with applications filed in fiscal year (FY) 1994 (October 1993-September 1994) (see discussion below).

Although the user-fee legislation will quicken the pace of, and involve hundreds of new personnel in, NDA reviews, it is unlikely to affect the nature of drug reviews. In many ways, the NDA review is similar to the IND review. The NDA is forwarded to the same division and, most likely, many of the same reviewers who evaluated the IND for the drug. And like the IND evaluation, the NDA review involves an evaluation of key medical/clinical, non-clinical pharmacology/toxicology, and manufacturing issues.

There are several fundamental differences between IND and NDA reviews, however:

- The NDA is a significantly larger and more complex document than the IND. Therefore, the NDA review absorbs far greater resources. Whereas INDs often comprise a few dozen volumes, NDAs for new molecular entities average over 200 volumes, according to an FDA study of NDAs submitted and approved during 1992.

- The FDA's evaluation of the NDA involves a detailed assessment of the drug's clinical safety and effectiveness, while the IND review involves only an assessment of the drug's likely clinical effects based on preclinical animal data (if available, data on previous human use will be used also).

- The implications of the actions proposed in an NDA are much greater than those proposed in an IND. Under a newly activated IND, a drug is used in patient pools of limited size and under carefully monitored conditions. When an NDA is approved, however, a drug may be prescribed for thousands of patients who comprise a group much larger and less homogeneous than the subjects who participated in the clinical trials. In addition, a marketed drug is often used under significantly less carefully monitored conditions than during the clinical testing phase.

A Profile of the NDA Review Process

Several factors make efforts to profile the FDA's NDA review process somewhat challenging. Although the agency documents many inspectional procedures in policy guidelines, CDER offers no such analysis of the NDA review process. More recently, several drug review divisions have described elements of the review process—particularly the clinical portion of the review—in their respective contributions to CDER's *CANDA Guidance Manual*. In the future, CDER's efforts to develop standards and guidelines for what center officials call "good review practices" may offer further insights.

Secondly, the various approaches to the NDA review by CDER's ten drug review divisions are likely to differ in some ways. Although all these units function under the same umbrella of laws and regulations, such differences are inevitable.

Still, the NDA review process is sufficiently uniform across the ten divisions to permit a general analysis. Following is a basic review of the NDA review process.

Initial Processing of the NDA

As it does for INDs, CDER's Central Document Room handles the initial processing of NDAs. This processing is largely administrative—staffers record information on the filing, including the sponsor's name, the drug, and the application's identification number, which is assigned by this office. Staffers also stamp the application with a receipt date, which starts the review time line applicable to the filing under the Prescription Drug User Fee Act of 1992 (see discussion below).

CDER's Central Document Room will also disassemble the various copies of the NDA for distribution to the various divisions that will evaluate the application. Although the bulk of the NDA review will take place within the drug review division responsible for the product, other divisions—such as the Division of Biopharmaceutics and the Division of Biometrics—also receive the technical sections relevant to their reviews.

According to Central Document Room staffers, the user-fee era has brought only one small change to initial NDA processing. With the NDA review copies, the staffers now forward a written form alerting the reviewers to the application's receipt date.

Processing Within the Drug Review Division

After initial processing of the NDA, CDER's Central Document Room forwards the application to a similar document control center within the review division responsible for the application's review. After the application is logged in, a division staffer prepares an acknowledgement letter for the sponsor. That letter informs the sponsor of the application's NDA number and date of receipt, and identifies the consumer safety officer (CSO) who will be the sponsor's FDA contact person—in most cases, the CSO assigned to a drug's IND will be assigned to the NDA as well. In many respects, the CSO functions as a coordinator for the NDA review, ensuring that the application is distributed and monitoring the status of the various technical reviews.

Upon receiving the NDA, the CSO performs an initial screening to ensure that the application is complete. If the application is found to be seriously incomplete, the division will refuse to file the NDA, and return the submission to the applicant with a letter describing the deficiencies.

If the NDA survives this initial screening, the application's technical sections are distributed to reviewers in the primary technical review disciplines—medical/clinical, pharmacology/toxicology, chemistry, and microbiology (i.e., for anti-infective drugs only). These individuals, along with consultancy reviewers (e.g., statistical and biopharmaceutics reviewers) within other divisions, form the NDA's review team.

Each reviewer then undertakes a more substantive or technical screening of the NDA, called a completeness review within some divisions. This evaluation ensures that sufficient data and information have been submitted in each area to justify "filing" the application—that is, initiating the formal review of the NDA.

Generally, the review team then convenes with division management in what is called a "45-Day Meeting" (so named because it takes place within 45 days of the NDA's submission) to determine whether the application should be filed or refused. If the team determines that the application should be filed, the meeting may then be used as a review planning session.

The FDA's Refuse-To-File Authorities

NDAs that the review team agrees are incomplete or deficient become the subject of a formal refuse-to-file (RTF) action. In such cases, the review division prepares a letter advising the applicant of the decision and the deficiencies that form its basis. The division will attempt to forward this letter within 60 days after the NDA receipt date.

For several reasons, the agency's RTF policies gained a significantly higher profile in 1993. First, RTF decisions will now carry a direct financial penalty for NDA sponsors—companies will have to surrender 25 percent of the full application fee when an NDA is refused.

In addition, with new pressures to take action on NDAs within the aggressive time lines specified by the Prescription Drug User Fee Act of 1992, CDER officials have warned that the application of the RTF policy will become more stringent. In a July 1993 RTF guidance document, CDER pointed out that, "In the past, decisions to refuse to file an application...generally were based on extreme deficiencies, e.g., the total omission of a needed section or the absence of any study that was even arguably an adequate and well-controlled study. More recently, applications have been refused when less extreme deficiencies existed, but when it was clear that the deficiencies were severe enough to make the application not approvable without major modification."

CDER's July 1993 RTF guidance document was, in most respects, almost a verbatim restatement of a revised draft statement released in 1992. The guidance states that CDER will exercise RTF authority under three circumstances: (1) omission of a section of the NDA required under federal regulations, or presentation of a section in so haphazard a manner as to render it incomplete on its face; (2) clear failure to include evidence of effectiveness compatible with the statute and regulations; and (3) omission of critical data, information, or analyses needed to evaluate effectiveness and safety or provide adequate directions for use. Most importantly, the document instructs CDER to continue basing RTF decisions "on omissions or inadequacies so severe as to render the application incomplete on its face. To be a basis for RTF, the omissions or inadequacies should be obvious, at least once identified, and not a matter of interpretation or judgement about the meaning of data submitted.... The RTF is not an appropriate vehicle for dealing with complex and close judgments on such matters as balancing risks and benefits, magnitude of drug effect, acceptability of a plausible surrogate marker, or nuances of study design (although designs that are obviously inadequate may lead to RTF...)."

Still, CDER's review divisions have considerable discretion regarding RTF decisions. For example, the document states that "Minor defects or omissions that could be repaired after the review commenced and that would not materially interfere with or delay review of the remainder of the application should not lead to RTF." Further, the RTF policy provides review divisions with the following discretionary powers:

- "The agency may, for particularly critical drugs, not use the RTF procedure, even where it could be invoked, or might review parts of a refused application if it believes that initiating the full review at the earliest possible time will better advance the public health."

- "Where an application contains more than one indication, it may be complete and potentially approvable for one indication, but inadequate for one or more additional indications. The agency may accept for filing those parts of an NDA that refer to the complete submissions for particular indications but refuse to file those parts that are obviously incomplete for other indications."

* "Each division may wish to develop its own checklist of points to consider regarding the fileability of an NDA in a particular drug class.... If any aspects of these checklists did more than clarify the general list, a means of conveying the additional points to pertinent sponsors should be developed." Several review divisions have developed their own RTF checklists.

The Preapproval Inspection   A division's decision to file an NDA triggers a few actions, including the beginning of the primary review process (see discussion below). It also triggers a division request for a preapproval inspection of the sponsor's manufacturing facilities. During such inspections, FDA investigators audit manufacturing-related statements and commitments made in the NDA against the sponsor's actual manufacturing practices. More specifically, the FDA has several motivations for conducting these inspections:

1. To verify the accuracy and completeness of the manufacturing-related information submitted in the NDA.

2. To evaluate the manufacturing controls for the preapproval batches upon which information provided in the NDA is based.

3. To evaluate the manufacturer's capabilities to comply with CGMPs and manufacturing-related commitments made in the NDA. In doing so, the FDA investigator will determine whether the necessary facilities, equipment, systems, and controls are functioning.

4. To collect a variety of drug samples for analysis by FDA field and CDER laboratories. These samples may be subjected to several analyses, including methods validation, methods verification, and forensic screening for substitution.

According to CDER policy, product-specific preapproval inspections generally are conducted for products: (1) that are new chemical or molecular entities; (2) that have narrow therapeutic ranges; (3) that represent the first approval for the applicant; or (4) that are sponsored by a company with a history of CGMP problems or that has not been the subject of a CGMP inspection over a considerable period. While the agency hopes to initiate preapproval inspections within 45 days of a filing decision, as of this writing, preapproval inspections were, on average, being conducted six or seven months after that decision is reached. More specific guidance on CDER's preapproval inspection program is available from the center's *Compliance Program Guide* 7346.832.

The Primary Review Process

Once the review team determines that an NDA is "fileable," the "primary" review begins. Here, the members of the review team sift through volumes of research data and information applicable to their reviewing expertise:

Clinical Reviewer: Evaluates the clinical data to determine if the drug is safe and effective in its proposed use(s). In determining the product's risk/benefit ratio, the reviewer assesses the clinical significance of the drug's therapeutic effects in relation to the possible adverse effects of the drug.

Pharmacology/Toxicology Reviewer: Evaluates the entire body of nonclinical data and analyses, with a focus on the newly submitted long-term test data, to identify relevant implications for the drug's clinical safety.

Chemistry Reviewer: Evaluates commercial-stage manufacturing procedures (e.g., method of synthesis or isolation, purification process, and process controls), and the specifications and analytical methods used to assure the identity, strength, purity, and bioavailability of the drug product.

Statistical Reviewer: Evaluates the pivotal clinical data to determine if there exists statistically significant evidence of the drug's safety and effectiveness; the appropriateness of the sponsor's clinical data analyses and the assumptions under which these analyses were used; the statistical significance of newly submitted nonclinical data; and the implications of stability data for establishing appropriate expiration dating for the product.

Biopharmaceutics Reviewer: Evaluates pharmacokinetic and bioavailability data to establish appropriate drug dosing.

Microbiology Reviewer (for anti-infectives): Evaluates the drug's effect on target viruses or other microorganisms.

Much of the primary review process involves reviewer attempts to confirm and validate the sponsor's conclusion that a drug is safe and effective in its proposed use. However, it is also likely to involve a reanalysis or an extension of the analyses performed by the sponsor and presented in the NDA. For example, the medical reviewer may seek to reanalyze a drug's effectiveness in a particular patient subpopulation not analyzed in the original submission. Similarly, the reviewer may disagree with the sponsor's assessment of evaluable patients and seek to retest effectiveness claims based on the reviewer-defined patient populations.

There is also likely to be considerable communication between review team members. If a medical reviewer's reanalysis of clinical data produces results different from those of the sponsor, for example, the reviewer is likely to forward this information to the statistical reviewer with a request for a reanalysis of the data. Likewise, the pharmacology reviewer may work closely with the statistical reviewer in evaluating the statistical significance of adverse drug effects in long-term animal studies (e.g., tumor rates).

Inevitably, the primary review produces the need for communication with, and clarification by, the NDA sponsor. In fact, sponsors must continue forwarding to the FDA new safety information during the entire NDA review. Through NDA "safety update reports," sponsors must provide periodic updates on any new safety-related information obtained from clinical studies, animal studies, or other sources. Sponsors must submit these reports four months after the original NDA submission, following the receipt of an "approvable" letter, and after an FDA request.

When the technical reviews are completed, each reviewer must develop a written evaluation of the NDA that presents his or her conclusions on, and recommendations regarding, the application. In most cases, the medical reviewer is responsible for evaluating and summarizing the conclusions of reviewers in all other scientific disciplines. The result is an action letter, which provides an approval/disapproval decision and a justification for that recommendation.

In reality, the reconciling of all reviewer conclusions and the development of a single course of action is likely to involve considerable dialogue between the medical reviewer and reviewers in the other disciplines. Since the ultimate decision hinges most directly on clinical safety, effectiveness, and risk/benefit issues, however, the medical reviewer is said to have the most influence in this process.

The results of the preapproval inspection may also figure into the final approval decision. When such inspections discover significant CGMP problems or other issues, the reviewing division may withhold approval until these are addressed and corrected. The division's response to such deficiencies is likely to depend on several factors, including the nature of the problem, the prognosis for the problem's correction, and the status of the NDA review.

The Final Approval of the NDA

The final channels through which an NDA must pass to obtain FDA approval will depend on issues such as the drug's novelty and importance. NDAs for NMEs, for example, need the approval of higher levels of FDA management than do marketing applications for less innovative products. Although federal regulations specify authority delegations for NDA "sign-off" powers (i.e., final approval authority), the regulations do give the FDA some flexibility to delegate these powers.

Once a single approval or disapproval recommendation is reached by the reviewers and their supervisors, the decision must then be evaluated and approved by the director of the applicable drug review division. For the director's review, the CSO assembles a "decision package" containing the action letter and any data, FDA memos, or other information supporting the reviewers' recommendation. Reviewers, their supervisors, and the division's director and deputy director then have an opportunity to examine the decision package.

After conducting what is sometimes called a "secondary review," the division director may begin a dialogue with the chemistry, medical, or pharmacology reviewers or their supervisors. Most often, the director will support the decision of the review group. For those drugs that are not considered particularly innovative or that are not seen as offering significant therapeutic advantages, the division director's decision generally serves as the final FDA ruling. In this respect, the division director is said to have "sign-off" authority for such drugs.

Other drugs, however, require an additional level of review to be considered approved. According to federal regulations, applications for new molecular entities require either CDER-level or office-level (i.e., ODE I or II) concurrence. In most instances, however, sign-off authorities for such products have been delegated to ODE I and ODE II. This office level review is sometimes called the "tertiary review."

Non-NME NDAs that present clinical issues beyond those presented by the previously approved versions of the subject drugs also revert to the office level for final approval. NDAs proposing major new indications or the first controlled-release dosage form of a previously approved drug are examples.

FDA Action Letters

The FDA communicates its official decision on an NDA through what is called an "action letter." Action letters are an important element in the agency's efforts to meet its review performance goals under the user-fee program—that is, the agency must "act on" NDAs within specific time frames. The FDA fulfills this requirement by issuing an action letter, which constitutes a complete action on the application, and which stops the review clock for the filing.

Three types of action letters—approval, approvable, and not-approvable—detail the FDA's decisions on NDAs. In some cases, knowing how and when to respond to an action letter can affect the ultimate approval decision on an application and how quickly that decision is made.

Approval Letter When the FDA sends an approval letter, the subject drug is considered approved as of the date of the letter. Generally, an applicant must submit final printed labeling before a drug is approved. However, if the FDA finds that the draft labeling is acceptable or if the agency requires only minor editorial changes, the NDA may be approved based on the draft labeling. In such cases, the FDA reminds the firm that marketing of the product with labeling other than that agreed to by the agency would cause the product to be viewed as an unapproved product.

Rarely, if ever, do drug sponsors receive an approval letter for an original NDA without first receiving an FDA request for more data or modification of the application in its originally submitted form. In many cases, an approvable letter precedes the approval letter.

Approvable Letter   According to the FDA's *Staff Manual Guide*, "The FDA will send the applicant an approvable letter if the application substantially meets the requirements for marketing approval and the agency believes that it can approve the application if specific additional information or material is submitted or specific conditions are agreed to by the applicant." Often, the FDA will request changes to the product's proposed labeling, and will require the submission of safety update reports and the product's final printed labeling.

Unless otherwise specified by the FDA, the sponsor has ten days after the date of the approvable letter to do one of the following:

• Amend, or acknowledge its intent to amend, the NDA. By choosing either of these two options, the sponsor automatically agrees to allow the FDA a 45-day extension period for the review of the amendment to be submitted.

• Withdraw the application. The FDA will consider the applicant's failure to respond to an approvable letter within ten days to represent the applicant's request to withdraw the application.

• For applications involving new drugs (not including antibiotics), ask the FDA to provide the applicant an opportunity for a hearing on whether grounds exist for denying the application's approval. Sponsors would make such a request when the FDA issues an approvable letter, but specifies in the letter marketing conditions that are unacceptable to the applicant. For example, the FDA may state in the letter that it considers only one of two indications proposed in an NDA to be "approvable" at that time. Should the FDA then refuse to approve the application under terms agreeable to the sponsor, the agency must give the applicant an opportunity for a hearing.

- For an antibiotic, file a petition or notify the FDA of an intent to file a petition proposing the issuance, amendment, or repeal of a regulation.

- Notify the FDA that the applicant agrees to a review period extension of a specified length so the applicant may give further consideration as to which of the previous four options it will pursue. The FDA will grant any reasonable request for an extension, and will consider the applicant's failure to respond during the extended review period to represent a request to withdraw the application.

Not-Approvable Letter   A not-approvable letter is forwarded to the applicant if the FDA believes the drug application is insufficient to justify approval. The letter describes the deficiencies in the application. Unless otherwise indicated by the FDA, the sponsor must do one of the following within ten days:

- Amend, or notify the FDA of an intent to amend, the NDA. The submission of the notification of amendment represents the sponsor's agreement to an extension of the review period.

- Withdraw the application. The FDA will consider the applicant's failure to respond within ten days to represent the applicant's request to withdraw the application.

- For applications involving new drugs (not including antibiotics), ask the FDA to provide the applicant an opportunity for a hearing on whether grounds exist for denying the application's approval. Should the FDA then refuse to approve the application, the agency will give the applicant an opportunity for a hearing.

- For an antibiotic, file a petition or notify the FDA of an intent to file a petition proposing the issuance, amendment, or repeal of a regulation.

- Notify the FDA that the applicant agrees to a review period extension of a specified length so the applicant may give further consideration to which of the previous four options the company will pursue. The FDA will grant any reasonable request for an extension, and will consider the applicant's failure to respond during the extended review period as a request to withdraw the application.

Final Printed Labeling

Labeling is usually the final major consideration in a drug's approval. Not until an NDA is virtually approved, or is judged to be "approvable," does labeling become the focus of FDA reviewers.

There are several practical reasons why labeling concerns are left until late in the drug review process. First, it is impossible to develop labeling with accurate accounts of indications, warnings, contraindications, and specific use instructions without conclusions drawn from pivotal clinical study data. Also, FDA reviewers will not invest significant time in evaluating proposed labeling until they are reasonably convinced that a drug is safe and effective, and that the drug's NDA is nearing approval.

Labeling becomes a principal concern once the agency issues an approvable letter, which, among other things, requests that the applicant forward its final printed labeling (i.e., all the labeling to appear on or to accompany a drug's package or container). At this point, only the labeling and possibly some minor deficiencies in an NDA stand between a drug and its approval.

Draft Package Labeling   Drug sponsors first propose labeling for a new pharmaceutical through what is called draft package labeling. Generally, draft labeling is submitted as part of the original NDA.

The specific labeling requirements facing a drug in its finished package form will depend on whether it is proposed for use as a prescription or as an over-the-counter (OTC) medicine. Principally because of dispensing differences, FDA labeling requirements for OTC and prescription drugs differ significantly.

Prescription Drug Labeling   According to federal regulations, prescription drug labeling must be "informative and accurate..., contain a summary of the essential scientific information needed for the safe and effective use of the drug...," and "be based, whenever possible, on data derived from human experience." In enforcing these and other requirements, the FDA has authority over the format and types of information that appear: (1) on the immediate drug container (i.e., manufacturer name, general brand name, lot number, etc.); and (2) on the outer carton in which the drug is shipped to physicians, hospitals, pharmacies, and other prescription drug dispensers.

A primary element in prescription drug labeling is the package insert. Drug manufacturers use prescription drug package inserts to meet the requirement that the physician or pharmacist be provided with the essential information needed to ensure the safe and effective use of the drug. Since the large body of information needed to satisfy this requirement cannot reasonably be placed on a prescription product's immediate container or package, manufacturers include it on a package insert. Such inserts generally consist of:

- a product description section describing the drug's dosage form, route of administration, ingredients, and therapeutic/pharmacologic effect;

- a clinical pharmacology section describing the action of the drug in humans and, if pertinent, its activity and effectiveness in animal and *in vitro* tests;

- an indications and usage section describing specific safety conditions and identifying indications supported by evidence of clinical effectiveness;

- a contraindications section;

- a warnings section describing potential safety hazards and steps to be taken if reactions occur;

- a precautions section discussing drug interactions and possible side effects in specific population groups such as pregnant women;

- an adverse reactions section;

- a drug abuse and dependence section, including a discussion of possible abuses and physical or psychological dependencies;

- an overdose section identifying specific signs, symptoms, complications, and laboratory findings that are associated with overdosage (this section might also specify the amount of the drug in a single dosage likely to cause overdosage symptoms and/or a life-threatening situation);

- a dosage and administration section identifying the recommended usual dose, safe upper dosage limit, and dosage modifications for children and the elderly; and

- a section describing how the drug is supplied (i.e., the drug's dosage form, strength, and unit availability).

Although the information on many inserts is reprinted in a publication called the *Physician's Desk Reference for Prescription Drugs*, consumers are generally not given this information directly when the prescription drug is dispensed. During 1993, however, the FDA seemed to be attempting to revive efforts to encourage industry to develop and supply patient package inserts for their prescription drugs.

OTC Drug Labeling OTC labeling requirements are, with regard to content, similar to those for prescription pharmaceuticals. Information regarding active ingredients, dosage and administration, indication, drug action, warnings, precautions, drug interaction, and overdosage must be provided.

However, because OTC products are self-prescribed, and because their use usually does not involve the guidance of a physician or pharmacist, OTC drug labeling must be structured differently. Much of the essential information provided to a pharmacist or physician through the package insert of a prescription drug must be detailed on the outer package of the container of the OTC product. In fact, all of the information that will allow the consumer to select and use the OTC product safely and effectively must appear on the outer package. This information must be presented in a manner suitable for the comprehension of the lay public.

The FDA's Review of Draft Labeling

When it becomes apparent that an NDA will be approved, agency reviewers evaluate the draft package labeling on at least two levels. First, the draft labeling is reviewed for its consistency with the regulatory requirements for applicable prescription or OTC drugs. Each important element of the proposed labeling (i.e., indications, use instructions, warnings, etc.) is then evaluated in view of conclusions drawn from nonclinical and clinical testing. All claims, instructions, and precautions must be based upon and accurately reflect the findings of the key test results, preferably clinical results.

If the FDA has major reservations about the draft labeling, the agency will usually forward to the sponsor a letter detailing its suggestions for revised labeling. In some cases, FDA reviewers themselves may revise a portion of the labeling, and instruct the sponsor to include the revision in the final printed labeling. Agency comments can relate to virtually any aspect of the proposed drug labeling, including:

- *Drug Indications.* The FDA and the applicant may disagree on the indications for which a drug was shown to be safe and effective in clinical trials.

- *General Wording.* FDA reviewers may believe that the proposed labeling is promotional or suggestive in nature and, therefore, may mislead physicians, pharmacists, or consumers.

- *Labeling Format.* The format must meet regulatory requirements, and must give proper emphasis to important elements of the labeling such as warnings and precautions.

- *Warnings/Precautions.* The warnings and precautions must directly reflect potential problem areas identified during human and/or animal testing.

The labeling "negotiation process," through which a drug's final approved labeling is agreed upon, can consume several weeks or several months. The length and complexity of the process will depend upon the nature and number of the FDA's comments, the degree to which the applicant is agreeable to making recommended revisions, and, of course, the applicant's desire to put the subject drug on the market.

In some cases, the sponsor will have to submit several revisions of its labeling before the FDA finds an acceptable version. Disagreements over labeling content, wording, and design are generally resolvable through either mail and telephone correspondence or through FDA-sponsor meetings.

Sponsor Rights During the NDA Review Process

Recent legislative and regulatory initiatives have affected several aspects of NDA sponsors' rights during the review of their applications. Companies should be aware of these rights and the courses of action available to them should these rights be violated. Sponsor rights during the NDA review process fall into roughly four categories:

- the right to a timely review;

- the right to confidentiality;

- the right to request meetings or conferences with the FDA; and

- the right to protest if the sponsor believes its rights are violated.

The Right to A Timely Review   Under the provisions of the Prescription Drug User Fee Act of 1992, the federal government has redefined the time frames for NDA reviews. For years, CDER has operated under legal requirements mandating the agency to review and act on NDAs within 180 days of their submission.

Most often, however, the 180-day time frame has been called a "phantom" requirement that CDER used as a goal or target, but seldom as a strictly enforced rule. All parties with a stake in the review process openly recognized that routine 180-day reviews were unreasonable given CDER's lack of resources and its need to make rational, informed decisions on new drugs.

The Prescription Drug User Fee Act of 1992 established a new series of drug review targets for the FDA, and provided the means—specifically, revenues derived from user fees—through which the agency could restaff and retool itself to meet these deadlines (for more on the user-fee component of the law, see Chapter 18). In reality, the review targets were developed by the agency itself, and were listed as agency commitments in a letter written by FDA Commissioner David Kessler, M.D., that was incorporated into the legislation. These review goals were to be phased in beginning in FY-1994 (October 1993-September 1994), and to be fully implemented by FY-1997. For applications submitted during FY-1994, the statute set out the following interim goals:

1. To review and act on 55 percent of NDAs within 12 months of submission.

2. To review and act on 55 percent of efficacy supplements within 12 months (for more on supplemental NDAs, see Chapter 14).

3. To review and act on 55 percent of manufacturing supplements within six months.

4. To review and act on 55 percent of resubmitted applications (i.e., after the applicant receives a not-approvable letter) within six months.

Under the provisions of the law, the FDA was to fulfill the "act on" requirement by issuing an action letter—approval, approvable, or not-approvable (see discussion above).

As will CDER staffing levels, the percentage targets rise each year through FY-1997: 70 percent in FY-1995; 80 percent in FY-1996; and 90 percent in FY-1997. Beginning in FY-1997, CDER must begin reviewing 90 percent of "priority" NDAs and efficacy supplements within six months, while the 12-month time frame will continue to apply to "standard" applications. Because of the different time frames applicable to standard and priority applications (i.e., beginning in FY-1997), the agency has introduced the following criteria for classifying original and supplemental submissions:

Priority Application. A priority application is for a product that "would be a significant improvement in the safety or effectiveness of the treatment, diagnosis, or prevention of a serious or life-threatening disease." The priority designation also applies to any drug that represents a significant improvement in the treatment, diagnosis, or prevention of a non-serious disease—for example, drugs showing documented improvement in patient compliance, drugs that eliminate or significantly reduce a treatment-limiting drug reaction, or drugs demonstrating safety or effectiveness in a new patient subpopulation.

Standard Application. All applications not qualifying as priority will be classified as standard submissions.

The applicable review time lines can be extended if the sponsor submits a "major" amendment to the original application during the review process. A major amendment involves the submission of a large amount of new, previously unreviewed data (e.g., new clinical or animal studies) or any submission that significantly affects the review process (e.g., a reanalysis involving multiple reviewing disciplines). When major amendments are submitted within three months of the action due date, the FDA will extend the review time frames by three months.

It will be at least a few years before the FDA's success in meeting its performance goals can be assessed to any significant degree. FDA officials concede that CDER's ability to meet the new review goals hinge on several key factors, including the center's ability to recruit and train new review staff; project management; performance and application tracking; and the establishment of accountability and reward systems for drug reviewers.

The Right To Confidentiality   Given the quantity of competitively sensitive data and information submitted in NDAs, confidentiality issues are of great importance to drug sponsors. Both the FDA and the federal government have policies and procedures designed to protect from public disclosure certain types of information submitted in the NDA. Under new regulations implemented in late 1993, however, the FDA does have limited rights to disclose certain NDA information to foreign drug regulatory agencies.

This initiative has not affected the public disclosure standards facing the FDA, however. The agency may not release any information or test data that qualify as trade secret or commercial or financial information. A trade secret is defined as "any formula, pattern, device, or compilation of information which is used in one's business and which gives him an opportunity to obtain an advantage over competitors who do not know or use it." To reflect relevant case law, the agency is in the process of revising its definition of trade secret information. This information, says the agency, has been defined by the courts as information relating to the making, preparing, compounding, or processing of trade commodities. In requiring a direct relationship between the trade secret and the productive process, this definition applies to a more narrow category of information than the current definition.

Commercial or financial information is "valuable data or information which is used in one's business and is of a type customarily held in strict confidence or regarded as privileged and not disclosed to any member of the public" by the company to which it belongs. Included in this definition is chemistry information and marketing assessments.

Non-confidential information (i.e., information not falling within one of the two definitions detailed above) may, at some point in the review process, be released by the FDA. However, the agency is restricted as to when it can publicly release such details as the NDA's existence, the name of the subject drug and its active ingredients, and other non-confidential information.

Non-confidential information is carefully guarded during the NDA review. However, the extent of protection given by the FDA depends on whether or not the existence of the NDA and any of its information have been previously disclosed or acknowledged publicly by the sponsor or another source. The FDA cannot announce the submission of an NDA or release any of the application's data if this information has not been previously disclosed.

When the NDA's existence and submission have been announced by the sponsor or discussed in a medical journal or other publication, a different set of confidentiality rules apply. In such cases, federal regulations state that the FDA may "disclose a summary of selected portions of the safety and effectiveness data that are appropriate for public consideration of a specific pending issue, for example, for consideration of an issue at an open session of an FDA advisory committee." The agency, however, is restricted in that it cannot make the sponsor's data or information directly available for public disclosure.

Many of the provisions restricting the FDA's public release of NDA-related non-confidential information apply only during the NDA review. More information is made publicly available once the FDA issues an approval letter to the applicant:

- a Summary Basis of Approval (SBA) document that provides a summary of the safety and effectiveness data and other information evaluated by the FDA;

- a non-confidential protocol for a test or study;

- adverse reaction reports, product experience reports, and consumer complaints;

- a list of all active ingredients and any inactive ingredients previously disclosed to the public; and

- a non-confidential assay method or other analytical method.

New FDA regulations released in late 1993 did provide the agency with greater powers to disclose nonpublic drug safety, effectiveness, and quality information to foreign regulatory agencies. The FDA sought to revise its regulations because previous standards for information disclosure were severely complicating its efforts to conduct cooperative drug reviews with foreign drug regulators (see Chapter 19)—principally the Canadian Health Protection Branch (HPB).

The specific issue of concern was the requirement that, if the FDA shared confidential commercial information with foreign regulatory officials, the agency was required to make the information publicly available as well. Because of this, the FDA and HPB had to develop special and time-consuming agreements and contracts—including the FDA's hiring of HPB reviewers as special U.S. government employees—to avoid the disclosure requirement. The need for such agreements, FDA officials contended, undermined the value of international drug reviews, which were intended to expedite drug reviews.

In response, the FDA published a November 1993 final rule that establishes conditions under which such information may be released to foreign regulatory officials without triggering public disclosure requirements. The FDA's new regulation establishes separate standards for the release of confidential commercial information and trade secret information.

According to the regulation, the FDA "may authorize the disclosure of confidential commercial information submitted to the Food and Drug Administration, or incorporated into agency-prepared records, to foreign government officials who perform counterpart functions to the Food and Drug Administration as part of cooperative law enforcement or regulatory efforts, provided that:

(i) The foreign government agency has provided both a written statement establishing its authority to protect confidential commercial information from public disclosure and a written commitment not to disclose any such information provided without the written permission of the sponsor or written confirmation by the Food and Drug Administration that the information no longer has confidential status; and

(ii) The Commissioner of Food and Drugs or the Commissioner's designee makes one or more of the following determinations: (A) The sponsor of the product application has provided written authorization for the disclosure; (B) Disclosure would be in the interest of public health by reason of the foreign government's possessing information concerning the safety, efficacy, or quality of a product or information concerning an investigation; or (C) The disclosure is to a foreign scientist visiting the Food and Drug Administration on the agency's premises as part of a joint review or long-term cooperative training effort authorized under [existing statutes], the review is in the interest of public health, the [FDA] retains physical control over the information, the [FDA] requires the visiting foreign scientist to sign a written commitment to protect the confidentiality of the information, and the scientist provides a written assurance that he or she has no financial interest in the regulated industry of the type that would preclude participation in the review of the matter if the individual were subject to the conflict of interest rules applicable to the Food and Drug Administration advisory committee members...."

With only two exceptions, the FDA will not authorize the disclosure to "government officials of other countries of trade secret information concerning manufacturing methods and processes...." First, the FDA will release trade secret information if the submitter has provided its "express written consent." Also, foreign scientists visiting the FDA will be given access to trade secret information "when such disclosures would be a necessary part of the joint review or training." These disclosures would be subject to the identical conditions as the FDA's sharing of confidential commercial information with visiting foreign scientists.

Despite industry criticism of this change, the FDA granted itself the authority to disclose confidential commercial information to foreign regulators without sponsor consent. In discussing its motivations, the FDA stated that, "There are situations in which it might be inappropriate to seek a sponsor's consent. For example, if communications and consultation with the submitters of the information have not resolved agency concerns, there may be circumstances in which FDA reviewers and investigators will want to consult with foreign government counterparts who are in the possession of similar submissions by the sponsor. It may even be that, during the course of an application review, FDA employees may discover problems with studies that raise the possibility that a sponsor or his employee had engaged in deliberate fraud or misrepresentation. Similarly, there are circumstances in which FDA investigators may wish to share with foreign counterparts confidential commercial information obtained through an FDA investigation for the foreign counterparts' use in their own regulatory efforts. This could include, for example, information in an open investigation concerning customer-supplier relationships or marketing plans. This type of information is customarily held in close confidence by businesses and therefore [is] usually protected from public disclosure by FDA in response to a [freedom-of-information] request. Disclosure of this information to foreign government counterparts, however, may facilitate efforts to keep unapproved, adulterated, counterfeit, or misbranded products off world markets as well as American markets." The FDA added, however, that it would seek sponsor authorization before most information exchanges.

The Right to Meetings The FDA communicates openly with sponsors about scientific, medical, and procedural issues that arise during the NDA review. These exchanges may take the form of telephone conversations, letters, or meetings, whichever is the most appropriate to discuss and resolve the relevant issue.

All sponsors have the right to at least one, and possibly several, conferences with the FDA during and after the NDA review. While the other forms of correspondence will occur routinely throughout the NDA review, the sponsor usually must make a written request before CDER will grant and schedule a conference. The number of meetings to which a sponsor is entitled may depend upon the subject drug and the priority given to it by the FDA. Under regulations codified in 1985, however, the agency claims to have made FDA-sponsor conferences more accessible to all applicants. These conferences include:

The 90-Day Conference. Approximately 90 days after it receives an NDA, CDER provides sponsors of certain drugs an opportunity to meet with officials and drug reviewers. Generally, such meetings are available only to sponsors of either NMEs or major new indications of currently marketed drugs. The purpose of the conference is to inform applicants about the general progress and status of their NDAs, and to advise them of deficiencies that have been identified but not yet communicated. However, the 90-day conference is not mandatory, and sponsors may choose not to request such a meeting. Also, the conference may be either a telephone or face-to-face meeting.

The End-of-Review Conference. The end-of-review conference is offered to all applicants after the FDA has issued either an approvable or not-approvable letter for an NDA. During this meeting, FDA officials discuss what further steps the sponsor must take before the application can be approved.

Other Meetings. Sponsors may request additional meetings to discuss scientific, medical, and other issues that arise during the review. Because of already heavy demands for its time, however, the FDA is likely to grant conferences only for more important issues. For resolving less significant issues, the agency will probably suggest communication by telephone or letter.

The Right to Protest   Although agency officials and shrewd industry officials tend to deny it, the NDA review process, in some senses, makes adversaries of the FDA and drug sponsors. The sponsor's goal—to obtain the most rapid approval possible for a product in which the company believes strongly—is not always consistent with the FDA's, which is to take the time necessary to ensure that the drug is both safe and effective before approving it. With such differing objectives, some disputes are almost certain to arise.

The FDA has a fairly sophisticated process for helping sponsors settle disputes. The process through which a particular dispute is resolved depends upon whether the problem is procedural/administrative or scientific/medical in nature.

Administrative and Procedural Disputes. Administrative and procedural disputes may involve problems such as sponsor difficulties in scheduling FDA meetings, obtaining timely agency responses to inquiries, and gaining timely reviews. The sponsor may also believe that the agency is not following procedures consistent with current laws or regulations.

When such problems arise, the FDA recommends that a sponsor first contact the CSO who is handling its application. Most CSOs are experts in the NDA review process, and are likely to have the most complete information about the status of a pending application. Because of this, and because CSOs work very closely with NDA reviewers, they can solve most procedural or administrative problems if the agency is at fault.

As of late 1990, sponsors of all FDA-regulated products have had another route to pursue their administrative/procedural disputes with the agency. In October 1990, the FDA created the position of FDA ombudsman, which the agency says is a position "designed to facilitate the investigation and resolution of complaints and disagreements that arise about the application of agency policy and procedures." With the exception of scientific and technical issues, sponsors can refer to the ombudsman problems for which there are "no other legal or established means of redress."

Scientific and Medical Disputes. The FDA believes that the 90-day and end-of-review conferences as well as the various other FDA-sponsor communications provide adequate vehicles for addressing and resolving scientific and medical disputes. The agency recognizes, however, that there are exceptions.

When the sponsor believes that conferences have proven inadequate, it may request a meeting with the management of the appropriate reviewing division. At that time, the sponsor may suggest that the FDA seek the advice of outside experts, such as consultants and other agency advisors. The sponsor may also invite its own consultant when such a meeting is granted.

If a specially scheduled meeting fails to resolve a dispute, the FDA may refer the matter to one of its standing advisory committees, which consist of non-FDA medical experts among others (see Chapter 11). The committee will review the issue and make recommendations. The FDA may then follow these recommendations or take its own course of action.

Chapter 10:
The FDA's Drug Classification System

As emphasized throughout this text, several factors can affect how quickly an NDA is reviewed and approved. Review division workload, an application's complexity, the nature of the scientific and medical issues presented by a drug, and the sponsor's ability to respond to FDA concerns are principal among these factors.

CDER's drug classification system assists reviewers in prioritizing their reviewing assignments. In doing so, the system is designed to help expedite the evaluation of drugs that offer particularly significant therapeutic benefits.

Under the existing classification system, each drug is placed into one of several categories based upon its chemical novelty and therapeutic potential relative to approved products. Drugs possessing novel and valuable therapeutic abilities are assigned a priority classification such as "1P," and are likely to receive a review priority higher than those drugs whose therapeutic promise is considered less significant.

Although some have argued that CDER's drug classification system was not particularly important in the past, it has become extremely relevant for drug reviews in the mid-1990s. Under its user-fee program, the FDA has new NDA review time frames that ultimately will be based solely on the classification of specific applications (see Chapter 9).

Chemical Novelty Rating

The classification code for any drug consists of at least one number and one letter designation (e.g., 2S). The number in the code represents the chemical novelty of a drug product's active ingredient. This rating indicates to FDA chemistry reviewers whether the active ingredient is new or is related to compounds already on the market.

According to internal CDER policy guide 4820.3, a drug is assigned one of the following seven chemical ratings:

Type 1–New Molecular Entity: "A drug for which the active moiety (present as the unmodified base [parent] compound, or an ester or a salt, clathrate, or other noncovalent derivative of the base [parent] compound) has not been previously approved or marketed in the United States for use in a drug product, either as a single ingredient or as part of a combination product or as part of a mixture of stereoisomers.

"The active moiety in a drug is the molecule or ion, excluding those appended portions of the molecule that cause the drug to be an ester, salt (including a salt with hydrogen or coordination bonds) or other noncovalent derivative (such as a complex, chelate, or clathrate) of the molecule, responsible for the physiological or [pharmacological] action of the drug substance. The active moiety is the entire molecule or ion, not the 'active site.'

"Ordinarily, an ester is not considered an active moiety as most ester linkages are rapidly broken, with the de-esterified molecule circulating in the blood. However, there can be exceptions to this where a stable ester is the active moiety, the de-esterified molecule being inert; an example of this is organic nitrates, where the nitrate esters are the active moieties. The organic base molecules (glycerol, isosorbide) are inert."

Type 2–New Ester, New Salt, or Other Noncovalent Derivative: "A drug for which the active moiety has been previously approved or marketed in the United States but for which the particular ester, or salt, clathrate, or other noncovalent derivative, [of] the unmodified base (parent) compound has not yet been approved or marketed in the United States, either as a single ingredient, part of a combination product, or part of a mixture of stereoisomers."

Type 3–New Formulation: "A new dosage form or formulation, including a new strength, where the drug has already been approved or marketed in the United States by the same or another manufacturer. The indication may be the same as that of the already marketed drug product or may be new.

208

"A drug with changes in its inactive ingredients such that clinical studies (as opposed to bioequivalence studies) are required is considered to be a Type 3 drug.

"A drug previously approved or marketed only as a part of a combination (either a manufactured combination or a naturally occurring mixture) or a mixture of stereoisomers will also be considered a Type 3 drug. A combination product all of whose components have previously been approved or marketed together in combination with another drug will also be considered to be a Type 3 drug.

"A change in the strength of one or more drugs in a previously approved or marketed combination is considered to be a new formulation, not a new combination."

Type 4–New Combination: "A drug product containing two or more active moieties that have not been previously approved or marketed together in a drug product by any manufacturer in the United States. The new product may be a physical or a chemical (ester or non-covalent) combination of two or more active moieties. A new physical combination containing one or more active moieties that have not been previously approved or marketed is considered to be a Type 1,4 drug.

"A chemical combination of two or more active moieties previously approved or marketed as a physical combination is considered to be a Type 1 drug if the chemical bond is a non-ester covalent bond. If the two moieties are linked by an ester bond, the drug is considered a Type 4 drug if the moieties have not been previously marketed or approved as a physical combination, and a Type 2 drug if the combination has been previously marketed or approved."

Type 5–New Manufacturer: "A drug product that duplicates a drug product (same active moiety, same salt, same formulation [i.e., differences not sufficient to cause the product to be a Type 3; may require bioequivalency testing, including bioequivalence tests with clinical endpoints, but not clinical studies], or same combination) already approved or marketed in the United States by another firm. This category also includes NDA's for duplicate products where clinical studies were needed because of marketing exclusivity held by the original applicant."

Type 6–New Indication: "A drug product that duplicates a drug product (same active moiety, same salt, same formulation, or same combination) already approved or marketed in the U.S. by the same or another firm except that it provides for a new indication."

Type 7–Drug Already Marketed But Without An Approved NDA: "The application is the first NDA for a drug product containing one or more drugs marketed at the time of application or in the past without an approved NDA. Includes (a) first post-1962 application for products marketed prior to 1938, and (b) first application for DESI-related products first marketed between 1938 and 1962 without an NDA. The indication may be the same as, or different from, the already marketed drug product."

Therapeutic Potential

The therapeutic rating is the second element of a product's classification, and is more relevant for purposes of the drug's review priority. In January 1992, the FDA simplified its three-tier therapeutic classification system into a two-tier system that categorizes drugs (and applications) as either priority (P) or standard (S).

It is this classification that determines CDER's target time frame for a product's review. Beginning in FY-1997, the agency will attempt to review most priority applications within six months and most standard applications within a year (see Chapter 9). With this at stake, the FDA has offered fairly detailed criteria for therapeutic classifications.

Priority Drugs   According to CDER's internal policy guide 4820.3, a priority drug is one that "appears to represent a therapeutic advance with respect to available therapy by [(a)]providing effective treatment or diagnosis for a disease not adequately treated or diagnosed by any marketed drug, or (b) providing improved treatment of a disease through greater effectiveness or safety (including decreased abuse potential), or (c) having a modest, but real, advantage over available marketed drugs, e.g., 1) significantly greater patient convenience (for example, the first less-frequent-dosing product for a class of drugs); 2) elimination of an annoying, but not necessarily dangerous, adverse reaction; 3) usefulness in a specific subpopulation of patients with the disease (for example, the elderly, pediatric patients, or those intolerant of already available drugs), etc."

After the implementation of user fees, several top FDA officials offered a similar definition for priority drugs. According to presentations made by these officials, a priority application is for a product that "would be a significant improvement in the safety or effectiveness of the treatment, diagnosis, or prevention of a serious or life-threatening disease." The officials also indicated that the designation also applied to drugs representing a significant improvement in the treatment, diagnosis, or prevention of a non-serious disease—for example, drugs showing documented improvement in patient compliance, drugs that eliminate or significantly reduce a treatment-limiting drug reaction, or drugs demonstrating safety or effectiveness in a new patient subpopulation.

Standard Drugs Under the FDA's user fee program, drugs that do not qualify as priority products are classified as standard therapies. According to CDER's policy guide 4820.3, a "standard" drug is one that appears to have therapeutic qualities similar to those of one or more already marketed drugs.

Special Situation Drugs The FDA may consider a conventional two-element rating code to be inadequate to properly identify a product's defining characteristics. In such cases, a review division may assign a drug one or more "special situation" ratings:

Type AA–AIDS Drug: "The drug is indicated for the treatment of AIDS or HIV-related disease."

Type E–Subpart E Drug: "The drug was developed and/or evaluated under the special procedures for drugs intended to treat life-threatening and severely debilitating illnesses" (see Chapter 17).

Type F–Fraud Policy Applies: "Substantive review of the application is deferred pending the outcome of a validity assessment of the submitted data as provided for by Compliance Policy Guide 7150.09. This code remains in the system throughout the audit and after when (a) the data are found to be not valid and a not approvable letter is issued or (b) the applicant withdraws the application before the audit is completed or after the audit is completed (data found to be not valid) but before a not approvable letter is issued."

Type G–Data Validated: "A validity assessment was performed on the application as provided for by CPG 7150.09, and the questions regarding the reliability of the data were satisfactorily resolved. (The G modifier replaces the F modifier previously associated with the application.)"

Type N–Non-Prescription Drug: "The drug has product labeling that provides for non-prescription (over-the-counter [OTC]) marketing. Applications will be labeled with an N designator whether all indications, or only some, are non-prescription."

Type V–Designated Orphan Drug: "The drug has officially received orphan designation…at the request of its sponsor/applicant" (see Chapter 15).

CDER's Prioritization Policy At Work

It is difficult to know precisely how CDER's drug review divisions use and implement the drug classification system. Perhaps the most detailed discussion appears in CDER's policy guide 4820.3: "The priority review policy is intended to direct attention and resources to the evaluation of applications for products that have the potential for providing some therapeutic advance (P) as compared to already marketed or approved products (S). When a reviewer has been assigned an NDA with a P classification, review of that NDA will take precedence over an NDA for a product that is considered to be substantially therapeutically equivalent to an already marketed or approved product (S). In addition, all NDA's for AIDS and HIV-related conditions will be classified as AA for priority purposes and will receive high priority review, regardless of their therapeutic potential.

"The priority review policy describes the overall approach to setting review priorities but is not intended to preclude work on all other projects. For example, there often will be opportunities to use relatively small amounts of time to complete ongoing actions. The fact that a reviewer is evaluating a 'P' application would not preclude use of some time to complete labeling or to answer questions from a supervisor about another NDA. Also, other work continues to be assigned while high priority NDA's are under review. A 30-day safety review for a newly submitted IND takes precedence over even a high priority NDA. Certain ad hoc special assignments may also take precedence. In the latter case, the supervisor is to advise the reviewer when an ad hoc assignment is to take precedence. As a general matter, if questions of priority arise, the reviewer should consult with the supervisor."

Chapter 11:

Advisory Committees and the Drug Approval Process

CDER's ten drug review divisions do not conduct their scientific and medical reviews of NDAs in a vacuum free from all outside input. In fact, throughout the review process the divisions have access to more than a dozen prescription drug advisory committees whose purpose is to provide advice on technical and medical issues related to the safety, effectiveness, testing, labeling, and use of new and approved drugs.

Today, CDER has 15 prescription drug advisory committees (see listing below) composed largely of leading scientists, most of whom are active researchers with academic appointments. In addition, CDER has two other advisory panels—the Nonprescription Drug Advisory Committee and the Generic Drug Advisory Committee—that can also become involved in prescription drug issues.

The advisory committees convene periodically to discuss issues that the FDA believes to be of major importance to the public health. Since 1964, CDER's new drug review divisions have looked to the advisory committees for recommendations on issues such as the approvability of specific drugs, the adequacy of drug development approaches (e.g., evaluating new guidelines or study design issues), and the status of certain marketed drugs. According to an internal CDER policy and practices memorandum, committee discussions of such issues bring "broader input to the decision-making process, provide access to technical expertise that may not be available within the agency and open FDA decision-making procedures to broader scrutiny."

CDER's Prescription Drug Advisory Committees

Division of Gastrointestinal and Coagulation Drug Products
• Gastrointestinal Drugs Advisory Committee

Division of Antiviral Drug Products
• Antiviral Drugs Advisory Committee

Division of Cardio-Renal Drug Products
• Cardiovascular and Renal Drugs Advisory Committee

Division of Neuropharmacological Drug Products
• Peripheral and Central Nervous System Drugs Advisory Committee
• Psychopharmacologic Drugs Advisory Committee

Division of Oncology and Pulmonary Drug Products
• Oncologic Drugs Advisory Committee
• Pulmonary-Allergy Drugs Advisory Committee

Division of Medical Imaging, Surgical, and Dental Drug Products
• Medical Imaging Drugs Advisory Committee

Division of Anti-Infective Drug Products*
• Anti-Infective Drugs Advisory Committee
• Dermatologic Drugs Advisory Committee

Division of Metabolism and Endocrine Drug Products
• Endocrinologic and Metabolic Drugs Advisory Committee
• Fertility and Maternal Health Drugs Advisory Committee

Pilot Drug Evaluation Staff
• Arthritis Drugs Advisory Committee
• Drug Abuse Advisory Committee
• Anesthetic and Life Support Drugs Advisory Committee

** Note: The effect of CDER's new Division of Topical Drug Products
is not reflected in this listing.*

Largely because advisory committee recommendations often have major medical and financial implications, the public profile of the committees has risen dramatically since the late 1980s. Although committee recommendations are not binding on the FDA, these recommendations are seen by the financial community and the pharmaceutical industry as forerunners of agency decisions on products. As a result, many committee meetings receive considerable attention from the financial community and trade press—a private firm now broadcasts the public segments of most important committee meetings live through satellite technology.

Although CDER's advisory committee program is three decades old, several emerging trends are changing the nature of committee roles and processes:

- *CDER's Reliance on Advisory Committees Is Rising.* After several years of little or no growth in meeting frequency, the number of advisory committee meetings surged 53 percent in fiscal year 1993 (see exhibit below). Although this surge is due, in part, to the founding of the Nonprescription Drug Advisory Committee, the use of existing committees rose considerably as well.

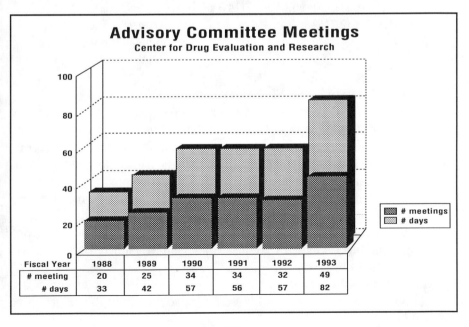

Advisory Committee Meetings
Center for Drug Evaluation and Research

Fiscal Year	1988	1989	1990	1991	1992	1993
# meeting	20	25	34	34	32	49
# days	33	42	57	56	57	82

- *Involvement of Advisory Committee Members Earlier and More Directly in the Drug Review Process.* Perhaps more frequently than ever, drug review divisions are bringing IND and clinical-stage (e.g., clinical protocols), rather than just approval-stage, issues before their advisors. Also, several divisions, including the Pilot Drug Evaluation Staff, increasingly involve advisory committee members directly in the review of drug applications. In some cases, committee members are invited to sponsor/FDA meetings early in the product development process.

- *Increasing Standardization.* At the request of FDA Commissioner David Kessler, M.D., the Institute of Medicine (IOM) undertook a comprehensive study of the agency's advisory committee program in late 1991. Although the IOM concluded that the FDA's advisory committee program is basically sound, it recommended that the agency standardize several aspects of the program, including member recruitment, conflict of interest policies, scheduling of meetings, and member training (see discussion below). The FDA is now revising an internal guide entitled *FDA Public Advisory Committees: A Handbook for Committee Members and Executive Secretaries (April 1988)* to incorporate many of these recommendations.

A Look at Committee Membership

The nature of an advisory committee's membership is a function of several factors, including the panel's charter and the technical expertise needed to evaluate the issues likely to come before the panel. Membership is comprised primarily of physicians, although qualified experts in such disciplines as epidemiology, nursing, biostatistics, pharmacology, toxicology, and psychology are also included. A technically qualified, consumer-nominated member may be designated as a voting member of a committee as well. Recently, the FDA revised the charters of its scientific advisory committees to allow the agency to supplement the committee's voting membership when necessary expertise is not available from existing members.

Nominated by professional or consumer organizations, other committee members, private individuals, or FDA staffers, advisors must be judged to be broadly trained and experienced, of established professional reputation and personal integrity, and committed to the public interest. Although the agency seeks balance in terms of gender, race, and geographic location, technical competence is the overriding consideration in selecting members. Because members serve four-year terms and, therefore, are likely to address a wide variety of issues during these periods, perhaps the ideal committee members are those who have recognized accomplishments and leadership within their fields, and have demonstrated abilities and interests in issues outside their specialties.

The FDA has several standards for ensuring the independence and objectivity of advisory committees. First, no FDA employees may serve as voting committee members. The FDA does, however, appoint an employee as an executive secretary for each committee. Although not a panel member, the executive secretary is the agency's liaison to the committee, and is responsible for all administrative planning and preparation for meetings.

The agency's dialogue with advisors is another aspect of the committee process that has been controversial at times. Some critics argue that agency staffers influence the views of advisors during such exchanges, an argument that top agency staffers openly reject. According to an internal CDER guide on policies and practices for center discussions with committee members, "It is never appropriate for either applicants or agency staff to lobby or negotiate with committee members about positions or conclusions the advisory committee should adopt on issues about to come before them. It is, however, appropriate for agency staff and corporate sponsors to provide members with background information on the issues at hand, and during meetings, to discuss the data and their own interpretation of the data with the whole committee."

Finally, the agency has stringent financial conflict-of-interest standards for its members. Committee members are screened for such conflicts when they are nominated. In addition, appointed members must file a statement disclosing their financial interests. Since many leading clinicians and scientists in academia work closely with product sponsors, conflict-of-interest concerns can be a severely limiting factor in recruiting committee members. However, individuals who have affiliations or investments that might present conflict-of-interest problems may be appointed to committees based on their qualifications. On a case-by-case basis, the agency will consider exclusions or waivers to allow the participation of such advisors in committee deliberations.

219

Committee members are paid $150 per day, and are reimbursed at the standard federal rate for travel, food, and lodging costs. Because of this cost structure, the advisory committee program is seen as a cost-efficient vehicle for obtaining input from many of the country's most knowledgeable, talented, and experienced scientists and clinicians.

When CDER Uses Advisory Committees

Given the limited number of advisory committee meetings, CDER must be careful to select for panel consideration issues with major implications for the public health. In fact, during 1991, CDER clarified its policies for selecting meeting topics in an internal document entitled *Policy and Procedure in Selection of Agenda to be Considered by Center for Drug Evaluation and Research Advisory Committees.*

According to that document, "Advisory committees are composed of committed but busy leading scientists, most of whom are active researchers with academic appointments. Participation in FDA deliberations does not free them of their other obligations. As meetings are usually 2 days long, occur 2 to 5 times per year, and involve substantial pre-meeting preparation, it is clear that, for many committee members, current meeting schedules represent a substantial commitment. Therefore, we must select issues for discussion in ways that maximize the valuable contribution of our advisors as a public health resource, as well as make efficient use of the agency's staff's time preparing for and participating in such meetings."

The internal policy guide defines the broad range of issues that may be considered by the committee, and general rules for selecting the most significant issues. Although this range includes general drug development issues (e.g., guidelines, study designs), emerging issues regarding marketed drugs (e.g., adverse reactions, labeling), and CDER's management of the drug evaluation process, the most important in the context of this discussion is committee deliberation on the approvability of specific drugs. In considering the data on a new drug or a significant new use of an already approved drug, the guide states that the committee might evaluate any of several issues, including:

• the adequacy of the design and conduct of studies intended to provide substantial evidence of effectiveness;

- the data supporting the proposed dose and schedule;

- critical studies;

- the appropriateness of surrogate endpoints for particular situations;

- the safety data base;

- the need for additional studies or special surveillance after marketing;

- the need to limit indications to a particular subset of the overall potential treatment population;

- the overall risk/benefit relationship of the new agent;

- the need for special labeling features, such as boxed warnings, limitations on use, monitoring requirements, or patient package inserts;

- the appropriateness of proposed prescription-to-OTC switches; and

- primary review of selected portions of NDAs.

In the internal guide, CDER attempts to specify general center policies for selecting issues for advisory committee deliberation:

"1. Applications for approval of the first entity in a pharmacological class will routinely be presented as well as any other new chemical entity whose evaluation poses special problems or raises issues of broader interest.

2. New drugs that are expected to have a major therapeutic impact, whether or not they are [new chemical entities] will ordinarily be presented. Similarly, major new uses of marketed drugs will ordinarily be presented to advisory committees. For drugs of particular urgency, this may require special or extra meetings. If these cannot be held, it may be necessary to present the advisory committee with reports of the agency's evaluation after the agency has taken action on the product.

3. Applications for initial [prescription] to OTC switches of a drug will routinely be presented to an advisory committee for their consideration.

4. Major safety concerns involving marketed drugs will usually be presented to advisory committees, if possible, before action is taken, although need for urgent action may require that the presentation take place after the agency's decision.

5. Clinical Guidelines will routinely be presented to the relevant committee for consideration before being adopted.

6. If the agency takes, or is planning to take, an action that conflicts with the explicit advice of an advisory committee on an important aspect of the committee's deliberations, the agency's position will ordinarily be summarized for the advisory committee with an explanation for the decision. Where the matter is likely to be controversial, this should be done before the decision.

7. Other issues may or may not be presented at the discretion of the [chairperson] and FDA staff, depending on the public health implications of the issue, the availability of time on the committee's calendar, and the need of the agency's review program for external advice on the issue. In general, requests by the Advisory Committee [chairperson] to have particular issues presented will be honored.

8. At least once a year, [a CDER] review division will present a program review of important and controversial drugs under development, and applications for [new chemical entities] that are pending. This shall specifically include an opportunity for the committee to advise the agency on the priority classification assigned to pending NDAs for [new chemical entities]."

The process for selecting issues often involves several steps. To identify potential topics for committee meetings, the executive secretary for each advisory committee periodically meets with the director of the drug review

222

division that the committee serves. These topics may be discussed during internal staff meetings.

It is important to note that CDER is not the only body involved in setting committee agendas. For example, drug sponsors may request that a pending issue involving its product be brought before a committee. Likewise, committee members themselves may request that certain issues of interest be considered.

Agenda items agreed to within CDER are then discussed with the committee chairperson to obtain his or her advice on which ones should be selected and how best to present the issues. Meeting agendas agreed to during this process are then published in the *Federal Register*.

How Advisory Committees Function

CDER officials are quick to point out that each advisory committee has its own personality and its own unique relationship with the review division that it serves. The committee's personality and method of functioning is influenced largely by the committee's chairperson. As noted above, the chairperson has input on which issues are selected for committee deliberation, and the presentation of these issues.

Although the product of the advisory committee process is generally a recommendation discussed and issued during a committee meeting, the process is considerably more involved. In fact, in many respects, periodic committee meetings represent the final stage of a lengthier and more complex process.

One of the fundamental principles of this process is that advisors be given access to sufficient information to allow them to provide informed recommendations during meetings. According to CDER's policy guide on committee discussions, "it is essential that the advisory committee collectively receive input from the agency regarding the staff's review of the data that will be presented to the committee. This provides committee members with the agency's expert analysis of the validity and organization of the data offered by sponsors, an analysis to which the agency usually brings more resources, expertise and experience than are available to the committee. It is also important that the committee have access to the agency's evaluation of the sponsor's data analyses, including the agency's evaluation of statistical techniques used, analysis of design issues, and assessment of the results of studies. Without such information, the committee may fail to address issues that will

223

be critical to the agency's reasoning when it formulates a final decision on the issue." Sponsors often provide "additional data, sometimes with additional documentation to focus discussion or assist an identified committee member serving as a primary or secondary reviewer of the drug."

Because they often play important roles during committee meetings, sponsors must also be informed of meeting agendas. "Every effort should be made to be sure the sponsor understands the issues that will be raised for discussion by agency reviewers. There are many ways to do this, including deficiency letters to sponsors, pre-meetings between the sponsor and agency in anticipation of any advisory committee discussions (it is useful to offer the sponsor an opportunity for such a meeting), and communicating to the sponsor any questions to be posed to the committee in advance of the meeting."

A review division assembles an information package and forwards it to the committee members at least two weeks before the scheduled meeting. Rarely, if ever, do committee members review an entire NDA or IND, although some committee chairpersons are encouraged to appoint a "committee reviewer"— a committee member who would either become involved in the evaluation of an application or would receive more detailed information on an application and make a separate report to the full committee.

Committee meetings, during which issues are discussed and recommendations are voted upon, are attended by committee members, key personnel from the relevant drug review division(s), and often representatives from the drug firm whose product is under discussion. A meeting will generally consist of two or more of the following segments:

- *Open Public Hearing.* Every advisory committee meeting includes an open hearing (at least an hour in duration), during which any interested person may present data, information, or oral or written views that are relevant to the advisory committee's agenda or other work.

- *Open Committee Discussion.* With limited exceptions, advisory committees are required to conduct their discussions of pending matters in open sessions. Although access to open discussions is not restricted, no public participation is permitted during this segment without the consent of the committee chairperson. External consultants and the drug sponsor may be asked, or may request the opportunity, to present data to the committee. Typically, sponsor and FDA presentations consume much of the time allocated to open committee discussions.

* *Closed Presentation of Data.* Data and information that are prohibited from public disclosure are presented to the advisory committee in a closed portion of the meeting. This policy applies to discussions involving information considered to be trade secrets by the sponsor, and the disclosure of personal information about clinical subjects. Only key FDA staffers, advisory committee members, agency consultants, and drug sponsors attend this segment of a meeting. This allows the sponsor to present and discuss sensitive information such as manufacturing processes without concern that competitors will gain access to that information.

* *Closed Committee Deliberations.* Committees may also choose to discuss issues in a closed session, in which attendance is limited to agency staff, committee members, and individuals invited by the committee chairperson. Such sessions are generally reserved for the discussion of existing internal documents whose premature disclosure might significantly impede proposed agency action.

Advisory committees are asked to make their recommendations as specific as possible, and to address key questions posed by the FDA. Depending on the nature of the question being considered, the committee may vote on an issue by a show of hands or a more in-depth discussion of individual member recommendations and the rationales for them.

How Influential Are CDER's Advisory Committees?

There is no real measure of advisory committee influence in the drug review process. Although committee recommendations are not binding on the FDA, there are few instances in which agency decisions contradict these recommendations. According to FDA statistics from 1975 to mid-1978, the agency followed 98.7 percent of advisory committee recommendations.

Still, it remains difficult to gauge whether committee decisions direct or simply support FDA decisions. As stated above, some critics of the process even suggest that FDA officials direct committee recommendations during pre-meeting communications.

It is also difficult to determine whether the agency would have reached the identical decision had the division not consulted an advisory committee. In fact, CDER's advisory committee policy guide acknowledges that a division may seek committee recommendations on a drug for which the division has already reached "a strong conclusion as to approvability."

In all likelihood, the influence of committee recommendations differs from case to case. Some FDA officials claim that the degrees of committee influence are best portrayed through several scenarios:

Scenario #1: The review division is faced with an issue that presents particularly complex technical issues about which it has not reached a decision. This might also include situations in which the advisory committee has expertise not available within the agency, or situations in which a drug's approval represents a "close call" given the risk/benefit profile of the product. In such situations, advisory committees are likely to have the most influence on FDA decision making.

Scenario #2: The review division has reached a preliminary decision, but wants advice on specific issues. For example, the division may have decided to approve a certain drug, but wants committee input on issues such as appropriate dosing, labeling, or the need for follow-up studies.

Scenario #3: The review division has made a decision, but would be more comfortable if an independent review supported the initial determination. For example, the FDA may have reached a not-approvable decision on an NDA, but may decide to bring the decision before an advisory committee to permit the sponsor to present its case to an outside review body. Although the division is open to reconsider its decision if so advised by the committee, recommendations offered in this context are less likely to affect agency decision making.

What Sponsors Should Know About Advisory Committees

Given the importance of advisory committee meetings, drug sponsors have much to gain in studying a committee before making a presentation to it. This is particularly important given the dynamic nature of the advisory committee process and the fundamental differences between the panels themselves.

Today, entire seminars are dedicated to preparing firms for advisory committee meetings. Although such detailed discussions cannot be presented here, there are several essential principles worth mentioning:

- Learn as much as possible about the committee members, particularly the chairperson. Each member's particular areas of expertise and interest are also extremely important. Some experts advise obtaining each member's curriculum vitae and research papers to gain insights about their interests, and to help anticipate possible concerns and questions.

- Gain a full understanding of the relevant issues as the review division views them. Division reviewers set the committee's agenda, and frame and phrase the specific questions to which the committee must respond.

- Learn how the committee functions, how meetings are conducted, how the committee reaches its decisions, and how much it values solicited and unsolicited input from the sponsor, clinical investigators, statisticians, outside consultants, and others.

- Research what topics are on the committee's agenda. This will affect the amount of time a drug sponsor will be given to present its case. For example, the Oncology Drugs Advisory Committee is known to move quickly through agenda topics, and to address two or more products at a single meeting. CDER provides agenda-related materials to all companies scheduled to participate in an upcoming meeting.

Recent Assessments of the Advisory Committee Process

As stated, the IOM convened a 17-person committee in late 1991 to evaluate the FDA's advisory committee program. This effort produced a 226-page report that included dozens of recommendations for improving all aspects of that program. These recommendations included the following:

- The FDA should adopt an agency-wide recruitment policy for its advisory committees, and should develop a more systematic approach to seeking nominations on a continuing basis.

- The FDA and the Office of the Special Council for Ethics within the Department of Health and Human Services should begin the process of codifying criteria for granting committee members waivers from conflict-of-interest standards, particularly with respect to institutional conflicts, research grants and contracts, and competing products and technologies.

- The FDA should develop, and require all agency professional staff who deal with advisory committees to take, a training program on conflict-of-interest issues. In addition, the agency should develop an orientation program for advisory committee members that includes "explicit attention" to conflict-of-interest issues.

- The FDA should develop criteria and procedures for identifying potential intellectual bias of advisory committee members, and for protecting the objectivity and impartiality of advisory committees.

- To eliminate unnecessary differences in the management of advisory committees, the FDA should develop uniform management guidelines.

- The FDA should adopt a policy of annual advance scheduling of committee meetings and of meeting agendas.

- The FDA should provide sponsors with the same materials that it sends to advisory committee members. Questions should be sent to committees and sponsors on the same schedule.

As of this writing, CDER was revising an internal guide entitled *FDA Public Advisory Committees: A Handbook for Committee Members and Executive Secretaries* (April 1988) to incorporate many of these recommendations. The revised handbook is expected to be released in 1994.

Chapter 12:

The FDA's Drug Listing and Establishment Registration Requirements

Since the early 1970s, industry submissions under the FDA's drug listing and establishment registration requirements have helped the agency to monitor, for compliance purposes, drug production and commercial distribution activities. These submissions provide the FDA with its most comprehensive account of drugs being distributed and of all facilities involved in the manufacture or processing of drugs in the United States.

Obviously, developing and maintaining these lists would be an unenviable, if not impossible, task for the FDA to face on its own. Therefore, in 1973, the Drug Listing Act of 1972 gave the FDA the authority to require, for the first time, both:

1. The registration of all facilities involved in the manufacture, preparation, propagation, compounding, or processing of a drug or drugs, including blood, blood products, and biologics.

2. The submission of the name of, and related information on, any drug in commercial distribution in the United States. Commercial distribution is defined as any distribution of a human drug except for investigational use. Internal or interplant transfer of a bulk drug substance between registered U.S. establishments within the same par-

ent, subsidiary, and/or affiliated company is not considered commercial distribution.

Drug listing and establishment registration play key roles in the FDA's enforcement of CGMP and NDA requirements. However, the listing of a drug or the registration of an establishment has little to do with, and does not exempt a company from, the requirements of the FDA's drug approval process. On the other hand, a company that sells or processes a drug must meet listing and establishment requirements for its product to be considered a legally marketed drug.

Drug listing and establishment registration differ in purpose and submission requirements.

Drug Establishment Registration

Drug establishment registration is a relatively simple procedure that requires little more than the submission of a facility's name and address, and the identification of the facility's owners/operators. The information identifies for the FDA those companies and facilities actively involved in manufacturing or processing pharmaceuticals. This can be important to the FDA's CGMP enforcement efforts, which involve the inspection of registered establishments.

But what is a drug establishment and who must register as one? Federal regulations define a drug establishment as a place of business under one management at one general physical location, including "among others, independent laboratories that engage in control activities for a registered drug establishment (i.e., 'consulting' laboratories), manufacturers of medicated feeds and vitamin products that are drugs..., human blood donor centers, and animal facilities used for the production or control testing of licensed biologicals, and establishments engaged in drug product salvaging."

Regardless of whether a company or facility seems to fall within the boundaries of this definition, establishment registration is required for:

- Owners/operators of U.S. facilities engaged in the manufacture, preparation, propagation, compounding, or processing of a drug or drugs, including blood, blood products, and biologicals.

- Owners/operators of U.S. facilities that repackage or otherwise change the container, wrapper, or labeling of any drug package during the distribution of the drug from the original place of manufacture to the person who makes the final delivery or sale. Private label and wholesale distributors are required to register only if they label, relabel, or otherwise change the product container, package, or wrapper.

Drug establishment registration involves the submission of *Form FDA 2656-Registration of Drug Establishment* and *Form FDA 2656E-Annual Registration of Drug Establishment*. These filings must provide the FDA with the following information:

- the name and address of the drug establishment;

- the name and signature of the establishment's authorizing official;

- the type of ownership or operator; and

- name of owners or operators of the establishment.

Establishment owner/operators must register a facility within five days after initiating the manufacture, preparation, propagation, compounding, processing, repackaging, or relabeling of any drug. If an establishment has not performed any of these operations previously, it must be registered within five days after the submission of an NDA, ANDA, medicated feed application, antibiotic application, or a biological product establishment license application. Annual registration must be completed within 30 days after the receipt of re-registration forms forwarded to the registered establishments by the FDA.

Drug Listing

Drug listing, which helps the FDA ensure that new drugs have met premarketing requirements, is slightly more complicated than establishment registration. The drug listing process involves the submission of specific product-related information for each establishment's commercially distributed drugs.

231

The applicability of drug listing requirements extends beyond registered drug establishments. Foreign manufacturers and processors, which are exempt from establishment registration requirements, must list each product shipped to the United States. Domestic firms that purchase bulk or finished drugs from foreign companies should inform representatives of those companies that all drugs imported into the United States must be listed by the foreign firm or its designated U.S. agent. In addition, all drugs exported by U.S. firms, whether in bulk or finished dosage forms, must be listed by the exporting firms.

To list a drug with the FDA, a firm must submit *Form FDA 2657–Drug Product Listing*, on which the following information must appear:

- A list of drugs, including finished dosage forms, bulk drug substances, and drug premixes by established and proprietary name, that are being manufactured, prepared, propagated, compounded, or processed for commercial distribution.

- The NDA number, ANDA number, or antibiotic application number for each drug that the firm believes is subject to the submission of these premarketing applications. A copy of all current labeling must be included.

- A copy of all current labels/labeling (only one representative container or carton label need be submitted where differences exist only in the quantity of contents statement), and a representative sampling of advertisements for each human prescription drug that the firm regards as not subject to legal requirements for new drugs, insulin-containing drugs, antibiotics, or biologicals.

- A copy of the label (only one representative container or carton label need be submitted when differences exist only in the quantity of contents statement), the package insert, and a representative sampling of any other labeling for each human over-the-counter (OTC) or animal drug that the firm regards as not subject to legal requirements for new, insulin-containing, antibiotic, animal, or biologic drugs.

- A quantitative listing of the active ingredient(s) for each prescription or OTC drug that the firm regards as not subject to legal requirements for new, insulin-containing, antibiotic, animal, or biologic drugs and that is not manufactured by a registered blood bank.

- The registration number of every drug establishment at which a drug is manufactured or processed.

- The National Drug Code (NDC) number of each drug. If the FDA has not assigned an NDC Labeler Code, the agency asks that a firm request an NDC Labeler Code by submitting *Form FDA 2656– Registration of Drug Establishment.*

After the initial listing, firms must update their product files twice yearly, at the end of June and December. Updating is also required when there is any material change in previously submitted information. Although companies can wait for the next semi-annual update to report newly manufactured drugs, the FDA prefers that firms inform the agency as soon as they begin manufacturing new drugs.

In addition to required drug listing information, the FDA encourages companies to submit other data on a voluntary basis. This includes the quantity of a drug being distributed, and a quantitative and qualitative listing of the inactive and active ingredients in all listed drugs.

Drug establishments are also required to list the drugs forwarded to distributors on *Form FDA 2658–Registered Establishment Report of Private Label Distributors.* However, if a distributor decides to list a drug itself and to certify that it has done so, the establishment is then exempt from the additional drug listing for the distributor. Like the manufacturer, distributors can list products by using *Form FDA 2657–Drug Product Listing.*

Exemptions from Drug Listing and Establishment Registration

The FDA offers several exemptions from drug listing and establishment registration requirements. A variety of exemptions exist for:

- pharmacies that operate under applicable local laws regulating the dispensing of prescription drugs, and that do not manufacture or process drugs for sale other than in the regular course of the practice of the profession of pharmacy, including dispensing and selling drugs at retail;

- hospitals, clinics, and public health agencies that maintain establishments in conformance with any applicable local laws regulating the practices of pharmacy or medicine, and that regularly engage in dispensing prescription drugs, other than human blood or blood products, upon the prescription of practitioners licensed by law to administer these drugs to patients under their professional care;

- practitioners licensed by law to prescribe or administer drugs and who manufacture or process drugs solely for use in their professional practice;

- persons who manufacture or process drugs solely for use in research, teaching, or chemical analysis;

- manufacturers of harmless inactive ingredients;

- persons who use drugs to prepare feed for their own animals;

- licensed manufacturers of a virus, serum, toxin, or analogous product intended for treatment of domestic animals; and

- carriers, in their receipt, carriage, holding, or delivery of drugs.

Chapter 13:

Beyond Approval: Drug Manufacturer Regulatory Responsibilities

A drug manufacturer's regulatory responsibilities certainly do not conclude with the FDA's approval of a new drug. In a real sense, a newly approved drug simply enters another stage of the product life cycle to which different regulatory standards apply.

But considering the fundamental differences between general marketing and comparatively tightly controlled clinical testing, the premarketing and postapproval responsibilities facing drug companies are remarkably similar in many respects. Just as the sponsor must ensure that its drug is produced according to accepted manufacturing standards during clinical testing, the sponsor must provide similar assurances when the product is marketed to the general public. Similarly, as the FDA calls upon sponsors to submit important test data during a drug's development, the agency also requires sponsors to report any postmarketing data or information that might cause the FDA to reassess a drug's safety and effectiveness.

In addition to abiding by the conditions of use (e.g., labeling, manufacturing commitments) detailed in its approved application, an NDA holder must fulfill several postapproval responsibilities in both the product reporting and manufacturing areas. Most postmarketing requirements fall into one of three general areas:

• General Reporting Requirements;

235

- Adverse Experience (AE) Reporting Requirements;

- Current Good Manufacturing Practice (CGMP).

General Reporting Requirements

According to federal regulations, sponsors of approved NDAs must develop and submit to the FDA several different types of reports and materials—field alert reports, annual reports, advertising/promotional labeling specimens, and "special" reports. Taken together with AE reports, these submissions allow the FDA to monitor the distribution and effects of the drug. The reports also alert the FDA to information that might represent grounds for regulatory action (e.g., product recall).

Field Alert Reports   Federal regulations require NDA holders to report, within three days of receipt, any information:

- "...concerning any incident that causes the drug product or its labeling to be mistaken for, or applied to, another article."

- "...concerning any bacteriological contamination, or any significant chemical, physical, or other change or deterioration in the distributed drug product, or any failure of one or more distributed batches of the drug product to meet the specifications established for it in the application."

Companies may provide this information by telephone or other rapid means, provided that the initial notification is followed by a prompt written follow-up report. The written report should be plainly marked "NDA-Field Alert Report," and be submitted to the FDA district office responsible for the reporting manufacturing facility.

Annual Reports   The annual report plays a few important roles in the FDA's monitoring of a marketed drug's safety and quality. First, the report provides the FDA with a convenient summary of research data, distribution information, and labeling changes. Also, the annual submission is the vehicle

236

through which manufacturers must report certain types of information that need not be provided in any other mandatory filing.

Annual reports must be filed with the FDA drug review division responsible for evaluating and approving a subject drug's NDA. These reports must be submitted each year within 60 days of the anniversary date of the drug's approval, and must be accompanied by a *Transmittal of Periodic Reports for Drugs for Human Use* (Form FDA-2252).

Annual reports must include the following types of information "that the applicant received or otherwise obtained during the annual reporting interval which ends on the anniversary date:"

Summary Data. A brief summary of the significant new information obtained during the previous year that might affect the safety, effectiveness, or labeling of the drug product. Also, the sponsor must detail any action it has taken or is planning to take in response to this new information (e.g., submitting a labeling supplement, adding a warning to the labeling, or initiating a new study).

Distribution Data. Information on the quantity of the product distributed, and the amounts forwarded to drug distributors. This section must provide the National Drug Code (NDC) number, the total number of dosage units of each strength or potency distributed (e.g., 100,000/5 milligram tablets, 50,000/10 milliliter vials), and the quantities distributed for domestic and foreign use.

Labeling. Labeling information and samples, including currently used professional labeling, patient brochures or package inserts (if any), a representative sample of the package labels, and a summary of product labeling changes implemented since the last report. If the manufacturer implemented no labeling changes, this should be stated in the report.

Chemistry, Manufacturing, and Controls Changes. Chemistry, manufacturing, and controls changes, including reports of any new experiences, investigations, studies, or tests involving chemical, physical, or other properties of the drug that may affect the FDA's previous conclusions on the product. The report should also provide a full description of all implemented manufacturing and controls changes that did not require a supplemental application.

New Drug Development: A Regulatory Overview

Nonclinical Laboratory Studies. Nonclinical laboratory studies, including copies of unpublished reports, summaries of published reports of new toxicological findings in animal studies, and *in vitro* studies conducted or otherwise obtained by the sponsor relating to the product's ingredients.

Clinical Data. Published clinical trials on the drug (or abstracts of them), including: data from trials on safety and effectiveness or new uses; biopharmaceutic, pharmacokinetic, and clinical pharmacology studies; and reports of clinical experiences pertinent to safety (e.g., epidemiologic studies) conducted or obtained by the sponsor. Also needed are summaries of completed unpublished clinical trials—a study is considered completed one year after its conclusion—or pre-publication manuscripts developed or obtained by the applicant. Supporting information should not be reported. Review articles, papers describing the use of the drug product in medical practice, papers and abstracts in which the drug is used as a research tool, promotional articles, press clippings, and papers that do not contain tabulations or summaries of original data should not be reported.

Status Reports. A statement on the current status of any postmarketing studies performed by, or on behalf of, the applicant.

Other Reports   Federal regulations state that sponsors must be prepared to file other reports, including:

Advertisements and Promotional Labeling. NDA holders must "submit specimens of mailing pieces and any other labeling or advertising devised for promotion of the drug product at the time of initial dissemination of the labeling and at the time of initial publication of the advertisement for a prescription drug product. Mailing pieces and labeling that are designed to contain samples of a drug product are required to be complete, except the sample of the drug product may be omitted. Each submission is required to be accompanied by a completed transmittal Form FDA-2253 (Transmittal of Advertisements and Promotional Labeling for Drugs for Human Use) and is required to include a copy of the product's current professional labeling."

Special Reports. The FDA may request that the applicant submit any of the reports profiled above at times different than those required under federal regulations.

Adverse Drug Experience (AE) Reporting Requirements

NDA holders must collect, analyze, and submit data on postmarketing adverse drug experiences (AE) so that the company and the FDA can continually reassess the product's risk/benefit relationship and the conditions under which the drug should be marketed and used.

As of this writing, CDER was in the process of revising several aspects of its postmarketing AE reporting requirements. In early 1994, CDER was expected to publish a proposal to incorporate changes introduced through the FDA's MedWatch Program, which is designed to "facilitate the reporting of adverse events and product problems for all FDA-regulated products." These changes include a new form for postmarketing AE reports and a new definition for "serious" AEs.

In the proposal, the agency was also expected to propose a series of changes to harmonize its postmarketing reporting requirements with those of the international community. When finalized, this initiative is expected to change the frequency of periodic AE reports and the formatting of both periodic and alert (e.g., 15-day and increased frequency) AE reports. Possible changes as a result of the MedWatch and harmonization initiatives are highlighted in the discussion of existing requirements below.

CDER's current postmarketing AE reporting requirements are a product of a series of revisions implemented in the mid- and late-1980s. These requirements are described in FDA regulations and CDER's *Guideline for Postmarketing Reporting of Adverse Drug Experiences* (March 1992).

Key Definitions for AE Reporting   Like many other areas of FDA regulation, AE reporting has a language very much its own. In fact, reporting requirements are directly linked to criteria outlined in the definitions of at least three important terms:

"Adverse Drug Experience." According to FDA regulations, *"Adverse drug experience* means any adverse event associated with the use of a drug in humans, whether or not considered drug related." Such experiences include the following: "an adverse event occurring in the course of the use of a drug product in professional practice; an adverse event occurring from drug overdose, whether accidental or intentional; an adverse event occurring from drug

abuse; an adverse event occurring from drug withdrawal; and any failure of expected pharmacological action."

"Unexpected Adverse Experience." Federal regulations define an unexpected AE as "an adverse drug experience that is not listed in the current labeling for the drug." This definition includes an event that may be symptomatically and pathophysiologically related to an event listed in the labeling, but that differs from the event because of greater severity or specificity.

"Serious Adverse Experience." Current regulations define "serious" AE as "an adverse drug experience that is fatal or life-threatening, is permanently disabling, requires in-patient hospitalization, or is a congenital anomaly, cancer, or overdose." Under the proposed regulation expected in early 1994, CDER was expected to propose amending its definition of "serious" AE to make it compatible with international definitions and with the definition promoted by the FDA's MedWatch Program. That proposal is expected to define a "serious" AE as "an adverse experience occurring at any dose that is fatal or life-threatening, results in persistent or significant disability/incapacity, requires or prolongs inpatient hospitalization, necessitates medical or surgical intervention to preclude impairment of a body function or permanent damage to a body structure, or is a congenital anomaly." However, the FDA will not require that companies implement the new definition until it publishes a final rule for the AE reporting changes.

The definitions above are critical in determining what types of AE reports a drug manufacturer must file, and when the company must file them. Current regulations specify two vehicles through which NDA holders must report AEs: 15-day alert reports and periodic reports.

15-Day Alert Reports Manufacturers are required to alert the FDA, within 15 working days, to: (1) all adverse drug experiences that are both serious and unexpected (unlabeled); (2) any significant increase in the frequency of an adverse drug experience that is both serious and expected; and (3) any significant increase in the frequency of therapeutic failures. The 15-day clock begins when the manufacturer first becomes aware of the AE.

Serious and unexpected AEs must be reported in a *Drug Experience Report* (Form FDA-1639), a document that has five components: (1) reaction information; (2) the suspect drug; (3) concomitant drugs and medical history; (4) manufacturer-related information; and (5) the reporter identifying the reaction. The submission of this form does not represent a sponsor's admission that the drug caused the adverse reaction.

Since the FDA unveiled its MedWatch Program in June 1993, the agency has encouraged sponsors to report postmarketing AEs on the newly developed FDA Form 3500A (see exhibit below), a common AE and problem reporting form for biologics, medical devices, drugs, and other FDA-regulated products. Ultimately, the new MedWatch Form will replace Form FDA-1639 as the vehicle for 15-day and other alert reports. Until the FDA can publish a final regulation mandating its use, however, manufacturers may continue to use the older AE reporting form. Sponsors may use alternate reporting formats that the FDA agrees to accept.

Sponsors must investigate each AE that is the subject of a 15-day Alert Report, and "submit follow-up reports within 15 working days of receipt of new information or as requested by FDA. If additional information is not obtainable, a follow-up report may be required that describes briefly the steps taken to seek additional information and the reasons why it could not be obtained. These 15-day Alert Reports and follow-ups to them are required to be submitted under separate cover and may not be included, except for summary or tabular purposes, in a periodic report" (see discussion below).

Unlike reports of serious and unexpected AEs, reports of any significant increase in therapeutic failures or the frequency of a serious and expected AE are made in narrative reports. These narratives must be submitted within 15 days of the applicant's discovery of any increase in the relative number of reports of serious labeled AEs or therapeutic failures (i.e., after suitable adjustments for marketing are made). FDA regulations require applicants to periodically review, at least as often as the periodic reporting cycle (see discussion below), the frequency of reports involving therapeutic failures or serious and expected AEs, regardless of source.

15-day Alert Reports based on information in the scientific literature must be accompanied by a copy of the published article. The alert reporting requirements for serious, unexpected AEs or therapeutic failures "apply only to reports found in scientific and medical journals either as case reports or as the result of a formal clinical trial." The alert reporting requirements for significant increases in the frequency of a serious, expected AE "apply only to

Form Approved: OMB No. 0910-0291 Expires 12/31/94
See OMB statement on reverse

MED**W**ATCH
THE FDA MEDICAL PRODUCTS REPORTING PROGRAM

For use by user-facilities, distributors and manufacturers for MANDATORY reporting.

Page ____ of ____

Mfr. report #

U.F. Dist. report #

FDA Use Only

A. Patient Information

1. Patient identifier

2. Age at time of event:
or
Date of birth:

In confidence

3. Sex
☐ female
☐ male

4. Weight
____ lbs
or
____ kgs

B. Adverse event or product problem

1. ☐ Adverse event and/or ☐ Product problem (e.g., defects/malfunctions)

2. Outcomes attributed to adverse event (check all that apply)
☐ death ____ (mo. day yr.)
☐ life-threatening
☐ hospitalization - initial or prolonged

☐ disability
☐ congenital anomaly
☐ required intervention to prevent permanent impairment/damage
☐ other ____

3. Date of event ____ (mo. day yr.)

4. Date of this report ____ (mo. day yr.)

5. Describe event or problem

6. Relevant tests/laboratory data, including dates

7. Other relevant history, including preexisting medical conditions (e.g., allergies, race, pregnancy, smoking and alcohol use, hepatic/renal dysfunction, etc.)

C. Suspect medication(s)

1. Name (give labeled strength & mfr/labeler, if known)
#1.
#2

2. Dose, frequency & route used
#1.
#2

3. Therapy dates (if known, give duration)
#1.
#2

4. Diagnosis for use (indication)
#1.
#2

5. Event abated after use stopped or dose reduced
#1.☐ yes ☐ no☐ doesn't apply
#2.☐ yes ☐ no☐ doesn't apply

6. Lot # (if known)
#1.
#2

7. Exp. date (if known)
#1.
#2

8. Event reappeared after reintroduction
#1.☐ yes ☐ no☐ doesn't apply
#2.☐ yes ☐ no☐ doesn't apply

9. NDC # - for product problems only (if known)

10. Concomitant medical products and therapy dates (exclude treatment of event)

G. All manufacturers

1. Contact offices-names/address(& mfring site for devices)

2. Phone number

3. Report source
(check all that apply)
☐ foreign
☐ study
☐ literature
☐ consumer
☐ health professional
☐ user facility
☐ company representative
☐ distributor
☐ other

4. Date received by manufacturer

5.
(A) NDA #
IND #
PLA #
Pre-1938 ☐ yes
OTC product ☐ yes

6. If IND, protocol #

7. Type of report
(check all that apply)
☐ 5-day ☐ 15-day
☐ 10-day ☐ periodic
☐ initial ☐ follow-up #

8. Adverse event term(s)

9. Mfr.report number

E. Initial reporter

1. Name, address & phone #

FDA

FDA Form 3500A (6/93)

Submission of a report does not constitute an admission that medical personnel, user facility, distributor, manufacturer or product caused or contributed to the event.

2. Health professional?
☐ yes ☐ no

3. Occupation

4. Initial reporter also sent report to FDA
☐ yes ☐ no ☐ unk

reports found in scientific and medical journals either as the result of a formal clinical trial, or from epidemiologic studies or analyses of experience in a monitored series of patients."

These requirements also apply to any person whose name appears on the drug product's label as a manufacturer, packer, or distributor. To avoid unnecessary duplication of reporting, however, federal regulations permit such "nonapplicants" to meet their reporting requirements by submitting all serious AE reports directly to the applicant rather than the FDA. In such cases, the nonapplicant must submit the reports within three working days of receiving the information. The NDA holder is required to make further reports (as described above) and maintain a record of this action.

Periodic Reports   NDA holders must develop and submit periodic drug experience reports at quarterly intervals for the first three years following a new drug's approval, and annually thereafter. The quarterly reports must be submitted within 30 days of the close of the quarter (i.e., the first quarter beginning on an application's approval date). Annual reports must be filed within 60 days of the anniversary date of the application's approval.

According to federal regulations, each periodic report must contain:

- a narrative summary and analysis of the information in the report, and an analysis of the 15-day Alert Reports submitted during the reporting interval (all 15-day Alert Reports being appropriately referenced by the applicant's patient identification number, adverse reaction term(s), and date of submission to the FDA);

- a Form FDA-1639 or FDA Form 3500A for each AE not reported in a 15-day Alert Report (i.e., non-15-day foreign study and literature reports), with an index consisting of a line listing of the applicant's patient identification number and adverse reaction term(s); and

- a history of actions taken since the last report because of adverse experiences (e.g., labeling changes or studies initiated).

In early 1994, CDER was expected to propose changes that would harmonize its periodic adverse experience reporting requirements with the recommendations of the Council for International Organizations of Medical Sciences (CIOMS). An independent body that provides a forum for manufacturers and regulators to develop and test uniform approaches for AE reporting, CIOMS has attempted to develop an AE reporting format and frequency that would enable a manufacturer to prepare a single report that would satisfy the requirements of national regulatory authorities throughout the world. The elements of the proposed periodic reporting requirements are expected to including the following:

- A six-month periodic reporting cycle.

- The submission of a periodic report within 45 days of the date on which the product was first licensed anywhere in the world (i.e., the product's international birth date).

- A "core data sheet" containing all relevant safety information. The core data sheet would enable a manufacturer to produce a periodic report acceptable to all participating countries.

- A report format that is based on CIOMS recommendations and that includes information on patient exposure and worldwide regulatory decisions concerning marketing, regulatory, or manufacturer actions taken for safety reasons.

Current Good Manufacturing Practice (CGMP)

Since 1962, federal drug law has required that firms producing drugs for administration to humans operate under standards called Current Good Manufacturing Practice (CGMP). The statutory requirement calls for all drugs—including drug products (i.e., finished dosage forms) and drug components (i.e., bulk ingredients)—to be made in conformance with CGMP to ensure that the items meet legal requirements of safety, and that they have the identity, strength, quality, and purity that they purport or are represented to possess.

When CGMP became a legal requirement, the FDA had envisioned as many as several different CGMPs, with separate standards for finished dosage forms, bulk ingredients, and other classes of products. To date, the FDA has published only one set of CGMPs, a regulation that applies solely to finished dosage forms. However, as such documents as the FDA's *Guide to Inspectors of Bulk Pharmaceutical Chemical Manufacturing* make clear, the general concepts of the existing CGMPs can be applied to other product classes.

It is worth noting that the applicability of CGMP standards is not restricted to approved medicines. As the FDA establishes in its *Guideline on the Preparation of Investigational New Drug Products* (Human and Animal) (March 1991), experimental drugs used in clinical testing are subject to certain CGMP requirements as well.

CGMP regulations seek to ensure the quality of drugs by setting minimum standards for all drug manufacturing facilities. The regulations establish standards in ten separate areas:

- organization and personnel;

- buildings and facilities;

- equipment;

- control of components and drug product containers and closures;

- production and process controls;

- packaging and labeling controls;

- holding and distribution;

- laboratory controls;

- records and reports; and

- returned and salvaged drug products.

Organization and Personnel　One of the most important CGMP requirements is that applicable to a facility's quality control unit, which each manufacturing facility must have to ensure compliance with CGMP.

According to federal regulations, the quality control unit assumes "the responsibility and authority to approve or reject all components, drug product containers, closures, in-process materials, packaging materials, labeling, and drug products and the authority to review production records to ensure that no errors have occurred or, if errors have occurred, that they have been fully investigated." In addition, the one-or-more-person quality control unit is responsible for approving or rejecting all procedures or specifications affecting the identity, strength, quality, and purity of the drug product.

Obviously, the professionals responsible for performing, supervising, or consulting on the manufacture, processing, packing, or holding of a drug must be adequate in number and sufficiently qualified by education, training, and experience to carry out their respective tasks. Facility staffers must be trained not only in their specific tasks, but in CGMP as well. The facility must document this training.

Buildings and Facilities   CGMP building and facility requirements are designed to ensure that any structures used to manufacture, process, pack, or hold a drug are of a suitable size, construction, and location to allow proper cleaning, maintenance, and operation. These requirements call for the separation of several plant operations (e.g., control and laboratory operations, packaging and labeling operations) to reduce the possibility of cross-contamination and other mishaps. Specific requirements for lighting, ventilation, heating and cooling systems, plumbing, sanitation, and maintenance are also provided.

Equipment   CGMP equipment requirements are generally concerned with equipment design, size, location, and maintenance. To ensure that drug product attributes are not adversely affected, surfaces that contact components, in-process materials, or drug products must not be reactive, additive, or absorptive. Lubricants and other substances required for equipment operations must not cause product contamination.

At predetermined intervals, all utensils and equipment must be cleaned, maintained, and sanitized according to specific written procedures. Filters and automatic, mechanical, and electronic equipment (including computers) face special validation requirements.

Components and Drug Product Containers and Closures

Controls   A facility must maintain detailed written procedures for the receipt, identification, storage, handling, sampling, testing, and approval/rejection of components and drug product containers and closures. Upon receipt, these materials must be inspected visually for appropriate labeling and contents, container damage, broken seals, and contamination. Before use, samples from each lot of components must be drawn, and the components tested for identity and conformity with purity, strength, and quality specifications. Drug product containers and closures must be tested for conformance to applicable written requirements.

Production and Process Controls   Manufacturing plants must maintain written procedures for production and process controls designed to ensure that the drug products have the identity, strength, quality, and purity they claim or are represented to possess. Special CGMP requirements exist for the charge-in of components, yield calculations, the identification of compounding and storage containers, processing lines, and the major equipment used in the production of a drug's batch, the sampling and testing of in-process materials and drug products, and the limiting of production times.

Packaging and Labeling Controls   All packaging and labeling materials must be sampled, examined, or tested before their use. Documented procedures must be established for the receipt, identification, storage, handling, sampling, examination, and testing of labeling and packaging materials. CGMP regulations also specify requirements for labeling issuances and accountability, packaging and labeling operations control and inspection, tamper-resistant packaging for OTC drugs, drug product inspection, and expiration dating.

Holding and Distribution Requirements   Facilities must maintain detailed written procedures describing the warehousing operations (including quarantine and special storage procedures) and distribution methods in use for a drug product. In most cases, facilities should implement the "first in, first out" (FIFO) principle in storing and distributing the product.

Laboratory Controls   Each organizational unit within a firm is required to maintain procedures for control mechanisms. These procedures and mechanisms, such as specifications, standards, sampling plans, and test procedures, are designed to ensure that components, drug product containers, closures, in-process materials, labeling, and drug products conform to appropriate standards of identity, strength, quality, and purity. Laboratory controls, which must be reviewed and approved by the quality control unit, include:

- the determination, through documented sampling and testing procedures, that each shipment lot of components, drug product containers, closures, and labeling conforms to relevant specifications;

- the determination, through sampling and testing procedures, that in-process materials conform to written specifications;

- the determination that the laboratory is complying with written descriptions of drug product sampling procedures and specifications; and

- the determination that instruments, apparatus, gauges, and recording devices have been calibrated at suitable intervals according to written procedures that provide specific directions, schedules, limits for accuracy and precision, and provisions for remedial action in the event accuracy and/or precision limits are not met.

A written program must be designed for stability testing procedures. The results of this testing are used to determine appropriate storage conditions and expiration dates for each drug. Reserve samples of drug substances and drug products must be retained for specific intervals.

Also included in the laboratory controls subpart of the CGMP regulations are requirements for: (1) the sampling, testing, and release for distribution of drug product batches; (2) the special testing for sterile, pyrogen-free, ophthalmic, and controlled-release drugs, reserve sample retention, laboratory test animals; and (3) testing for penicillin contamination.

Records and Reports   Facilities must retain records for all drug components, drug product containers, closures, and labeling for at least one year after the expiration date of the drug product for which they were used. Certain OTC drugs do not require expiration dating because they meet specific exemption criteria. For these drugs, records must be kept for three years after distribution of the last lot of drug product incorporating the component or using the container, closure, or labeling. CGMP regulations also specify requirements for master and batch production records, laboratory records, distribution records, and complaint files.

Returned and Salvaged Drug Products   Any returned drug products must be identified and held. A manufacturer must destroy such products if there is any doubt about their safety, identity, strength, quality, or purity, but may reprocess the products if the resultant drug can meet applicable standards, specifications, and characteristics. Drugs subjected to improper storage, including extremes in temperature, humidity, smoke, fumes, pressure, age, radiation due to natural disasters, fires, accidents, or equipment failures, may not be salvaged and returned to the marketplace. Facilities must undertake reprocessing according to written and company-approved procedures.

The Enforcement of CGMP

While some critics have claimed that CGMP provisions are too general and difficult to enforce, the FDA has an active program designed to ensure manufacturer compliance. Enforcement responsibilities fall mainly on the FDA's district offices located throughout the United States. These offices police the industry by inspecting each drug manufacturing facility within their regions at least once every two years.

CGMP inspections are conducted on an impromptu basis—that is, the facility to be inspected is generally not given advance warning by the FDA field office. The CGMP inspector arrives at the plant and, after the presentation of credentials and a notice of inspection, must be given immediate access to the building.

This procedure, however, is not applicable to the inspection of non-U.S. drug manufacturers. For foreign manufacturing facilities, the FDA makes only CGMP inspections that are pre-arranged with the manufacturers several months in advance. The most frequent subjects of foreign CGMP inspections are bulk active ingredient manufacturers.

In recent years, the FDA's international surveillance activities have increased considerably. With vastly increased funding targeted for foreign inspections, FDA officials were hoping to double the agency's inspectional assignments for foreign manufacturing facilities during the mid-1990s.

When a foreign or domestic inspection is completed, the manufacturer is alerted to any detected CGMP violations. Minor violations are generally handled by the FDA's district offices, which provide the manufacturer a period of time within which to eliminate the detected violations. For major violations, the district office files a report with FDA headquarters, which will review the case and decide on proper regulatory action.

Legal sanctions available to the agency include product seizure, injunction, and prosecution. When necessary, the FDA proposes such actions to the U.S. Justice Department, which may then file cases with the appropriate U.S. district court.

Chapter 14:
The Supplemental NDA

Following an original NDA's approval, its owner can access and supplement the application's data to seek FDA authorization to market variations of the drug beyond those provided for in the approved NDA. In many cases, this authorization is obtained through what is called a supplemental new drug application (SNDA).

SNDAs are submitted to the FDA when a sponsor wants to change an approved drug (e.g., dosage form, strength), its manufacturing processes, its indication, or certain elements of its labeling. Federal regulations require that, "The applicant...notify the Food and Drug Administration about each change in each condition established in an approved application beyond the variations already provided for in the application."

In practice, SNDAs are submitted to obtain regulatory authorization for a wide variety of modifications to approved drugs. These include proposed changes to an approved drug's:

- manufacturing and control methods (manufacturing supplement);

- dosage form or route of administration;

- indication (efficacy supplement);

- ingredients or strength;

- dosage schedule;

- labeling; and

- container and closure system.

251

The nature of the modification specified in the SNDA determines whether the sponsor must await the agency's approval before implementing the change. An approved supplement is required before a sponsor may institute changes to the drug substance, drug product, or significant aspects of the product's labeling (e.g., indications). Sponsors may implement less significant changes immediately upon reporting the changes to the FDA in a supplemental application (see discussion below). The least significant of changes do not even require an SNDA, but must be described in an annual report to the NDA.

When To Submit Supplemental versus Original NDAs

For drug changes that require FDA approval before implementation, sponsors traditionally have had the option of submitting either full or supplemental NDAs. Some maintain that SNDAs have certain advantages over full submissions, while others believe that original NDAs should be submitted whenever possible.

Consider, for example, a sponsor that seeks to market its approved drug for a new indication. Although the drug would be considered a "new" drug for this unapproved indication, the sponsor may submit either a full NDA or an SNDA for the new use. If the SNDA route is chosen, the supplemental application need provide only those new data—probably new clinical data at a minimum—necessary to prove the safety and effectiveness of the drug in its newly proposed indication. Provided there is a rational scientific and medical basis, the sponsor can take full advantage of the data in the approved NDA that support the safety and efficacy of the drug in its new indication. The sponsor can do this simply by referencing the previously submitted data in the SNDA. Obviously, the relevance of the data in the approved NDA depends directly on how closely related the newly proposed use and use conditions are to the approved indications and conditions.

Others maintain that sponsors should submit full applications because they perceive that SNDAs receive a lower priority than original NDAs.

Such debates may have been mooted by new policies instituted under the FDA's user-fee program. Because different fees apply to certain original and supplemental NDAs, the agency specifies when each should be used. In an interim guidance document entitled *Separate Marketing Applications and Clinical Data for Purposes of Assessing User Fees Under the Prescription*

Drug User Fee Act of 1992, the FDA specifies when original and supplemental NDAs are appropriate:

1. Changes in the composition of an approved product to support a change in the dosage form or route of administration should be submitted in full NDAs. Exceptions would include route of administration changes in which the new product remains quantitatively and qualitatively identical to the approved product in composition (e.g., an injectable liquid dosage form intended for use by the intravenous and intraperitoneal routes). Also eligible for SNDAs would be dosage form changes in which the new product is identical to the approved product in quantitative and qualitative composition (e.g., a sterile liquid in a single dose vial that is intended for use as either an injectable or an inhalation solution).

2. Modifications to an approved product that are based on chemistry, manufacturing, or controls data and bioequivalence or other studies (e.g., safety and immunogenicity) and that change the strength or concentration, change the manufacturing process, equipment or facility, or change the formulation (e.g., different excipients) should be submitted as supplements to an approved application. Ordinarily, such modifications do not warrant a new original application unless they involve a change in the dosage form or route of administration.

3. Requests for approval of a new indication, or a modification of a previously approved indication, should each be submitted individually in a separate supplement to an approved NDA. According to the FDA, "Each indication is considered a separate change for which a separate supplement should be submitted. The policy allows FDA to approve each indication when it is ready for approval rather than delaying approval until the last of a group of indications is ready to be approved."

The FDA's user-fee policies have several other implications for SNDAs. First, sponsors of supplements requiring FDA approval must pay user fees for such applications (see Chapter 18).

But the FDA's user-fee program also provides SNDAs with a significantly higher level of priority. In fact, the agency has set specific performance goals regarding SNDA reviews. Under that program, the agency has committed to eliminating its backlog of overdue efficacy and manufacturing supplements within 18 months of the program's implementation. And the agency has specific review time lines for SNDAs submitted on or after October 1, 1993 (see Chapter 9).

Supplemental NDA Submission Requirements

No standard SNDA data submission requirements exist. The change proposed in an SNDA directly determines testing and submission requirements. Federal regulations state that: "the information required in the supplement is limited to that needed to support the change."

Obviously, changes to a drug's indication, ingredients, or route of administration are likely to need new clinical data to prove the product's safety and effectiveness. In contrast, minor changes to manufacturing or control methods often require little more than a thorough explanation of the change. Therefore, SNDAs can range from a minor abbreviated filing to a document longer and more complex than some NDAs. All SNDAs, however, are required to provide an archival copy and a review copy that include an application form, appropriate technical sections, samples, and labeling.

The type of change proposed in an SNDA also determines when the application must be submitted. In its regulations, the FDA has categorized most types of changes into one of three regulatory classes. The first category, which includes changes that might affect the FDA's conclusions about the drug's safety and effectiveness, requires the submission, and FDA approval, of an SNDA before being instituted. The second category includes less important changes that may be instituted prior to FDA approval, but which must be immediately reported to the agency through an SNDA. All remaining types of changes fall into the final category, and must be described in the sponsor's annual report rather than an SNDA submission.

Supplements Needing Prior FDA Approval

Changes to an approved drug substance, drug product, or important elements of drug labeling require FDA approval before being instituted. If the sponsor believes that any delay in making the change would impose an extraordinary hardship, it can request that the FDA expedite its review of the application by marking the SNDA with the heading "Supplement-Expedited Review Requested."

Drug Substance Changes   Drug substance changes requiring FDA approval include any modifications that would:

- relax the limits for a specification;

- establish a new regulatory analytical method;

- delete a specification or regulatory analytical method;

- change the synthesis of the drug substance, including a change in solvents and a change in the route of synthesis; or

- involve a different facility or establishment in the manufacture of the drug substance, where: (a) the manufacturing process in the new facility or establishment differs materially from that in the former facility or establishment; or (b) the new facility or establishment has not received a satisfactory current good manufacturing practice (CGMP) inspection within the previous two years covering that manufacturing process.

Drug Product Changes   Drug product changes requiring FDA approval include any modifications that would:

- add or delete an ingredient, or otherwise change the composition of the drug product, other than the deletion of an ingredient intended only to affect the color of the drug product;

- relax the limits for a specification;

- establish a new regulatory analytical method;

- delete a specification or regulatory analytical method;

- change the drug product's method of manufacture, including changing or relaxing an in-process control;

- use a different facility or establishment, including a different contract laboratory or labeler, to manufacture, process, or pack the drug product;

- change the container and closure system for the drug product (for example, glass to high density polyethylene—HDPE—or HDPE to polyvinyl chloride), or change a specification or regulatory analytical method for the container and closure system;

- change the size of the container, except for solid dosage forms, without a change in the container and closure system;

- extend the expiration date of the drug based on data obtained under a new or revised stability testing protocol that has not been approved in the application; or

- establish a new procedure for reprocessing a batch of the drug product that fails to meet specifications.

Significant Labeling Changes   All significant drug labeling changes must be approved by the FDA before implementation. Although some labeling changes of lesser importance can be made prior to approval (see discussion below), the following modifications require FDA clearance:

- the addition of new indications;

- changes in dosage strengths;

- changes in dosage form; and

- changes in recommended dosage schedules.

SNDAs for new indications are more visible than most other types of supplements. Because these "efficacy supplements," as they often are called, propose important new uses for approved drugs, the FDA has developed a system for prioritizing their reviews within the agency. Efficacy supplements receive one of the following six classifications:

SE1 (highest priority): A supplement proposing a new indication or a significant modification of an existing drug indication.

SE2: A supplement proposing a new dosage regimen, including an increase or decrease in daily dosage, or a change in frequency of administration.

SE3: A supplement proposing a new route of administration.

SE4: A supplement proposing a comparative efficacy or comparative pharmacokinetic claim naming another drug.

SE5: A supplement proposing a change expected to significantly affect the size of the patient population to be given the drug by broadening or narrowing the population.

SE6 (lowest priority): A supplement proposing a prescription-to-OTC marketing switch.

SNDAs Not Requiring Prior FDA Approval

A sponsor may institute certain changes to an approved drug, its manufacturing process, or its labeling before submitting or obtaining FDA approval for an SNDA. When any of these changes are made, however, the sponsor must submit a supplemental application. The filing must "give a full explanation of the basis for the change, identify the date on which the change is made, and, if the change concerns labeling, include 12 copies of final printed labeling." Such changes include:

- changes that add a new specification or test method or that modify the methods, facilities (except a change to a new facility), or controls used to provide increased assurance that the drug will have the characteristics of identity, strength, quality, and purity that it purports or is represented to possess;

- labeling changes to add or strengthen a contraindication, warning, precaution, or adverse reaction;

- labeling modifications to add or strengthen a statement about drug abuse, dependence, or overdosage;

- labeling changes intended to promote the safe use of the product by adding or strengthening an instruction about dosage and administration;

- labeling changes to delete false, misleading, or unsupported indications for use or claims for effectiveness; and

- changes involving the use of a different facility or establishment to manufacture the drug substance, where: (a) the manufacturing process in the new facility or establishment does not differ materially from that in the former facilities or establishments; and (b) the new facility or establishment has received a satisfactory CGMP inspection within the previous two years covering that manufacturing process.

For such changes, the SNDA and its mailing cover should be marked: "Special Supplement-Changes Being Effected."

Changes Not Requiring SNDAs

To avoid the submission of unnecessary SNDAs and the burdens that these applications would place on agency reviewing resources, the FDA exempts several types of minor changes from supplemental filing requirements. These modifications, however, must be reported and described in a sponsor's annual report. Exempted changes include:

- any modification made to comply with an official compendium;

- a change in the labeling regarding the description of the drug or the information about how it is supplied (changes in dosage strength or dosage form do not qualify);

- an editorial or other minor change in labeling;

- the deletion of an ingredient intended only to affect the drug's color;

- extension of the expiration date based upon full shelf-life data obtained from an approved protocol;

- a change in the container and closure system for the drug (except a change in container size for nonsolid dosage forms) based upon a showing of equivalency to the approved system under a protocol approved in the application or published in an official compendium;

- the addition or deletion of an alternate analytical method; and

- a change in the size of a container for a solid dosage form, without a change from one container and closure system to another.

Chapter 15:

The FDA's Orphan Drug Development Program

Although orphan drugs represent only a minor percentage of the medicines prescribed in the United States annually, these products have gained an exceptionally high profile in recent decades. Early in the 1980s, for example, orphan drugs became not only the subject of major legislation, but the focus of an FDA office devoted solely to their development as well.

More recently, regulatory, legal, and commercial controversies surrounding better-known orphan drugs, such as Genentech's human growth hormone and Amgen's erythropoietin, have done much to bring widespread attention to orphan products and industry efforts to develop and market these medicines. In part representing the government's response to these controversies, FDA regulations implementing the key elements of the orphan drug laws were released in December 1992.

The special problems and issues facing orphan product development are now well known. The products are unique because they are potentially useful drugs, biologics, and antibiotics that have limited commercial value. There are several reasons why they may lack profit potential—a product may be used to treat a disease with a small patient population, it may be used only in minute doses, or it may have an unfavorable patent status.

In the past, few companies were willing to invest in an experimental drug whose potential sales did not justify, or whose actual sales might not even recover, these expenditures. Individuals suffering from such rare conditions as Turner's Syndrome, central precocious puberty, acute graft v. host disease

(GVHD), and cystinosis were caught between the medical reality that few others shared their plight, and the economic reality that a drug's development can cost more than $200 million.

However, thanks to orphan drug legislation and the FDA's own efforts to shepherd the products through the development process, the 1980s and early 1990s brought no dearth of firms willing to invest in orphan products. According to a U.S. Pharmaceutical Manufacturers Association (PMA) survey, 132 companies were developing 189 orphan drugs during 1992.

The FDA and Orphan Drugs: A Brief History

During the late 1970s, government leaders became increasingly concerned that the therapeutic abilities of many drugs went unexplored while millions of patients with one of an estimated 5,000 rare or orphan diseases went untreated. A 1979 report by the FDA-organized Interagency Task Force on Significant Drugs of Limited Commercial Value stated that, "Whenever a drug has been identified as potentially life-saving or otherwise of unique major benefit to some patient, it is the obligation of society, as represented by government, to seek to make that drug available to that patient." The formal government response to the problem came several years later in the form of the Orphan Drug Act of 1983, a law that provides incentives for manufacturers to develop and market orphan products, including drugs, antibiotics and biologics.

Responsibility for administering the law was given to the FDA's Office of Orphan Product Development (OPD), which was founded in 1982. Today, the 20-person office continues to encourage orphan drug development by awarding financial incentives available under the law to sponsors of qualifying products, coordinating the efforts of investigators and drug companies, acting as a mediator between orphan sponsors and the FDA's drug and biologic review divisions, administering a grant program, and performing other promotional and educational activities.

The Importance of Orphan Drug Designation

The incentives offered under the Orphan Drug Act are seen as the keys to the development of future orphan products. The law provides major financial and marketing incentives to companies and investigators willing to research and develop qualified products. But before outlining the orphan incentives themselves, it is worthwhile discussing orphan drug designation, a status that drugs must attain to become eligible for the most valuable of these incentives.

Tax advantages and marketing exclusivity are perhaps the two most important incentives that the U.S. Congress made available to orphan product sponsors through the Orphan Drug Act of 1983. Since Congress did not want these incentives to be awarded indiscriminately, it wrote into law that only products meeting specific criteria would be eligible for the two principal benefits.

Today, there are at least five basic eligibility criteria for orphan drug designation. To be eligible, a product:

- *Must be a drug, biologic, or antibiotic.* Medical devices, medical foods, and other products do not qualify for designation.

- *Must have a sponsor that is testing or is planning to test the product for use in a rare disease or condition.* According to the Orphan Drug Act, a rare disease or condition is one that: "A) affects less than 200,000 persons in the United States, or B) affects more than 200,000 persons in the United States but for which there is no reasonable expectation that the costs of developing and making available in the United States a drug for such disease or condition will be recovered from sales in the United States for such drug." The under-200,000 provision applies not only to diseases or conditions with a total patient prevalence of less than 200,000, but to subpopulations of more common diseases as well. The FDA insists that sponsors of orphan products for such indications be able to test the product in, and clearly label the product for, use in the relevant subpopulation. For prophylactic products such as vaccines and blood products, the figure of 200,000 applies to the number of patients per year receiving the product.

- *Must not have been previously approved under a new drug application (NDA) or product license application (PLA) for the disease or condition for which the sponsor is seeking orphan status.* In other words, eligible products include both new chemical entities (NCE)—substances never before approved as medicines in the

263

United States—and products that have been approved for any indication other than the indication for which the sponsor is seeking orphan designation. When granted by the FDA, designation applies only to the subject product for use in the specific rare disease or condition.

- *Must be shown to have an adequate pharmacologic rationale for use in the orphan indication.* This requirement is not one that the FDA enforces rigidly. Dr. Marion Finkel, former director of the FDA's Office of Orphan Products Development, stated in a 1984 speech that: "A plausible hypothesis backed by some experimental evidence would be sufficient for orphan drug designation."

- *Must not be the subject of a submitted marketing application prior to the filing of an orphan status request.* This requirement was added in mid-1988 through the Orphan Drug Amendment Act of 1987. The amendment was an attempt by Congress to reserve marketing exclusivity and tax incentives for those firms whose initial intentions were to develop orphan drugs, and to withhold the incentives from companies that pursue designation simply as an afterthought to optimize the profitability of their products.

Congress gave the FDA the authority to determine which drugs meet these criteria. To have its product designated, a firm must submit to the FDA an application called a *Request for Designation of a Drug as an Orphan Drug*. The FDA's 1992 orphan drug regulations specify nine basic submission requirements for designation requests. According to those regulations, a sponsor must submit two copies of a completed, dated, and signed designation request that contains the following:

- A statement that the sponsor requests orphan-drug designation for a rare disease or condition, which must be identified with specificity.

- The name and address of the sponsor; the name and address of the sponsor's primary contact person and/or resident agent, including the person's title, address, and telephone number; the drug's generic and trade name (if any); and the name and address of the source of the drug if it is not manufactured by the sponsor.

- A description of the rare disease or condition for which the drug is being or will be investigated, the proposed indication or indications for the drug, and the reasons why such therapy is needed.

- A description of the drug, and a discussion of the scientific rationale for the use of the drug for the rare disease or condition, including all data from nonclinical laboratory studies, clinical investigations, and other relevant data that are available to the sponsor, whether positive, negative, or inconclusive. Copies of pertinent unpublished and published papers are also required.

- When the sponsor of a drug that is otherwise the same as an already-approved orphan drug seeks orphan-drug designation for the same rare disease or condition, an explanation of why the proposed variation may be clinically superior to the first drug (see discussion below).

- When a drug is under development only for a subset of persons with a particular disease or condition, a demonstration that the product's use in this patient subset is medically plausible.

- A summary of the regulatory status and marketing history of the drug in the United States and in foreign countries (e.g., IND and marketing application status and dispositions; what uses are under investigation in each country; for what indication is the drug approved in foreign countries; and what "adverse regulatory actions" have been taken against the drug in any country).

- Documentation, with appended authoritative references, to demonstrate: (1) that the disease or condition for which the drug is intended affects fewer than 200,000 people in the United States or, if the drug is a vaccine, diagnostic drug, or preventive drug, that the persons to whom the drug will be administered in the United States are fewer than 200,000 per year as specified in federal regulations, or (2) for a drug intended for diseases or conditions affecting 200,000 or more people, or for a vaccine, diagnostic drug, or preventive drug to be administered to 200,000 or more persons per year in the United States, that there is no reasonable expectation that costs of research and development of the drug for the indication can be recovered by sales of the drug in the United States (e.g., cost data, a statement and justification of future development costs the sponsor expects to incur, and an estimate and justification for the expected revenues from drug sales during its first seven years of marketing).

- A statement as to whether the sponsor submitting the request is the "real party in interest" in the development and the intended or actual production and sales of the product.

Drug sponsors may request orphan drug designation any time prior to the submission of a marketing application for the product. Once a request for designation is submitted, the FDA's OPD has 60 days to issue a decision. In most cases, the office handles the review itself, although it may refer certain technical or scientific questions to one of the agency's drug or biological product review divisions. Within 14 months after a drug is designated, and annually thereafter, the sponsor must submit to OPD a brief progress report that includes a short account of the progress of drug development, the investigational plan for the coming year, and any changes that may affect the product's orphan-drug status.

When OPD denies these designation requests, the reasons range from poorly prepared designation request documents to a sponsor's selection of invalid subpopulations. Before sponsors submit designation requests, OPD officials recommend that companies educate themselves about designation request submission requirements, and have a defined rationale for the use of a drug for a selected indication, a reasonable strategy for the product's development, and a highly specific indication and patient population that can be studied and for which the drug can be labeled if ultimately approved.

The practical advantages of orphan drug designation essentially are limited to tax incentives and marketing exclusivity. Although some believe that designation makes FDA drug reviewers more aware of a specific orphan drug, there are probably no real advantages during the drug approval process.

FDA staffers claim that many sponsors are surprised to learn that orphan drug designation itself affords no competitive advantages. For example, a drug's designation does not stop another firm from requesting and obtaining a designation for the same drug and indication. Also, the seven-year marketing exclusivity is awarded to the first designated orphan drug to obtain marketing approval, not designation.

There seem to be few, if any, disadvantages to obtaining orphan drug designation. Having to prepare a designation request and having general information published about the drug upon designation are, in many cases, small inconveniences when compared to the benefits designation offers.

Still, some drug firms do not pursue designation when developing a product that qualifies as an orphan drug. In some cases, these firms do not seek orphan designation because they view it as their corporate responsibility as a health-care company to develop these products. Others speculate that companies, knowing that orphan drugs may prove useful in additional, more profitable ways, do not want the possible public relations burden of profiting from a drug developed using public monies.

A Look at Orphan Drug Incentives

Currently, the Orphan Drug Act and the FDA offer orphan drug sponsors four primary incentives: marketing exclusivity, tax credits, protocol assistance, and grants and contracts.

Marketing Exclusivity Marketing exclusivity may be the single most important incentive to orphan drug sponsors. Under the law, the first sponsor to obtain marketing approval for a designated orphan drug is awarded a seven-year period of marketing exclusivity for the product. During that period, no other sponsor can obtain FDA approval for the drug for the orphan indication. The agency can, however, approve identical versions of the drug for other indications.

The rewards of marketing exclusivity are linked directly to FDA approval. Although orphan designation makes a drug eligible for exclusivity, that exclusivity is not awarded until a product's NDA or PLA is approved. Therefore, several identical products could be designated for the same orphan indication, but only the first company to receive approval will obtain marketing exclusivity rights.

Marketing exclusivity has at least two main advantages over traditional patent protection. First, designation and product approval are virtually the only eligibility requirements for exclusivity. The product need not be new or unobvious, or meet any of the criteria used in determining a product's patent eligibility. Because of this, natural substances and other products that are unable to receive any form of patent protection are eligible for marketing exclusivity.

The second significant advantage marketing exclusivity has over patent protection is that its life begins on the date of approval. Although a patent award grants a 17-year monopoly, a product's patent life begins on the date the patent is awarded, and several years of that life are generally lost during the drug testing and evaluation process. Since exclusivity is awarded upon approval, its seven-year life is not eroded in such ways.

While marketing exclusivity may be the most important orphan drug incentive, it is also the most complex. In the past, some critics have argued that the FDA's inability or unwillingness to deny marketing approval to drugs that are similar in structure to drugs that have already been awarded marketing exclusivity unfairly denied orphan product innovators the protection afforded to them under the Orphan Drug Act.

In fact, during the late 1980s, the FDA faced a few widely publicized situations—involving two human growth hormone products and two erythropoietin products—that tested its criteria for determining when two drugs were considered identical. The issue, in both cases, involved the FDA's then-unpublished criteria for differentiating between medical compounds, particularly biologics and biotechnology products, for the purposes of marketing exclusivity. The FDA's December 1992 regulations were the first to detail the conditions under which the agency would consider two drugs to be the same and, therefore, take action to block the approval of the second designated product:

"(i) If it is a drug composed of small molecules, a drug that contains the same active moiety as a previously approved drug and is intended for the same use as the previously approved drug, even if the

particular ester or salt (including a salt with hydrogen or coordination bonds) or other noncovalent derivative such as a complex,
chelate or clathrate has not been previously approved, except that if
the subsequent drug can be shown to be clinically superior to the
first drug, it will not be considered to be the same drug.

(ii) If it is a drug composed of large molecules (macromolecules), a
drug that contains the same principal molecular structural features
(but not necessarily all of the same structural features) and is
intended for the same use as a previously approved drug, except
that, if the subsequent drug can be shown to be clinically superior, it
will not be considered the same drug. This criterion will be applied
as follows to different kinds of macromolecules:

(A) Two protein drugs would be considered the same if the
only differences in structure between them were due to
post-translational events, or infidelity of translation or tran-
scription, or were minor differences in amino acid sequence;
other potentially important differences, such as different gly-
cosylation patterns or different tertiary structures, would not
cause the drugs to be considered different unless the differences were shown to be clinically superior.

(B) Two polysaccharide drugs would be considered the same
if they had identical saccharide repeating units, even if the
number of units were to vary and even if there were post-
polymerization modifications, unless the subsequent drug
could be shown to be clinically superior.

(C) Two polynucleotide drugs consisting of two or more distinct nucleotides would be considered the same if they had an
identical sequence of purine and pyrimidine bases (or their
derivatives) bound to an identical sugar backbone (ribose,
deoxyribose, or modifications of these sugars), unless the
subsequent drug were shown to be clinically superior.

(D) Closely related, complex partly definable drugs with similar therapeutic intent, such as two live viral vaccines for the same indication, would be considered the same unless the subsequent drug were shown to be clinically superior."

Tax Credits   Designated orphan drugs are eligible for a 50 percent tax credit for funds spent on clinical development. Therefore, a firm can subtract directly from its annual tax bill one-half of the money spent on the clinical testing of an orphan drug.

However, there are several important limitations to the tax credit incentive:

- Sponsors can receive credits only for clinical testing conducted within the United States. The one principal exception to this is a situation in which the sponsor must go outside the United States to find the patients necessary to conduct the trial.

- The credits can be used only for clinical testing actually paid for and conducted by the sponsor. For example, a sponsor could not receive credits for another company's testing that is referenced in the sponsor's drug application.

- The credits are available only for products that are formally designated by the FDA.

- The credit can be applied only to testing conducted for the orphan indication for which a drug is designated.

- Tax credits do not apply to nonclinical testing. OPD staffers claim that this can be a problem, since basic animal toxicity and carcinogenicity testing alone can cost well over a million dollars.

Unfortunately for many biotechnology and other fledgling companies, there is one more notable limitation to the Orphan Drug Act's tax incentives: tax credits are only beneficial to companies that are profitable. Under current law, orphan product tax credits can be applied against taxes on profits, but an unprofitable company cannot use the tax credits to increase its losses. Stated differently, a profitable company can use the tax credits to reduce its annual tax bill, but an unprofitable firm cannot use the tax credits to increase its annual tax refund.

What makes the orphan tax credit a particularly inflexible incentive is that the cost of clinical research on an orphan product cannot be moved forward or backward to different tax years. In other words, the costs of clinical research on an orphan product incurred in 1994 cannot, like many corporate losses, be declared in any year other than 1994. Therefore, if the sponsor was unprofitable in 1994, tax benefits the firm would have received from clinical trial costs for the orphan drug are lost even if the drug is designated.

Protocol Assistance Protocol assistance is an incentive for which orphan designation is unnecessary. If a sponsor can show the FDA that a drug will ultimately be used for a rare disease or condition, the agency provides written recommendations on the nonclinical and clinical studies needed for the product's approval.

To obtain protocol assistance, a sponsor must submit a formal request providing information on the drug, including its intended use, available test data, regulatory and marketing status, and proposed testing plans. The FDA's 1992 orphan drug regulations specify 16 content requirements for such requests. OPD staffers warn that, unless sponsors ask specific questions in these requests, firms are likely to receive extremely vague recommendations. Protocol recommendations are made by product review divisions within CDER.

FDA Grants and Contracts The Orphan Drug Act authorizes the U.S. Congress to appropriate funds for grants and contracts to physicians, companies, and others who are developing orphan drugs. In fiscal year 1994, Congress appropriated $12 million for such purposes.

More common than contracts, grants are awarded to university-based investigators for the clinical testing of orphan drugs, while contract funds are available to investigators and companies that agree to conduct testing for a drug or in a therapeutic area of particular interest to the FDA.

The FDA Approval Process: Advantages for Orphan Drugs?

Generally, orphan products receive no preferential treatment in terms of testing and submission requirements, and face the same safety and effectiveness

271

criteria and review processes as undesignated products. FDA staffers do claim, however, that the agency will modify the drug testing and approval process for orphan products when appropriate. In the past, issues such as the availability of patients with orphan conditions and the lack of available competitive therapies have forced the agency to consider alternative testing requirements and review criteria.

NDAs and PLAs submitted for orphan products are reviewed within one of the FDA's drug or biological review divisions. There, reviewers evaluate products strictly on the basis of safety, efficacy, and risk-benefit analyses. Although the product's status as an orphan drug may appear to be of little or no benefit, OPD staffers do work to make agency reviewers more sensitive to the special issues that orphan products present.

One advantage that many orphan drugs have over other products is that they often receive prioritized reviews. This is related not to the fact that they are orphan drugs, but that they are often the only treatment available for certain conditions. Because of this, the FDA frequently classifies them as high priority drugs, and expedites their review. However, the FDA did, in mid-1989, deny a petition requesting that all orphan drugs automatically receive the FDA's highest review priority.

According to FDA statistics, approval times for orphan drugs compare favorably with those of conventional drugs. In 1992, CDER approved NDAs for nine orphan drugs in an average of 17.6 months, compared to a 32.6-month average for all NDAs approved in that year.

What is the OPD's role in the review of an orphan drug? The office actively monitors the progress of orphan reviews, but has no formal authority in product approvals or real influence in the decisions of FDA reviewers. However, OPD staffers do attend FDA-orphan sponsor meetings and act as mediators to help resolve special regulatory problems presented by orphan drugs.

Chapter 16:

CDER's Bioresearch Monitoring Program

Since its regulatory decisions are based directly on research data, CDER has a vested interest in the accuracy and validity of clinical and nonclinical study results. Under CDER's Bioresearch Monitoring Program, agency investigators conduct on-site inspections of laboratories, clinics, and offices where scientific data are developed and stored.

Specifically, CDER inspects clinical investigators, drug firms, IRBs, and nonclinical laboratories to ensure: (1) that data submitted in product applications are accurate and valid; and (2) that the rights and welfare of human subjects are protected in clinical studies. During these inspections, FDA investigators evaluate how well sponsors, monitors, IRBs, and clinical and nonclinical investigational site staff have fulfilled their respective responsibilities and commitments under GCP, research protocols, and related standards and regulatory requirements.

While clinical investigators are the focus of most CDER bioresearch inspections, there are several reasons why inspection results are of great importance to clinical trial sponsors. First, drug sponsors are ultimately responsible for the conduct of clinical studies, and FDA inspections are designed to determine how well sponsors perform in that role. Secondly, these inspections, should they uncover serious problems, can result in the agency's rejection of data essential to a drug's approval.

A Brief History of the Bioresearch Monitoring Program
The origin of the FDA's authority to inspect research data and related records is in the Food, Drug and Cosmetic (FD&C) Act. The law states that every

person required to maintain records must, upon the FDA's request, allow access to clinical data for review and copying. FDA regulations—specifically, Form FDA-1572, which clinical investigators sign before undertaking the study of an investigational drug—state that "...the investigator will make such records available for inspection and copying."

Because of physicians' importance in the development and collection of clinical safety and efficacy data, inspections of investigators represent the core of the FDA's Bioresearch Monitoring Program. FDA inspections of clinical investigators began in 1962, although only three inspections were conducted by 1965. The agency expanded its efforts in the years following and established a four-person office to organize and conduct inspections. But because government authorities outside the FDA believed that only physicians should inspect other physicians, inspectional activities were limited (i.e., only seven or eight inspections were conducted annually).

By 1972, the U.S. government had gained a new respect for the importance and abilities of FDA inspectors. As a result, the FDA initiated a survey of 162 commercially sponsored clinical investigators, 70 noncommercial clinical investigators, and 15 manufacturers. The results of this multi-year study, and increased FDA staff and budget, led to the founding of the agency's Bioresearch Monitoring Program in June 1977.

Although this chapter focuses on clinical investigator and sponsor/monitor compliance activities, today's Bioresearch Monitoring Program consists of four separate compliance inspection programs, each designed to evaluate the activities of a key figure in the conduct of a scientific study:

- Clinical Investigator Compliance Program;

- Sponsor/Monitor Compliance Program;

- Institutional Review Board (IRB) Compliance Program; and

- Nonclinical Laboratory Compliance Program (*for information on the inspection of nonclinical laboratories, see Chapter 3*).

These four inspectional programs are managed by several branches within CDER's Division of Scientific Investigations: the Clinical Investigations

Branch, the Nonclinical Laboratory Branch, the Institutional Review Branch, and the Regulatory Management Branch.

The Clinical Investigator Compliance Program

As stated previously, inspections of clinical investigators represent the core of CDER's Bioresearch Monitoring Program. CDER has three separate investigator inspection programs:

• Data Audit Program;

• "For Cause" Inspection Program; and

• Bioequivalency/Bioavailability Inspection Program.

Data Audit Program   The Data Audit Program is a routine surveillance initiative that involves the inspection of about 200 clinical investigators per year. During these inspections, an FDA field inspector looks at the conduct of the study and performs a data audit. In evaluating the investigator's conduct of a clinical study, the inspector considers several factors:

• what the investigator, each of his/her staffers, and others did during the study;

• the degree of delegation of authority;

• when and where specific aspects of the study were performed;

• how and where data were recorded;

• how the drug substance was stored and accounted for;

• the monitor's interaction with the physician;

• evidence that proper informed consent was obtained from subjects; and

• evidence that IRB approval was obtained for studies performed.

275

In the typical audit, data submitted in an application are compared with the on-site records that should support their validity. On-site records to which an FDA inspector must be given access include a physician's office records, hospital records, and various laboratory reports. Records obtained prior to the initiation, and following the completion of, the study may be reviewed and copied.

When the FDA has targeted key clinical studies for inspection, agency staffers send a field inspector an "assignment package," which includes copies of a representative number of case reports, the protocol, and other pertinent information. Due to the nature of physicians' work and schedules, inspections are made by appointment. Therefore, investigators are alerted as

---

Targeting Investigators and Studies for Data Audits

Inspection assignments for the data audit program are made by an application's reviewing medical officer in consultation with CDER's Division of Scientific Investigations. To determine which clinical investigators and studies should be inspected, the FDA uses a stratified sampling system that has the following priorities (listed in descending order):

1) studies important to the evaluation of a pending NDA;

2) studies submitted in support of new claims in supplemental NDAs;

3) important studies submitted in support of over-the-counter (OTC) drug claims;

4) studies conducted under maturing INDs;

5) studies conducted to upgrade labeling claims for old drugs found to be less than effective; and

6) studies conducted under noncommercial INDs.

---

to which study is to be audited, and are given the opportunity to locate and prepare all relevant records.

Because sponsors increasingly are relying on foreign data in their drug applications, CDER is now averaging several inspections of foreign clinical investigators per year. Since 1977, the center has conducted 92 foreign inspections, over half in just three countries: Canada (27 inspections), The Netherlands (10 inspections); and Sweden (10 inspections). However, CDER generally will inspect a foreign-based investigator only when data from that foreign site are pivotal to a drug's approval.

"For Cause" Inspection Program   The "for cause" inspection of an investigator is, in most respects, similar to the data audit inspection. For cause inspections are not routine, however, and may be initiated for one or more of several reasons:

- the investigator is suspected of impropriety;

- the investigator is responsible for a large volume of work, particularly if that work involves different medical disciplines;

- the investigator has done work outside his/her specialty;

- the investigator reports effectiveness for a drug that appears to be too optimistic when compared to the reports of other physicians studying the same drug;

- the investigator reports no toxicity or few adverse reactions when other physicians report numerous reactions of a certain type;

- the investigator seems to have too many patients with a given disease for the locale or the setting in which he or she practices;

- the investigator reports laboratory results that are consistent beyond the usual biologic variation or which are inconsistent with results submitted by other investigators;

- representatives of the sponsor have reported to the FDA that they are having difficulty getting case reports from the investigator, or that they have found the investigator to be deficient in some other manner;

- a routine audit revealed problems too serious to be handled by correspondence;

- the investigator has conducted a pivotal study that merits in-depth examination because of its importance to the approval of the NDA; or

- the FDA receives letters or phone calls claiming violations of subject's rights, variations in protocol, or some other violation or noncompliance.

During "for cause" inspections, an FDA scientist generally accompanies the field investigator. Although the procedures used parallel those of routine inspections, the inspection team probably reviews more data. For instance, the inspector and agency scientist will probably evaluate more case reports—sometimes for the entire study—and may audit studies of more than one drug. Patient interviews may be conducted when there are questions as to whether a subject participated in a study, whether the subject had the condition being studied, or whether informed consent was obtained.

Bioequivalency/Bioavailability Inspection Program Bioequivalency/bioavailability inspections involve the inspection of both a clinical and an analytical facility. According to FDA staffers, these inspections are more important for the verification of biopharmaceutic data submitted for generic drugs than for new drugs. An FDA field inspector and an FDA laboratory scientist qualified in the evaluation of analytical techniques conduct this audit.

During the inspection of a biopharmaceutic facility, where a drug is administered to, and blood samples are then taken from, human volunteers, the inspection team will verify that IRB approval was given for the study and that all regulatory requirements were met. The inspector might review such records and factors as drug accountability records, prescreening laboratory data, the presence of medical supervision, the handling of biological samples, and the assessment of situations in which the health and safety of the subjects are placed at risk.

In the analytical audit, the inspection team reviews standard operating procedures for the technology utilized, the status of the samples to be analyzed, qualifications of the personnel performing the analyses, raw documentation of the reported results, and the presence of quality control techniques such as the use of standard curves.

Post-Inspectional FDA Actions   At the conclusion of all three types of inspections, the FDA inspector conducts what is called an "exit interview" with the clinical investigator. During this time, the two individuals discuss the inspector's findings, which will be reported to the FDA in the form of an *Establishment Inspection Report* (EIR).

In some cases, the inspector may leave the investigator with a written statement of his/her observations on Form FDA-483, the *Inspectional Observation* form. This statement identifies the relevant deviations from regulations, protocols, or accepted procedures. If the form becomes too involved, the FDA inspector will generally return to the clinical site to discuss its content with the clinical investigator. CDER provides a detailed discussion of the Clinical Investigator Compliance Program in its *Compliance Program Guidance Manual for Clinical Investigators* (7348.811).

The Sponsor/Monitor Compliance Program

Historically, CDER's Sponsor/Monitor Compliance Program has not been one of the center's most active monitoring programs. FDA officials claim that this is due to several factors, including relatively broad regulations on sponsor requirements and CDER's greater concerns about investigator activities and compliance.

Nonetheless, CDER does initiate about 20 sponsor inspections annually to determine: (1) if a sponsor, a sponsor's employee, or a contract research organization (CRO) is monitoring a clinical investigation adequately; and (2) if the sponsor is fulfilling each of its requirements as outlined in existing federal regulations. The clinical sponsor and its research-related activities are the primary focus of inspections conducted under this program. It is worth mentioning, however, that two other entities, because they may assume some of the sponsor's responsibilities during a clinical study, may also be investigated by the FDA:

- *Clinical Monitors.* Monitors are those individuals selected by either a sponsor or contract research organization to oversee the progress of the clinical investigation. The monitor may be an employee of the sponsor, a contract research organization, or a consultant.

- *Contract Research Organization (CRO).* CROs are organizations or corporations that enter into contractual agreements with sponsors to perform one or more of the sponsor's duties in the clinical research process. Sponsors may delegate several of their responsibilities to a CRO, including the design of a protocol, the monitoring of clinical studies, the selection of investigators and study monitors, the evaluation of reports, and the preparation of materials to be submitted to the FDA.

The FDA's Scientific Investigations Branch manages the sponsor/monitor compliance program, as it does each of the other bioresearch monitoring efforts. Staffers within this office decide which sponsors are to be inspected, what a particular inspection will consist of, and what actions the FDA will take in response to an inspector's report.

The agency conducts mostly "routine surveillance" inspections, although, in rare cases, "for cause" inspections are performed when there are indications that a sponsor is not fulfilling its responsibilities. Given their prevalence in the clinical research field, CROs have become an increasingly common focus of such inspections, according to center officials.

Generally, a drug sponsor that is selected for inspection meets two criteria: (1) the company is the sponsor of a pending NDA or active IND (i.e., an IND under which a firm is conducting clinical studies); and (2) the company has not been the subject of an inspection under the Sponsor Compliance Program within the past two years. Unless the FDA suspects the existence of a problem, clinical sponsors whose headquarters are located outside the United States are generally not inspected.

After determining which firms satisfy these criteria, the FDA's Division of Scientific Investigations forwards an inspection assignment to the relevant FDA regional office—the office that oversees the district in which the sponsor's headquarters are located. The assignment package tells an FDA field inspector the name and address of the sponsor, and provides instructions on which study or studies are to be investigated.

The Inspection of Drug Sponsors   Sponsor inspections take place at the company's headquarters, and generally involve the evaluation of records from recently conducted or active studies. According to the FDA's *Compliance Program Guidance Manual for Sponsors, Contract Research Organizations, and Monitors* (7348.810), the field inspector evaluates at least six elements of a clinical study: (1) the selection of and directions to a monitor; (2) test article accountability; (3) assurance of IRB approval; (4) the adequacy of facilities; (5) continuing evaluation of data; and (6) records retention.

Monitor Selection and Directions. In this aspect of the inspection, the FDA investigator determines if the clinical monitor is adequately qualified, and whether the sponsor has given the monitor sufficient direction. Specifically, the inspector must determine:

- whether at least one individual has been charged with monitoring the progress of the investigation (if there are two or more monitors, the inspector must determine how the responsibilities are divided);

- what training, education, and experience qualify the monitor to oversee the progress of the clinical investigation;

- whether written procedures in addition to the protocol have been established for the monitoring of the clinical investigation; and

- whether the sponsor has assured that the monitor has met his or her obligations.

Test Article Accountability. The inspector must evaluate whether the sponsor maintained adequate drug accounting procedures before, during, and, if applicable, after a clinical investigation. The inspector is instructed to make six separate determinations:

- whether the sponsor maintained accounting procedures for the test article, including records showing (1) the shipment dates, quantity, serial, batch lot or other identification number of units sent, (2) the receipt dates and the quantity of returned articles, and (3) the names of investigators;

- whether the records are sufficient to allow a comparison of the total amount of the drug shipped against the amounts used and returned by the investigator;

- whether all unused or reusable supplies of the test article were returned to the sponsor when either (1) the investigator discontinued or finished participating in the clinical investigation, or (2) the investigation was terminated;

- if all unused or reusable supplies of the test article were not returned to the sponsor, a determination of the alternate disposition of the test article and a description of how the sponsor determined the manner in which the investigator accounted for unused or reusable supplies of the test article dispensed to a subject and not returned to the investigator;

- whether the alternate disposition was adequate to ensure that humans or food-producing animals were not exposed to experimental risk; and

- whether records were maintained for alternate disposition of the test article.

Assurance of IRB Approval. For a clinical investigation subject to IRB approval, the FDA inspector must determine whether the sponsor maintains documentation showing that the clinical investigator obtained IRB approval before any human subjects were allowed to participate in the investigation.

Ascertaining the Adequacy of Facilities. The FDA inspector must determine whether the monitor assessed the adequacy of all facilities used by the study investigator (e.g., office, clinic, hospital).

Continuing Evaluation of Data. The inspector must examine records to evaluate the clinical sponsor's efficiency in reviewing data submitted by the investigator and in responding to reports of adverse reactions. In this aspect of the inspection, the investigator must make six determinations:

- whether the sponsor reviews all new case reports and other data received from the investigator regarding the safety of the test article within ten working days after receipt;

- whether all case reports and other data received from the investigator are periodically evaluated for effectiveness as portions of the study are completed (included in this determination are the practices of the monitor);

- what actions are taken in response to incomplete case report forms;

- whether there is a system for tabulating the frequency and character of adverse reactions;

- whether existing evidence indicates that the sponsor's present data receipt system is operating satisfactorily; and

- whether any deaths occurred among study subjects, and what actions were taken to determine whether the deaths were related to the use of the test article.

Record Retention. Finally, the inspector must determine the sponsor's compliance with whichever of the following two record retention requirements is applicable: (1) records must be retained for a period of two years after a drug's marketing application is approved; or (2) records must be retained for a period of two years following the date on which the sponsor discontinues the shipment and delivery of the drug for investigational use and so notifies the FDA.

Chapter 17:
Accelerated Drug Approval/Accessibility Programs

During the 1980s and early 1990s, the AIDS crisis thrust the FDA into a crucible of victim desperation and public and political pressure. Ultimately, the realities and politics of AIDS spurred the FDA to develop and implement several plans under which promising new therapies could reach desperately ill patients more quickly.

From 1987 through 1992, the FDA developed and implemented four principal drug access programs: the treatment IND, a mechanism that provides patients with access to promising experimental-stage drugs for serious and life-threatening diseases; parallel track, a plan that provides patients suffering from AIDS or AIDS-related diseases with early access to experimental-stage therapies; an accelerated drug development program for drugs designed to treat life-threatening and seriously debilitating diseases; and an accelerated drug approval program for products designed to treat serious or life-threatening illnesses.

In developing such programs, the FDA has acknowledged that the traditional drug development process is a compromise in many respects, and that the system can be particularly costly to those in dire need of new therapeutic alternatives. After all, it is during this process that potentially valuable drugs are often withheld from many who need them while clinical testing and the NDA review move forward. While critics have charged that some aspects of the drug approval process are unethical and even cruel, the FDA has maintained that the randomized, placebo-controlled clinical trial remains the single most efficient vehicle for determining whether new drugs are safe and effective.

285

For at least two reasons, the desperation and public pressure that prompted government action seemed to subside in late 1993. First, victims of AIDS and AIDS-related conditions had several approved therapeutic options to treat their conditions. Secondly, increasing numbers of experts began to question the wisdom of providing early and expanded access to therapies whose risks and benefits have not been characterized in traditional drug development processes. In 1992, at least one study questioned the relevance of the surrogate endpoints on which the approval of the first AIDS therapies were based.

Further, some agency advisors pointed to several patient deaths during a Phase 2 trial involving the hepatitis B treatment fialuridine (FIAU) as both a warning about the dangers of expanded access plans and a confirmation of the value of traditional drug development schemes. Although FIAU was not used in an expanded access program, members of the FDA's Antiviral Drugs Advisory Committee pointed out that, if the drug had shown early activity against AIDS, it might have been used in such a program. Five trial-related deaths might have become dozens or even hundreds under an expanded access program, they speculated during a 1993 meeting. One member of the committee, which reviews AIDS treatments as well, suggested that the pendulum has begun to swing away from early drug access plans and back toward conventional drug development programs.

The Treatment IND

Although the FDA has been pressured to reform clinical testing methodologies in the past, the unique issues posed by AIDS demonstrated the shortcomings of the drug development process as never before. As Burroughs Wellcome's AZT, or Retrovir, emerged as the first therapy to show promise in treating AIDS, victims of the disease not fortunate enough to be enrolled in clinical trials refused to die silently in the name of science. The intense public debate that followed was often bitter, but was not unproductive. After early clinical studies of AZT showed promising results, the FDA quickly approved what it called a treatment IND, under which more than 4,000 patients were allowed access to AZT while the drug underwent final FDA review.

The realities of AIDS first brought formal changes to FDA regulations on May 22, 1987, when the agency published a final rule allowing the treatment use and sale of investigational drugs intended to treat desperately ill patients.

Specifically, the regulations were "intended to facilitate the availability of promising new drugs as early in the drug development process as possible...to patients with serious and life-threatening diseases for which no comparable or satisfactory alternative drug or other therapies exist."

In many respects, the treatment IND was a compromise that attempted to satisfy those who believed that the desperately ill should have unmitigated access to an emerging therapy, and those who believed that a developmental-stage drug should be withheld from patients outside the clinical trial setting until such testing is completed and is judged to have demonstrated the drug's safety and effectiveness. Under a treatment IND, desperately ill patients gain access to a promising drug while the all-important clinical development and FDA review of a drug continue.

Although it was the AIDS crisis that eventually brought the FDA to formalize the treatment IND as it is now known, agency officials point out that the treatment IND has its roots in the 1960s and 1970s. At that time, applications commonly referred to as "compassionate INDs" were used to make unapproved antiarrhythmics, calcium channel blockers, and beta blockers accessible to patients intolerant to other therapies. In the early 1980s, FDA regulations formally recognized the treatment IND, allowing its use in cases in which: (1) there was sufficient evidence of safety and effectiveness; (2) the potential benefits outweighed the risks; and (3) the medical condition under study was a serious disease with no satisfactory therapies.

The 1987 regulations took a relatively loose concept and, for the first time, defined the treatment IND's purpose, established more specific criteria for FDA approval, and described how and when the treatment IND could be used. The regulations specify the point in a product's development at which treatment use may begin, a key factor since preapproval accessibility was the primary goal of the treatment IND.

To qualify for treatment use under the FDA's treatment IND program, a drug must meet four principal criteria. According to federal regulations, "FDA shall permit an investigational drug to be used for a treatment use under a treatment protocol or treatment IND if: (i) The drug is intended to treat a serious or immediately life-threatening disease; (ii) There is no comparable or satisfactory alternative drug or other therapy available to treat that stage of the disease in the intended patient population; (iii) The drug is under investigation in a controlled clinical trial under an IND in effect for the trial, or all clinical trials have been completed; and (iv) The sponsor of the controlled trial is actively pursuing approval of the investigational drug with due diligence."

The second criterion noted above is worth a short discussion, primarily because the entire treatment IND concept is designed for desperately ill individuals with no therapeutic alternatives. Responding to concern about its interpretation of the "no comparable or satisfactory alternative drug or other therapy available" requirement for treatment IND eligibility, the FDA has clarified that this standard is met "when there are patients who are not adequately treated by available therapies, even if the particular disease does respond in some cases to available therapy. This criterion would be met, for example, if the intended population is for patients who have failed on an existing therapy (i.e., the existing therapy did not provide its intended therapeutic benefit or did not fully treat the condition); for patients who could not tolerate the existing therapy (i.e., it caused unacceptable adverse effects); or for patients who had other complicating diseases that made the existing therapy unacceptable (e.g., concomitant disease making available therapy contraindicated) for the patient population."

In reality, FDA regulations provide for two different treatment IND vehicles: one for drugs designed to treat immediately life-threatening illnesses, and the other for drugs intended to treat serious diseases. The timing of, and FDA criteria for granting, treatment INDs for the two types of indications differ considerably.

Treatment Use for Immediately Life-Threatening Conditions
Under the May 1987 regulations, the FDA defined "immediately life-threatening disease" as a stage of a disease in which there is a reasonable likelihood that death will occur within a matter of months or in which premature death is likely without early treatment. The agency claims that it will apply a common sense definition so that death within more than a year would not normally be considered immediately life-threatening, but that death within several days or even several weeks would fall under the definition.

For illustrative purposes, the FDA identified in the regulations nine diseases that would "normally" be considered immediately life-threatening: advanced cases of AIDS, advanced congestive heart failure (New York Heart Association Class IV), recurrent sustained ventricular tachycardia or ventricular fibrillation, herpes simplex encephalitis, most advanced metastatic refractory cancers, far advanced emphysema, severe combined immunodeficiency syndrome, bacterial endocarditis, and subarachnoid hemorrhage.

Provided that a drug meets the four principal criteria outlined above, the FDA may only deny a treatment IND "if the available scientific evidence, taken as a whole, fails to provide a reasonable basis for concluding that the drug: (A) May be effective for its intended use in its intended patient population; or (B) Would not expose the patients to whom the drug is to be administered to an unreasonable and significant additional risk of illness or injury." The rather vague efficacy standard was discussed just briefly in the regulation's preamble, which stated that, "...the level of evidence needed is well short of that needed for a new drug approval—and may be less than what would be needed to support treatment use in diseases that are serious but not immediately life-threatening."

One of the more hotly debated aspects of the treatment IND regulations was the timing of treatment programs for drugs used against immediately life-threatening conditions. Some regarded the FDA's criteria as too liberal, and claimed that these criteria allow general accessibility before a drug development program can be expected to provide sufficient evidence of safety and/or effectiveness. The FDA, however, held to the provisions of its early proposals, and now allows drugs for immediately life-threatening conditions to be "made available for treatment use...earlier than Phase 3, but ordinarily not earlier than Phase 2."

But the FDA stresses that available scientific evidence, rather than simply the phase of development, is more important to its decision-making process: "FDA expects that data from controlled clinical trials will ordinarily be available at the time a treatment IND is requested. However, FDA is committed to reviewing and considering all available evidence, including results of domestic and foreign clinical trials, animal data, and, where pertinent, *in vitro* data. FDA will also consider clinical experience from outside a controlled trial, where the circumstances surrounding an experience provide sufficient indication of scientific value."

Treatment Use for Serious Conditions   The FDA's criteria for granting treatment INDs for serious conditions were considerably less controversial than those for immediately life-threatening illnesses. Interestingly, however, the FDA provided no specific definition of "serious" in either the treatment IND proposal or final rule. The agency did give examples of serious conditions: Alzheimer's disease, advanced multiple sclerosis, advanced Parkinson's disease, transient ischemic attacks, progressive ankylosing spondylitis, active advanced lupus erythematosus, certain forms of epilepsy, nonacidotic or hyperosmolar diabetes, and paroxysmal supraventricular tachycardia.

To qualify for treatment use, drugs intended to treat serious illnesses must meet a tougher, if more vague, safety and effectiveness standard than that described above for life-threatening conditions. The FDA "may deny a request for treatment use...if there is insufficient evidence of safety and effectiveness to support such use."

Considering this requirement, it is not surprising that treatment INDs for serious illnesses are more likely to be granted later in the clinical development process than are therapies for immediately life-threatening conditions: "In the case of serious diseases, a drug ordinarily may be made available for treatment use...during Phase 3 investigations or after all clinical trials have been completed; however, in appropriate circumstances, a drug may be made available for treatment use during Phase 2."

Obtaining FDA Permission for Treatment Use   Both drug sponsors and practicing physicians may pursue FDA approval for a treatment use. The sponsor of a drug's IND may do so through a treatment protocol, while "licensed practitioners" must submit a treatment IND.

According to FDA regulations, a sponsor-submitted treatment protocol must provide:

- the intended use of the drug;

- an explanation of the rationale for use of the drug, including, as appropriate, either a list of what available regimens ordinarily should be tried before using the investigational drug, or an explanation of why the use of the investigational drug is preferable to the use of available marketed treatments;

- a brief description of the criteria for patient selection;

- the method of administration and the dosages of the drug; and

- a description of clinical procedures, laboratory tests, or other measures designed to monitor the effects of the drug and to minimize risk.

Additionally, a treatment protocol must "be supported" by an informational brochure for each treating physician, technical information relevant to the safety and effectiveness of the drug for the intended treatment purpose, and a commitment by the sponsor to ensure the compliance of all participating investigators with informed consent requirements.

Like a traditional IND submission, a treatment protocol becomes active 30 days after the FDA receives the protocol, or on earlier notification by the FDA that the treatment use may begin. Of course, treatment protocols are also subject to clinical holds any time after submission.

If a practicing physician wants to obtain for treatment use a drug whose sponsor will not establish a treatment protocol for this purpose, the practitioner must submit his or her own treatment IND. Such applications must contain:

- a cover sheet (Form FDA 1571);

- information (when not provided by the sponsor either directly or through the incorporation-by-reference of information in the existing IND) on the drug's chemistry, manufacturing, and controls, and prior clinical and nonclinical experience with the drug;

- a statement of the steps taken by the practitioner to obtain the drug from the drug sponsor under a treatment protocol;

- a treatment protocol containing all the information required for such a submission (see discussion above);

- a statement of the practitioner's qualifications to use the investigational drug for the intended treatment use;

- the practitioner's statement of familiarity with information on the drug's safety and effectiveness derived from previous clinical and nonclinical experience with the drug; and

- the practitioner's commitment to report to the FDA safety information in accordance with current regulations.

The licensed practitioner who submits a treatment IND is the "sponsor-investigator" for such an IND, and is responsible for meeting all applicable sponsor and investigator responsibilities. Like standard INDs and treatment protocols, treatment INDs may be initiated 30 days after submission or upon early notification by the FDA.

The Sale of Investigational Drugs   The FDA's treatment IND regulations also contain provisions that allow sponsors to sell investigational drugs under some conditions. However, drug sponsors may not "commercialize an investigational drug by charging a price larger than that necessary to recover costs of manufacture, research, development, and handling of the investigational drug."

According to federal regulations, a sponsor may charge for an investigational drug under a treatment protocol or treatment IND, provided that: "(i) There is adequate enrollment in the ongoing clinical investigations under the authorized IND; (ii) charging does not constitute commercial marketing of a new drug for which a marketing application has not been approved; (iii) the drug is not being commercially promoted or advertised; and (iv) the sponsor of the drug is actively pursuing marketing approval with due diligence."

At least 30 days prior to selling an investigational drug, a sponsor must notify the FDA in writing and, with this notification, include a certified statement that the requested price is not greater than the amount necessary to recover costs associated with the drug's manufacture, research, development, and handling. If the FDA does not contact the sponsor within the 30-day review period, the sponsor is free to begin selling the drug.

A sponsor may also sell a drug in any clinical trial, provided the sponsor can gain the FDA's prior approval. To obtain this approval, the sponsor must provide an adequate explanation of why sale of the drug is necessary to either begin or continue a trial.

Unfortunately, the final regulations give few details on how a company can show that the sale of a drug is necessary or how this necessity should be determined. The regulation's preamble states that: "...charging for investigational drugs during a clinical trial would normally not be allowed.... FDA believes that cost recovery is justified in clinical trials only when necessary to further the study and development of a promising drug that might otherwise be lost to the medical armamentarium. The agency believes that this situation is most likely to arise in the context of new products derived through biotechnology which are produced by small, medium and large firms alike." Since the treatment IND regulations were published, the FDA has approved the sale of certain investigational products.

Although more than two dozen treatment INDs have been approved, the submission and approval of treatment INDs have diminished markedly since 1991. Since that time, the agency has granted only a handful of treatment INDs. The reasons, many observers believe, are related partly to continuing ambivalence within the pharmaceutical industry toward the treatment IND program. It is also obvious that the FDA's current leadership has not been as aggressive in recruiting treatment INDs as was Frank Young, M.D., who was the FDA commissioner when the program was introduced.

Critics of the treatment IND program continue to view the plan as little more than an FDA effort to relieve public and political pressure. These critics hold that the treatment IND brought nothing to what the FDA could have and has done using "compassionate use" protocols, open-label studies, and other flexible, if informal, drug accessibility plans.

The FDA's Accelerated Drug Development Program

By mid-1988, the FDA had successfully implemented several initiatives designed to make drugs more accessible through both preapproval availability plans and speedier reviews. At that time, the treatment IND regulations were in effect, and seven experimental therapies had been available to patients with AIDS, cancer, Parkinson's disease, and other life-threatening conditions. In addition, the agency had established a new level of review priority for all AIDS products, and had created a new drug review division to focus on evaluating these therapies. The FDA credited such initiatives with the rapid availability and review of AZT, which the FDA approved only 107 days after Burroughs Wellcome submitted its NDA for the antiviral drug.

In August 1988, then-Vice President George Bush, in his capacity as the chairman of the Presidential Task Force on Regulatory Relief, asked the FDA to build on these "successes" by developing procedures for expediting the marketing of new therapies intended to treat AIDS and other life-threatening illnesses. In the two months that followed, FDA officials met with representatives from other government agencies, AIDS groups, and consumer, health, and academic organizations to obtain input on developing this program.

On October 21, 1988, the FDA released such a plan: its Interim Rules on Procedures for Drugs Intended to Treat Life-Threatening and Severely Debilitating Illnesses, or Subpart E procedures. The interim rule, which the FDA claims is based on its experience with AZT, is described by the agency as an attempt "to speed the availability of new therapies to desperately ill patients, while preserving appropriate guarantees for safety and effectiveness. These procedures are intended to facilitate the development, evaluation, and marketing of such products, especially where no satisfactory therapies exist. These procedures reflect the recognition that physicians and patients are generally willing to accept greater risks or side effects from products that treat life-threatening and severely debilitating illnesses than they would accept from products that treat less serious illnesses. These procedures also reflect the recognition that the benefits of the drug need to be evaluated in light of the severity of the disease being treated. The procedures apply to products intended to treat acquired immunodeficiency syndrome (AIDS), some cancers, and other life-threatening and severely debilitating illnesses."

Like the treatment IND, the FDA's accelerated development plan was announced with considerable fanfare and, in turn, was met by some degree of skepticism. Even officials within the FDA review units responsible for the approval of AIDS and cancer therapies claimed that the plan's primary elements—close sponsor consultation and an accelerated clinical testing scheme—were already common practice.

But because it provided for a drug's approval before its sale, the accelerated development program had three key advantages over the treatment IND, according to the FDA: (1) no limitations are put on the pricing or profitability of FDA-approved drugs; (2) consumers who buy FDA-approved drugs are eligible for third-party reimbursement, for which patients under treatment INDs cannot qualify; and (3) FDA approval confers some liability protection to manufacturers.

Essentially, there are four key components to the FDA's expedited development plan: (1) early and increased FDA and sponsor consultation aimed at formulating agreements on the design of preclinical and clinical studies needed for marketing approval; (2) the "compression" of Phase 3 clinical trials into Phase 2 testing; (3) the FDA's adoption of a modified medical risk-benefit analysis when assessing the safety and effectiveness of qualifying drugs; and (4) the use of Phase 4 postmarketing studies to obtain additional information about drug risks, benefits, and optimal use.

Eligibility for Accelerated Development Eligibility was perhaps the most fascinating aspect of the interim regulation when it was first released. Recognizing the great opportunities that expedited approval could offer, the drug industry quickly turned to the agency for guidance on which products might qualify for the plan.

In general terms, the expedited approval program applies to new drugs, antibiotics, and biologics being studied for their safety and effectiveness in treating life-threatening or severely debilitating diseases. As is that of every other regulation, the scope of this interim rule is subject to FDA interpretation, which the agency bases on two primary definitions:

- *Life-Threatening Conditions.* For the purposes of the plan, "life-threatening" illnesses include: "(1) Diseases or conditions where the likelihood of death is high unless the course of the disease is interrupted; and (2) Diseases or conditions with potentially fatal outcomes, where the end point of clinical trial analysis is survival." Any disease whose progression is likely to lead to death, particularly in a short period (e.g. six months to one year), would also fall under this definition, as would any "condition on which a study is to be carried out to determine whether the treatment has a beneficial effect on survival (e.g., increased survival after a stroke or heart attack)."

- *Severely Debilitating Conditions.* The FDA has defined "severely debilitating" illnesses as "diseases or conditions that cause major irreversible morbidity," such as severe function deficits in multiple sclerosis, Alzheimer's disease, or progressive ankylosing spondylitis, and blindness due to cytomegalovirus infection in AIDS patients. The agency cautioned that accelerated approvals would be relevant only for studies that "will examine the treatment's capacity to prevent or reverse what would otherwise be irreversible damage such as putting ankylosing spondylitis into remission and stopping joint damage and deformity, or preventing blindness."

Despite these definitions, eligibility remained a widely discussed issue in the months following the interim rule's publication. To help educate industry as well as its own staff, the FDA completed a retrospective review of approximately 200 new molecular entities (NME) approved during the 1980s to determine which of these would have been eligible under the new rules. The agency also reviewed its existing inventory of approximately 10,000 drug INDs, and reportedly contacted the sponsors of qualifying drugs.

The Cornerstone of Accelerated Development: Early FDA-Sponsor Consultation Despite serious questions about whether the agency should involve itself in the research process, FDA officials have maintained that early consultation is the single most critical element of this program. The FDA believes that the insights it has gained in reviewing both acceptable and unacceptable drug applications could prove invaluable to sponsors, and that close consultation will allow the agency to share its expertise in the planning and design of both preclinical and clinical development programs.

According to the FDA's interim rule, FDA-sponsor consultations would take two forms:

- *Pre-Investigational New Drug Application (IND) Meetings.* Prior to an IND submission, the sponsor may request a meeting "to review and reach agreement on the design of animal studies needed to initiate human testing. The meeting may also provide an opportunity for discussing the scope and design of Phase 1 testing, and the best approach for presentation and formatting of data in the IND."

- *End-of-Phase 1 Meetings.* In the FDA's ideal accelerated drug development program, Phase 3 clinical trials are "compressed" into Phase 2 studies, which then provide the data on which the drug is to be approved. Therefore, after Phase 1 data are available, the sponsor may again request a meeting to "review and reach agreement on the design of Phase 2 controlled clinical trials, with the goal that such testing will be adequate to provide sufficient data on the drug's safety and effectiveness to support a decision on its approvability for marketing."

Restructuring Clinical Trials   In attempting to use data derived from Phase 2 trials as the basis for the final approval of a new drug, the FDA brought about, in theory at least, a reasonably significant departure from the traditional drug development and approval path. Interestingly, however, the FDA drug review divisions responsible for evaluating AIDS and cancer therapies claimed to have approved desperately needed new drugs based upon Phase 2 clinical data well before the plan's introduction.

Under the accelerated development scheme, Phase 3 trials are "compressed" into Phase 2 studies, with Phase 1 trials taking on the significance of conventional Phase 2 studies. According to the interim rule: "To increase the likelihood that phase 2 testing can provide sufficient results, sponsors could need to plan phase 2 studies that are somewhat larger and more extensive than is currently the norm, including a mode for replication of key findings. Moreover, to avoid missing an effect by using too little drug, or to avoid studying a dose that proves toxic, it may be necessary to study several doses in the first formal trials, an approach that may require a larger study but can plainly save time, thereby enabling physicians to treat patients with life-threatening illnesses more rapidly. However, it should be appreciated that if a drug has only minor or inconsistent therapeutic benefits, its positive effects may be missed in this stage of clinical testing, even if the drug ultimately proves to be beneficial following more extensive phase 3 trials."

On the issue of the quantity of data needed for approval, the FDA has stated that, in most cases, two pivotal Phase 2 studies will be necessary: "...the agency cautions that persuasively dramatic results are rare and that two entirely independent studies will generally be required." The approvals of the first AIDS drugs under the accelerated program, however, indicate that the FDA is willing to base the approval of desperately needed drugs on a single pivotal study.

Other Provisions of the Interim Rule   The FDA's interim rule contains key provisions in several other areas, including the following:

• *Treatment IND.* The accelerated approval plan was not meant to eliminate the need for treatment INDs. In fact, when the preliminary analyses of Phase 2 results appear promising, the FDA may ask the sponsor to submit a treatment IND, under which the test drug could be made available while the sponsor prepares, and the FDA reviews, the NDA.

• *FDA Risk-Benefit Analysis.* According to the interim rule, the "FDA will consider the seriousness of the disease being treated in balancing risks and benefits.... Clearly, for a life-threatening illness, a relatively high level of known risks and some uncertainty about potential risk from the drug can be acceptable in exchange for the improved survival provided by effective drug treatment for a condition that, if left untreated, would result in death. Similarly, for the same life-threatening illnesses, evidence of effectiveness must be weighed against risks of the drug and the knowledge that death would result in the absence of treatment."

• *Phase 4 Testing.* Although FDA officials state that approvals granted under the accelerated plan are in no way conditional on sponsor willingness to conduct postmarketing testing, the agency says that it "...may seek agreement from the sponsor to conduct certain postmarketing (phase 4) studies to delineate additional information about the drug's risks, benefits, and optimal use. These studies could include, but would not be limited to, studying different doses or schedules of administration than were used in phase 2 studies, use of the drug in other patient populations or other stages of the disease, or use of the drug over a longer period of time."

Accelerated Drug Approval Program

With its 1988 accelerated drug development program already in place, the FDA wanted to take "additional steps...to facilitate the approval of significant new drugs...to treat serious or life-threatening diseases." The agency took these steps under a final regulation published in December 1992.

Unlike the FDA's accelerated development program, which focused largely on expediting the drug testing process, the 1992 regulations focused on accelerating the agency's review and approval of promising therapies. The regulation attempted to do so by modifying the criteria on which the agency can base marketing approval for desperately needed new drugs, and by giving the agency greater authority regarding the study and use of the drugs following approval.

Specifically, the accelerated approval program allows the agency to base marketing approval on a drug's effect on a surrogate endpoint or on a clinical endpoint other than survival or irreversible morbidity. According to the regulation, "FDA may grant marketing approval for a new drug product on the basis of adequate and well-controlled clinical trials establishing that the drug product has an effect on a surrogate endpoint that is reasonably likely, based on epidemiologic, therapeutic, pathophysiologic, or other evidence, to predict clinical benefit or on the basis of an effect on a clinical endpoint other than survival or irreversible morbidity. Approval under this section will be subject to the requirement that the applicant study the drug further, to verify and describe its clinical benefit, where there is uncertainty as to the relation of the surrogate endpoint to clinical benefit, or of the observed clinical benefit to ultimate outcome. Postmarketing studies would usually be studies already underway. When required to be conducted, such studies must also be adequate and well controlled."

In its April 1992 regulatory proposal for the accelerated approval plan, the FDA discussed the benefits of not requiring companies to study the effects of desperately needed new drugs on primary endpoints (i.e., mortality or morbidity). "Approval of a drug on the basis of a well-documented effect on a surrogate endpoint can allow a drug to be marketed earlier, sometimes much earlier, than it could if a demonstrated clinical benefit were required.... Approval could be granted where there is some uncertainty as to the relation of that endpoint to clinical benefit, with the requirement that the sponsor conduct or complete studies after approval to establish and define the drug's clinical benefit."

The regulations also permit the FDA to accelerate its approval processes if the agency "concludes that a drug product shown to be effective can be safely used only if distribution or use is restricted." Under the program, the agency may apply postmarketing restrictions commensurate with the relevant safety concerns regarding the product. These restrictions may include: (1) restricting distribution to certain facilities or physicians with special training or experience; or (2) making drug distribution conditional on the performance of specified medical procedures.

Eligibility for Accelerated Approval   Under the FDA's regulations, the accelerated approval program "applies to certain new drug and antibiotic products that have been studied for their safety and effectiveness in treating serious and life-threatening illnesses and that provide meaningful therapeutic benefit to patients over existing treatments (e.g., the ability to treat patients unresponsive to, or intolerant of, available therapy, or improved patient response over available therapy)."

Although the agency stated in its April 1992 proposal that it would apply the terms "serious" and "life-threatening" as it has in its treatment IND program and other programs, the FDA did discuss their application once again in the context of the accelerated approval plan. "The seriousness of a disease is a matter of judgement, but generally is based on its impact on such factors as survival, day-to-day functioning, or the likelihood that the disease, if left untreated, will progress from a less severe condition to a more serious one. Thus, acquired immunodeficiency syndrome (HIV) infection, Alzheimer's dementia, angina pectoris, heart failure, cancer, and many other diseases are clearly serious in their full manifestations. Further, many chronic illnesses that are generally well-managed by available therapy can have serious outcomes. For example, inflammatory bowel disease, asthma, rheumatoid arthritis, diabetes mellitus, systemic lupus erythematosus, depression, psychoses, and many other diseases can be serious for certain populations or in some or all of their phases."

The Parallel Track Program
In mid-1989, National Institute of Allergy and Infectious Diseases (NIAID) Director Anthony Fauci, M.D., publicly proposed a new experimental drug accessibility plan called "parallel track." As proposed, the plan would allow the availability of experimental AIDS therapies earlier than ever in clinical development.

The federal government officially unveiled the parallel track program in April 1992 as a plan "intended to make promising new investigational drugs for AIDS and other HIV-related diseases more widely available as early as possible in the drug development process."

The new approach called for AIDS drugs to be made available after the completion of Phase 1 studies to subjects who are unable to enroll in the controlled trials or are unable to benefit from current therapies. Although similar to the treatment IND concept, parallel track is a more liberal mechanism in that it can provide for expanded drug access when the evidence of a drug's effectiveness cannot meet the threshold necessary to qualify for a treatment IND.

There are other, if more subtle, differences between the two experimental access programs. While the treatment IND requires approval at the commissioner's office level, parallel track is technically a protocol amendment, which needs the approval of review division directors. Also, sponsors can submit their parallel track proposals for review by the AIDS Research Advisory Committee of the National Institute of Allergy and Infectious Diseases in addition to the FDA.

In October 1992, Bristol-Myers Squibb's AIDS drug d4T (stavudine) became the first drug made available under parallel track. The company established the parallel track arm during Phase 2/3 trials, and at a time when the controlled trials were enrolling rapidly. Just six weeks into the parallel track program, the company's controlled trials were fully enrolled, while the parallel access arm had enrolled several hundred patients.

The almost routine nature of Bristol-Myers Squibb's parallel track experience seemed to contrast sharply with the company's treatment IND program for ddI, the existence of which many observers felt hurt enrollment efforts for ddI's controlled clinical trials. Early on, company officials credited the availability of other approved and experimental AIDS treatments for their early success with the parallel track program.

Chapter 18:

The FDA's Prescription Drug User Fee Program

When the Prescription Drug User Fee Act of 1992 was signed into law on October 29, 1992, it became the next great hope for expediting the FDA's drug review process. Under the historic legislation, the FDA committed to review drug applications within specific and ambitious time frames (see Chapter 9). To provide the FDA with the additional resources necessary to meet the new review goals, the pharmaceutical industry agreed to pay a series of user fees to be levied on drug applications, drug products, and manufacturing establishments.

From FY-1993 through FY-1997, the FDA expects to collect more than $325 million in user-fee revenues that will be split between CDER and CBER. Over that period, CDER hopes to recruit about 300 additional drug reviewers and support staff, to acquire new office space to accommodate its expanded ranks, and to streamline drug reviews through the expanded use of computer technology.

User fees are not new to the FDA—the agency has collected user fees for color and insulin certifications for more than 40 years. Further, the federal government has proposed collecting drug user fees at various times over the past 20 years. But finally, in 1992, an FDA badly in need of additional resources, and a pharmaceutical industry craving speedier drug reviews, reached agreement on a workable user-fee concept. At the core of this consensus was the idea that user-fee revenues would supplement, rather than replace, existing FDA appropriations (unlike previous proposals), would be fully dedicated to the drug and biologics review process, and would be accompanied by a long-term government commitment to improve the drug review process.

The Basics of User Fees

Although early drafts of the statute proposed that fees be charged on a wide range of FDA-regulated products, the final draft authorized fees only for prescription drugs and biologics. Large-volume parenterals and generic drugs were among the drug products exempted from the fees, while whole blood products, drugs made from bovine blood products, allergenic extract products, and *in vitro* diagnostics were among biologics exempted.

Under the user-fee legislation, the FDA levies three different user fees:

Annual Fees on Drug Manufacturing Establishments. A "prescription drug establishment" is defined as a foreign or domestic "place of business at one general location with buildings within 5 miles of each other manufacturing one or more prescription drug products in final dosage form which is not the same as a product subject to an approved [abbreviated new drug application]." Also, the establishment must be "under the management of a person that is listed as the applicant" in at least one application for a prescription drug product manufactured at the facility. Therefore, contract manufacturers not holding an approved application for a prescription drug product would not be assessed an annual establishment fee.

Annual Fees on Prescription Drug Products. For the purposes of user fees, a prescription drug product is a specific strength or potency of a drug in final dosage form for which a human drug application has been approved. The term includes neither generic nor OTC drugs. An annual fee is required for each strength of a product.

Application Fees. Sponsors of several types of human drug applications are assessed user fees: (1) full NDAs; (2) "paper" NDAs for which clinical data are not required; and (3) supplemental NDAs for which clinical data other than bioavailability or bioequivalence data are required (i.e., primarily effectiveness supplements proposing new uses, dosage regimens, etc.). Therefore, manufacturing supplements (regardless of whether they include bioequivalence data) and other supplements that do not need clinical data for approval are not subject to fees. The fees are applicable to filings for new prescription drugs, nonprescription drugs, and prescription-to-OTC switches.

The legislation specified annual revenue targets for FY-1993 through FY-1997, and mandated that each of the three categories of fees account for one-third of the total annual fee revenues. In FY-1993, for example, the FDA was to collect a total of $36 million, with application fees, establishment fees, and product fees each accounting for $12 million of the total (see chart below). This ensures that no single fee is "exceedingly" large (i.e., something that would be prohibitive for smaller companies), and provides the FDA with some degree of predictability in projecting fee revenues (i.e., since NDA submissions vary from year to year).

Based on projections regarding NDA submissions, manufacturing facilities, and marketed drug products, the FDA has estimated user fees for each fiscal year through FY-1997 (see chart below). At the beginning of each fiscal year, the FDA must adjust the three fees based on updated projections and on estimated federal employee salary increases.

Projected FDA User Fees

	FY93 (actual)	FY94 (actual)	FY95	FY96	FY97
Annual Establishment Fee	$60,000	$93,800	$126,000	$131,000	$138,000
Annual Product Fee	$6,000	$9,400	$12,500	$13,000	$14,000
Drug Application Fees:					
Full NDA	$100,000	$162,000	$208,000	$217,000	$233,000
Supplements With, NDAs Without, Clinical Data	$50,000	$81,000	$104,000	$108,000	$116,000

As the chart above indicates, the fee amount assessed to an application depends on the nature of the filing. The FDA has created a two-tiered application fee structure to reflect the review resources an application is likely to consume. Therefore, full NDAs with clinical data will be assessed a larger fee than either NDA supplements or those NDAs without clinical data. Establishment and product fees are assessed uniformly among marketed drugs and facilities for which the fees are applicable.

The Complexities of User Fees

Implementing a user-fee program has required a massive initiative by the FDA. One of the most significant FDA efforts was to develop guidance that would explain the user-fee concept and how the agency would implement user fees.

Like that of any new legislation, the implementation of the Prescription Drug User Fee Act of 1992 is based largely on agency interpretations of the law's provisions. For example, since the fee assessed to an application depends on whether or not the application includes clinical data, what would the FDA consider to comprise clinical data for the purposes of such assessments? Also, to what degree would the FDA, as it has in the past, allow drugs for different indications, dosage strengths, and dosage forms, to be "bundled" into a single NDA, thereby allowing the sponsor to avoid the assessment of multiple application fees?

To provide insights on these and dozens of other issues regarding its user-fee program, the FDA released a series of guidance documents during mid-1993:

Payment Procedures Under the Prescription Drug User Fee Act of 1992. As implied by its title, this document instructs sponsors on methods for paying user fees. One-half of the total application fee must be paid upon the submission of an NDA or supplement, with the balance due when the FDA acts on the submission. The FDA will accept no application for filing until the initial fee and any other outstanding fees are paid. These payments should not accompany applications, but should be forwarded in U.S. currency, by check, draft, or U.S. postal money order, to: FDA, P.O. Box 7777-W7745, Philadelphia, PA 19175-7745. The FDA will invoice companies for annual establishment and product fees. Payment must be made within 30 days from the date of these annual invoices.

Application, Product, and Establishment Fees: Common Issues and Their Resolution. In this document, the FDA describes its rationale in resolving several important fee assessment issues. Many of these are "special case" issues, such as situations in which products are transferred from one NDA holder to another, when products are manufactured in the United States but are only marketed abroad, and cases in which foreign manufacturing facilities make products for marketing under an approved NDA.

Interim Guidance: Separate Marketing Applications and Clinical Data For Purposes of Assessing User Fees Under the Prescription Drug User Fee Act of 1992. This document describes the FDA's application "bundling" policy, and provides a working definition of clinical data for the purpose of assessing user fees. According to this guidance document, each of the following products require separate original applications:

- every active ingredient (including different salts, esters, complexes, etc. of the same active moiety) or combination of two or more different active ingredients;

- products to be marketed as both a racemic mixture and a single enantiomer;

- drug substances purified from mixtures with multiple constituents of an active ingredient (e.g., enantiomers, polymorphs);

- products to be administered using different routes of administration, unless the product(s) for use by all routes in a given application are quantitatively and qualitatively identical (drugs) or alike (biologicals) in composition (e.g., an injectable liquid dosage form intended for use by the intravenous and intraperitoneal routes);

- products with different dosage forms, unless the products are identical (drugs) or alike (biologicals) in quantitative or qualitative composition (e.g., a sterile liquid in a single dose vial that is intended for use as either an injectable or an inhalation solution);

- pharmacy bulk packages and products for prescription compounding (these products should also have their own package inserts);

- single entity or combination drug products with quantitatively or qualitatively different excipients that require separate clinical studies for safety and effectiveness; and

- topical products with different excipients that require separate *in vivo* demonstrations of bioequivalence.

The FDA also provided examples of products that should be bundled in a single application:

- drugs with different indications and uses, but with the same dosage form and route of administration (regardless of dose, duration of use, schedule of administration, target population, or the condition for which the product is indicated);

- different strengths or concentrations of one drug substance, active biological product, or combination product, provided that they involve the same dosage form, are intended for the same route of administration and general indication(s), and are qualitatively identical in composition;

- single entity or combination products with excipients that differ qualitatively or quantitatively to accommodate different container sizes and configurations, or that differ qualitatively or quantitatively with respect to: colors, flavorings, adjustment of pH or osmolality, or preservatives (provided the products do not otherwise meet relevant criteria requiring separate submissions); and

- different container sizes and configurations (e.g., filled syringes, ampules, sealed vials) of one finished pharmaceutical product intended for use in the same route of administration and for the same indication(s).

As stated above, the presence or absence of clinical data in original and supplemental NDAs has implications for the assessment of user fees. Therefore, the FDA specified in the guidance document the types of clinical data relevant to the user-fee program: "User fees will be assessed for original applications (NDAs and PLAs) and supplements containing the following types of clinical data required to form the primary basis for approval:" (1) "study reports or literature reports of what are explicitly or implicitly represented by the applicant to be adequate and well-controlled trials; or" (2) "reports of comparative activity (other than bioequivalence and bioavailability studies), immunogenicity, or efficacy, where those reports are necessary to support a claim of comparable clinical effect."

Conversely, the following types of clinical data and applications will not trigger user fees:

- data used to modify labeling to add a restriction that would improve the safe use of the drug (e.g., to add an adverse reaction, contraindication, or warning to the labeling);

- NDA supplements based solely on bioequivalence studies or studies of bioavailability of a drug, even if the studies include clinical endpoints; and

- supplements to PLAs in support of a process or site change that uses safety, biochemical equivalence, and/or limited comparative product equivalence data generated in animals or humans as the supportable basis for such a change.

Interim Guidance: Applicability of User Fees To: (1) Applications Withdrawn Before Filing Decision; or (2) Applications the Agency Has Refused to File and That Are Resubmitted Over Protest. This interim guidance describes how the FDA intends to assess user fees if the sponsor files an application over protest, or withdraws an application before a decision is made on its fileability. If the FDA refuses to file an application or the application is withdrawn before filing, the agency will refund one-half the fee submitted with the application. If the sponsor subsequently resubmits the application or requests that the application be filed over protest, "the following principles will apply:

a. If, after withdrawing the application, the applicant resubmits the unamended application, or amends and resubmits the application, the agency will treat the resubmission as a new original application and it should be accompanied by the fees applicable to a new submission.

b. If the applicant decides to file the application over protest, the filing of the application over protest will be regarded by the agency as a new original application for user-fee purposes. Therefore, it should be accompanied by the fees applicable to a new submission."

Interim Guidance Document For Waivers of and Reductions in User Fees. The Prescription Drug User Fee Act permits the FDA to grant certain waivers from, and reductions in, user fees "under limited circumstances." Under the act, the FDA can grant waivers from, or a reduction in, one or more of the three types of fees when it finds any of the following: (1) that such a waiver or reduction is necessary to protect the public health; (2) that the assessment of the fee would present a significant barrier to innovation because of limited resources available to such person or other circumstances; (3) that the fees to be paid will exceed the FDA's anticipated present and future costs incurred in reviewing the application; or (4) assessment of the fee for an original or supplemental application would be inequitable because an application (e.g., an abbreviated new drug application) for a product containing the same active ingredient filed by another person cannot be assessed a fee.

In the interim guidance, the FDA segments commercial pharmaceutical companies into six categories for the purpose of evaluating waivers based on the first two grounds listed above. The agency states that it "expects to grant most of the fee waivers and reductions...to [companies classified as small and very small] whose ability to pay fees is limited by the entity's resources. Although there is no express threshold for defining a small entity, FDA generally considers an entity with less than $10 million in annual gross revenues and no corporate parent or funding source with annual gross revenues of $100 million or more...as less likely to be able to continue to provide products that benefit the public health and to develop innovative technology because of user fees."

The act also provides for both a reduction and deferral of the application fee "for any business which has fewer than 500 employees, including employees of affiliates, and which does not have a prescription drug product introduced or delivered for introduction into interstate commerce." A qualifying small business need pay only one-half the amount of the fee for an original human drug application. In addition, no fee is due until one year after the date of the application's submission.

Chapter 19:

FDA Initiatives to Speed Drug Reviews

While the FDA's user-fee program is the most ambitious government initiative to reduce drug review times, it represents only one of a wide range of efforts to accelerate product reviews. Since the late 1980s, CDER has experimented with many novel drug review approaches, ranging from process tinkering to fundamental system changes, in response to public and political pressure to slash NDA review times that averaged about 2.5 years through the early 1990s.

Experimental approaches such as NDA Days and computer-assisted new drug applications (CANDA) have not been embraced by all CDER review divisions. Regardless, these and other methods are seen as contributing substantially to the FDA's ability to approve increasing numbers of NDAs extremely quickly. Of the 26 new molecular entities approved in 1992, for example, more than one-third were reviewed in 18 months or less. And five NMEs were approved in less than one year. It is also worth noting that, in several of these cases, the rapid approvals extended beyond simply drugs for AIDS and cancer.

This chapter focuses on four of CDER's more significant initiatives to expedite product reviews: NDA Days, CANDAs, external application reviews, and cooperative international product reviews. The FDA's user-fee program and accelerated development/approval programs for drugs to treat serious and life-threatening conditions are profiled in separate chapters.

NDA Days

The NDA Day is a relatively recent concept that has been welcomed by some drug review divisions and rejected by others. In general terms, an NDA Day involves an intensive one- or two-day session that assembles key scientists from the drug sponsor and an application's primary, secondary, and tertiary reviewers to address the pending issues regarding a submission late in the evaluation process. The sessions are designed to accelerate drug reviews by condensing a process that would ordinarily involve months of intermittent discussions into a meeting that consumes as little as one day.

The inaugural NDA Day was held in 1988 between CDER's Pilot Drug Evaluation Staff and Ciba-Geigy, which was pursuing approval for Voltaren (diclofenac). Ciba-Geigy officials speculate that the meeting reduced the Voltaren review by as much as six months. The agency approved Voltaren in just over three months following the NDA Day.

As of January 1, 1994, CDER had participated in a total of 32 NDA Days. The center's Pilot Drug Evaluation Staff has participated in no less than 27 of these sessions. The Division of Neuropharmacological Drug Products and the Division of Cardio-Renal Drug Products have each held two NDA Days, while the Division of Anti-Infective Drug Products has participated in one NDA Day.

These statistics reveal that most of CDER's drug review divisions have not been as receptive to this approach. Some emphasize that the intensity of work needed to prepare adequately for such meetings diverts too many divisional resources away from other drug reviews. Others believe that the NDA Day creates the perception that the agency is focusing more on review speed than quality.

NDA Days can range from fairly straightforward sponsor-FDA meetings to more ambitious sessions involving advanced computer and communications technologies and dozens of sponsor and FDA representatives. A modest NDA Day session may involve a few key sponsor and FDA staffers, for instance. The applicant may station several scientists back at its headquarters with dedicated computer data bases and faxes to provide immediate responses to questions that arise during the meeting.

At the other end of the spectrum was an NDA Day held for Burroughs Wellcome's Nuromax. This meeting involved not only the sponsor and CDER's Pilot Drug Evaluation Staff, but an FDA advisory committee as well. The meeting's agenda included dose-related drug effects, the importance of demographic factors on efficacy parameters, and the relationship between single and multiple-dose pharmacokinetics and pharmacodynamics. To provide data and analyses on these issues, Wellcome established computer links between FDA local area networks (LAN) and the company's own mainframe computers. In addition, the firm used satellite technology to transmit audio/visual signals and computer data from company headquarters to the meeting site. During several months of preparation for the meeting, Wellcome formed a 50-person internal task force, and participated in a mock NDA Day in which outside consultants played the role of FDA reviewers and advisory committee members. Nuromax was approved six weeks following the session.

Such involved NDA Days may be increasingly rare, however, since even the most experienced review divisions are seeking to streamline these efforts. For example, the Pilot Drug Evaluation Staff is attempting to shorten and focus NDA Day meetings, and to involve only division personnel who are essential to the issues at hand. And the unit has scaled-back earlier plans to hold NDA Days for each drug reviewed by the division. Such changes, however, are a function of limited resources rather than a lack of success in NDA Days.

Computer-Assisted New Drug Applications

Outside of the user-fee program, CANDAs represent the greatest hope for accelerating drug reviews. In fact, many FDA officials believe that the effective use of CANDAs is essential if CDER is to meet its ambitious NDA review time lines under that program. Further, the FDA has stated that all NDAs must be computerized by 1995.

The agency defines CANDA as "any application using computer technology to improve the transmission, storage, retrieval, and analysis of data submitted to FDA as part of the drug approval process."

The FDA now has about a decade of experience in reviewing CANDAs. Over this period, CANDAs have evolved from mainframe-based to mostly PC-based systems, from fixed format to interactive submissions, and in several other key ways that reflect emerging technological trends and the growing knowledge and experience base within industry and the FDA.

Although there is considerable variability within the latest generation of CANDAs, computer submissions consist of one or more of three core components:

Word Processing Files. Much of an NDA, including the summary sections, study summaries, and product labeling, consists of narrative text that can be provided in a standard word processing file. After evaluating an NDA, a reviewer develops a review document, an estimated 80 percent of which consists of text taken verbatim from the narrative sections of an NDA submission. Therefore, providing the reviewer with the ability to "cut and paste" text from the NDA's key sections without having to rekey the text can save considerable time during NDA reviews.

Optical Images. In many CANDAs, sponsors provide reviewers with access to optical images of the entire NDA submission and/or patient case report forms (CRF). The advantage of document imaging is the ease of storing and speed of retrieving these documents. Typically, when a reviewer wanted to view an original CRF, he or she had to request either that the sponsor forward the CRF or that the document be retrieved from FDA storage facilities. In either case, the momentum of the review was interrupted. With an optical disk system, however, the reviewer can quickly retrieve the document electronically to view on the screen or, alternatively, to print the CRF in hardcopy form.

Interactive Data Bases. An estimated 80 percent of an NDA consists of clinical data and analyses, the evaluation of which is the most demanding and rate-limiting element of the NDA review process. Given this, it is not surprising that sponsors are applying advanced data base technologies to facilitate the clinical review process. By providing clinical data in a data base that drug reviewers can query and manipulate, sponsors eliminate the need for reviewers to rekey the data into computerized tools, or to contact the sponsor to perform new analyses. Most experts believe that interactive clinical data bases hold the most potential for reducing NDA review times.

Trends in CANDA Submissions   As of June 30, 1993, drug companies had submitted 101 CANDAs. But participation in CANDA projects has been anything but uniform within the drug industry. One third or more of CANDAs were developed by just a handful of drug companies, including Pfizer, Marion Merrell Dow, Upjohn, and Glaxo.

CANDA involvement has been uneven across CDER's drug review divisions as well. In recent years, the Division of Anti-Infective Drug Products has been the most active in the CANDA arena. From 1989 through mid-1993, for example, the division had received 28 CANDAs, almost 40 percent of all CANDAs submitted during that period (see exhibit below). Conversely, the Division of Medical Imaging, Surgical and Dental Drug Products is the only division not to have participated in a single CANDA review.

CANDA Submissions By Division, 1989–1993*

Division	1989	1990	1991	1992	1993*
Pilot Drug Evaluation Staff	0	2	5	1	0
Division of Cardio-Renal Drug Products	3	1	1	1	2
Division of Neuropharm- acological Drug Products	1	2	5	0	0
Division of Oncology and Pulmonary Drug Products	0	0	2	1	0
Division of Medical Imaging, Surgical and Dental Drug Products	0	0	0	0	0
Division of Gastrointestinal Drug Products	2	2	1	0	1
Division of Metabolism and Endocrine Drug Products	0	0	3	1	0
Division of Anti-Infective Drug Products	4	8	10	6	0
Division of Antiviral Drug Products	2	1	0	2	1
Total	*12*	*16*	*27*	*12*	*4*

* through June 30, 1993.

Source: FDA

Overall, CANDA submissions have been on a significant downward trend since 1991, when they hit a high of 27 submissions. In 1992, new CANDA submissions dropped by more than 50 percent. Further, data from mid-1993 suggested that 1993 submissions would drop by another third.

There is considerable speculation that the cause of the downturn is industry frustration over the lack of FDA direction regarding CANDAs. Although CDER has developed a *CANDA Guidance Manual*, such efforts have only started the process that will ultimately define specifications for CANDA hardware, software, and/or data interfaces.

CANDA sponsors must continue to tailor their CANDAs to the needs, preferences, and abilities of individual drug reviewers. Significant differences between reviewers are what make this process, as well as CDER's own efforts to define standard CANDA specifications, so difficult.

Several other factors may be contributing to the reduction in CANDA submissions. These include the FDA's long-term effort to develop a comprehensive information architecture as part of its Submission Management And Review Tracking (SMART) initiative, and uncertainty regarding the implications that this will have for CANDA efforts.

Still, FDA officials claim that a regulation expected in proposal form during early 1994 will jump-start the CANDA program. By establishing the "legal submissibility" of electronic filings as official agency records, the regulation will represent a first step toward a change in agency orientation from paper-based to computer-based submissions. Also, it will form the regulatory basis for something that agency officials claim is essential if CANDAs are to become standard working practice at the agency: the role reversal of CANDAs from just a working NDA copy to both an official record and working copy, and the relegation of the hard copy submission to a limited working copy.

Do CANDAs Reduce Review Time?   Resource investments directed to CANDA efforts were made under the presumption that CANDAs would reduce drug review times. However, several factors have complicated efforts to verify this presumption, including difficulty in classifying certain submissions as either paper-based or CANDA submissions.

Although there have been several attempts to compare CANDA and hardcopy NDA reviews, the FDA's own analyses may be the most meaningful and promising. In its studies, the agency includes only applications whose computer components were submitted simultaneously with the hard copy versions of the application (i.e., hard copy versions are required for all NDAs, even CANDAs). An FDA analysis of applications approved in 1992 found that CANDAs were approved in an average of 18.8 months, compared to 32.6 months for non-CANDA applications. Further, the agency reviewed the 26 CANDAs approved from 1989 through 1992 in an average of 21.3 months.

Cooperative International Drug Reviews

With a history of working closely with its foreign counterparts on drug compliance issues, the FDA has moved to widen the scope of international regulatory cooperation to include drug reviews in recent years. Specifically, the FDA and Canada's Health Protection Branch (HPB) have completed at least five "joint" or "cooperative" reviews of AIDS-related drugs. Officials at both agencies seem anxious to expand the program to include drugs other than AIDS-related therapies and, in the future, to involve other regulatory authorities as well.

Bristol-Myers Squibb's AIDS medication Videx (didanosine, ddI) was the first drug to undergo joint FDA/HPB review. Officials from both authorities agreed that the ability to pool information and share assessments of clinical and preclinical data helped to speed the Videx review.

However, FDA officials concede that the first three joint efforts—involving Videx, Hoffmann La Roche's ddC (dideoxycytidine), and Adria's Mycobutin (rifabutin)—were largely parallel, rather than joint, reviews. Although the FDA and HPB review teams held occasional face-to-face meetings and communicated by telephone, they each evaluated the applications independently.

With the review and approval of Burroughs Wellcome's Mepron (atovaquone) in 1992, FDA officials believe that the agencies took their first steps toward a true joint review. In this effort, an HPB reviewer was the primary reviewer for one of Wellcome's three principal clinical studies, while FDA reviewers handled the other two. The Division of Antiviral Drug Products relied on the HPB's evaluation of the third principal study as well as its own clinical reviews of the remaining studies in reaching an approval decision. In addition, the HPB reviewer presented the results of his review at an FDA advisory committee meeting on Mepron.

More recently, the FDA and HPB completed a cooperative review for U.S. Biosciences' NeuTrexin (trimetrexate glucuronate), which received FDA approval in December 1993. This review was similar to the Mepron model, and involved an HPB reviewer in the evaluation of two supportive clinical studies.

The FDA and HPB, each of which actively monitor the drug development pipeline for cooperative review candidates, are said to be involved in other joint reviews. The agencies were hoping to initiate reviews for two cancer drugs in 1993, and to consider central nervous system medications for treating Alzheimer's disease and Parkinson's disease as well.

Obviously, however, the willingness of the two regulatory bodies to engage in a joint review is only one of the necessary conditions essential to FDA/HPB efforts. A drug sponsor must have plans to seek approval in the United States and Canada, and must be able to submit largely equivalent premarketing applications simultaneously. Currently, the HPB accepts new drug submissions (NDS) in NDA format, provided the company can show that it will take three months or more to reformat its submission according to Canadian guidelines.

FDA officials believe that a November 1993 regulation, which gives the agency greater freedom to share confidential commercial information with foreign regulators, removes a key impediment to international cooperative reviews. The regulation incorporates several safeguards to ensure that any information exchanges with foreign authorities will not be disclosed further. In most cases, the FDA will seek a sponsor's approval before sharing information with foreign regulatory bodies during cooperative product reviews (see Chapter 9).

Despite participation in international harmonization and educational/training efforts, the FDA has not conducted any cooperative reviews with European regulatory authorities. Given Europe's continuing efforts to form a common market, FDA officials believe that cooperative reviews will be handled through Europe's regional drug regulatory authority rather than by member countries.

CDER's External Drug Review Program

During early 1992, CDER began an "external review" program in an attempt to alleviate the backlog of original and supplemental NDAs in several therapeutic areas, including anti-allergy, anti-infective, anti-inflammatory, and analgesic drugs. The program was designed to obtain qualified experts from outside the government to review what the agency termed "routine types of applications [and drugs]...whose review is not expected to pose major problems—for example, those similar to ones already approved." While the agency retains final approval authority over applications reviewed externally, contract reviewers were to handle the initial data analyses and make recommendations based on these analyses.

As part of the program, the FDA contracted with the MITRE Corporation, which was to review several applications under the terms of the agreement. As the only contractor under the program, MITRE had handled all external application reviews as of this writing. According to FDA officials, these reviews have involved several straightforward efficacy supplements.

Compared to CANDAs and NDA Days, the external review program has not been widely discussed. Some believe that the program, which was partly a product of a Bush Administration initiative to reduce government regulatory burdens, was unpopular with many FDA officials.

The agency has provided little information on the workings of the process outside of an April 1992 press release announcing the program. The release states that, "The FDA, contract reviewers, and if necessary, the drug sponsor will communicate regularly to review the progress and identify problem issues that may arise during the review. The contract reviewers will submit a comprehensive written report containing a recommendation on approval or nonapproval of the drug, 120 days after receiving the [application]. The FDA will then assess the quality, completeness and validity of the data review and if necessary, present the data to an FDA expert advisory committee. The sponsor will be notified by FDA 180 days after initiation of the review as to whether or not the drug is approvable."

As of this writing, there was no available analysis on the success of the external review program. However, FDA officials claim that the contract reviewers consistently have met the 120-day deadlines for conducting their reviews and submitting comprehensive reports to the agency. It is not known whether CDER has approved any of the efficacy supplements that have undergone external reviews.

In late 1993, FDA officials had serious doubts about the future of the external review program. Since monies collected under the user-fee program may not be used to fund external reviews, they must be funded by existing agency appropriations. And with FDA budget cutbacks, some within the agency believe that this program makes an easy target, particularly given that the program is reported to be unpopular with some FDA officials.

Index

-A-

Accelerated Drug Development and Approval: *see Procedures for Accelerated Approval of Drugs to Treat Life-Threatening and Severely Debilitating Illnesses and Parallel Track*

Action Letters, 189-192
approvable letters, 190-191
approval letters, 189-190
not-approvable letters, 191-192

Advisory Committees: *see FDA Advisory Committees*

Adverse Drug Experiences,
postmarketing reporting of, 239-244
premarketing reporting of, 68-72

Animal Testing: *See Nonclinical Testing*

Approvable Letters: *see Action Letters*

Approval Letters: *see Action Letters*

-B-

Bioresearch Monitoring Program, 273-285
clinical investigator compliance program, 275-279
history of, 273-275
sponsor-monitor compliance program, 279-283

-C-

CANDA: *see Computer-Assisted New Drug Applications*

Carcinogenicity Testing: *see Nonclinical Testing*

CDER: *see Center for Drug Evaluation and Research*

Center for Drug Evaluation and Research,
functions of, 76-77
structure of, 77-90
workload of, 80

CGMP: *see Current Good Manufacturing Practice*

FD&C Act: *see Federal Food, Drug and Cosmetic Act*

Federal Food, Drug and Cosmetic Act, 3-4

Final Printed Labeling, 192-195
FDA review of, 195-196

FPL: *see Final Printed Labeling*

-G-

Good Clinical Practices, 129-143
informed consent requirements, 139-141
investigator responsibilities, 136-139
IRB responsibilities, 141-143
sponsor responsibilities, 130-136

Good Laboratory Practice, 7, 35-43
FDA enforcement of, 41-43
history of, 36
major provisions of, 37-41
common violations of, 43

Good Manufacturing Practice: *see Current Good Manufacturing Practice*

-H-

Health Protection Branch (HPB), 319-320

-I-

ICH: *see International Conferences on Harmonization*

IND: *see Investigational New Drug Application*

Informed Consent, 139-141

International Conferences on Harmonization,
effects on clinical testing, 115, 125
effects on nonclinical testing, 18-31
effects on postmarketing adverse experience reporting, 239-244

International Harmonization Initiatives: *see International Conferences on Harmonization*

Investigational New Drug Application, 7-8, 45-74
annual reports to, 72-74
applicability of, 48-49
content requirements for, 50-66
emergency use IND, 46-48
exemptions from, 48-49
FDA review of, 8-10, 92-95
information amendments to, 74
investigator IND, 46
status categories for, 98-99
treatment IND, 48, 286-293
types of, 46-48
updating requirements for, 66-74

Investigator's Brochure, 55-56

Not-Approvable Letters: *see Action Letters*

-O-

Orphan Drugs, 261-272
    designation of, 262-267
    grants and contracts for, 271
    history of, 262
    marketing exclusivity for, 267-270
    protocol assistance for, 271
    tax credits for, 270-271

Over-the-Counter (OTC) Drug Labeling, 194

-P-

Parallel Track, 300-301

Phase 1-4 Clinical Testing: *see Clinical Testing*

Pilot Drug Evaluation Staff, 84-86

Pivotal Clinical Trials: *see Clinical Testing*

Pharmacoeconomic Clinical Studies, 127

Postmarketing Requirements, 235-250
    adverse drug experience reporting requirements, 239-243
    general reporting requirements, 236-238

Preapproval Inspections, 185-186

Preclinical Testing: *see Nonclinical Testing*

Pre-NDA Meetings, 175-176

Prescription Drug Advisory Committees: *see FDA Advisory Committees*

Prescription Drug User Fees, 2, 5-6, 196-198, 303-311
    basics of, 304-305
    FDA guidance on, 306-311

Primary Endpoints: *see Clinical Endpoints*

Priority Drugs, 210-211

Procedures for Accelerated Approval of Drugs to Treat Life-Threatening and Severely Debilitating Illnesses, 285-301

Protocols: *see Clinical Protocols*

-R-

Refuse-To-File Actions, 183-185

-S-

Secondary Endpoints: *see Clinical Endpoints*

SNDA: *see Supplemental NDA*

Standard Drugs, 211-212